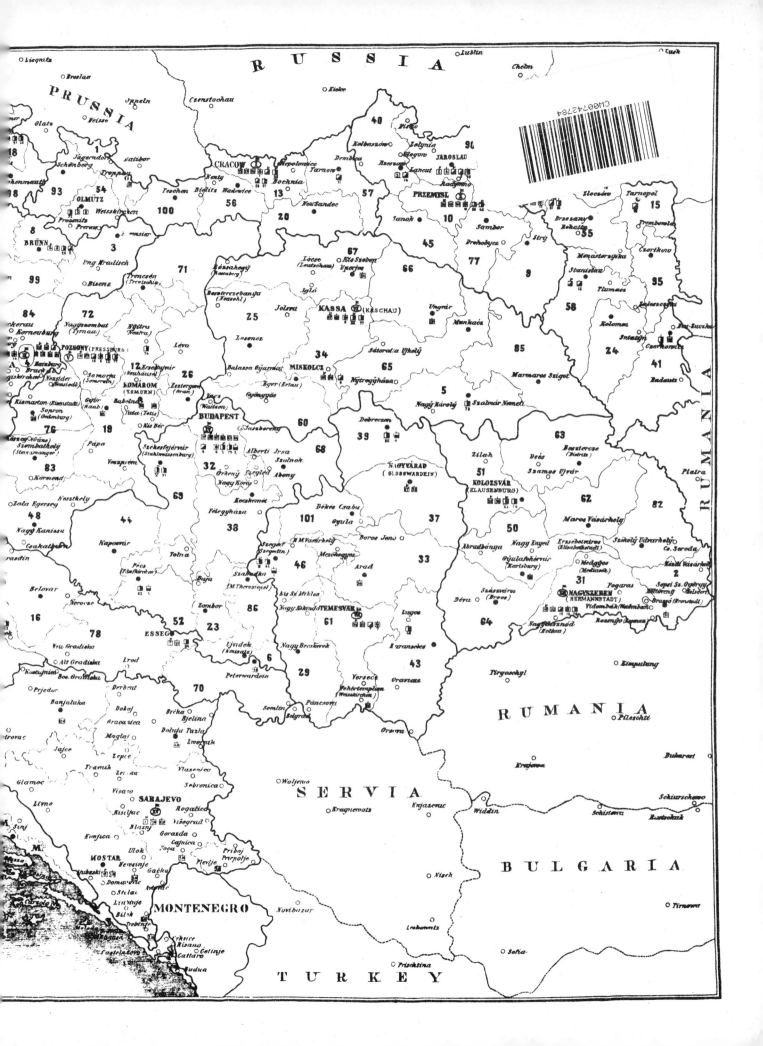

Fighting Troops
of the
Austro-Hungarian
Army
1868-1914

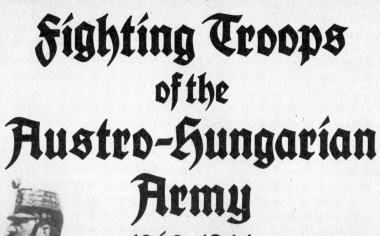

Fighting Troops
of the
Austro-Hungarian
Army
1868-1914

James Lucas

HIPPOCRENE BOOKS INC

New York

SPELLMOUNT LTD

Tunbridge Wells, Kent

In the Spellmount Military list:
The Uniforms of the British Yeomanry Forces 1794-1914 Series:
The Sussex Yeomanry
The North Somerset Yeomanry
The Yorkshire Hussars
Westmorland and Cumberland Yeomanry
3rd County of London (Sharpshooters)
Duke of Lancasters Own Yeomanry
Yorkshire Dragoons
Lovat Scouts

The Yeomanry Regiments—A Pictorial History
The Territorial Battalions 1859-1985—A Pictorial History
Over the Rhine—The Last Days of War in Europe
Riflemen Form
History of the Cambridge University OTC
Yeoman Service
Intelligence Officer in the Peninsula

In the Nautical list:
Sea of Memories

In the Aviation list:
Diary of a Bomb Aimer

First published in the UK 1987 by
Spellmount Ltd
12 Dene Way, Speldhurst
Tunbridge Wells, Kent TN3 0NX
ISBN 0-946771-04-9

First published in USA 1987 by
Hippocrene Books Inc,
171 Madison Avenue,
New York, NY 10016
ISBN 0-87052-362-7

British Library Cataloguing in Publication Data
Lucas, James
   The fighting troops of the Austro-Hungarian army 1868-1914.
   —(Militaria pictorial history)
   1. Austria—Armed Forces—History
   I. Title   II. Series
   355′.009436   UA670

Designed by Words & Images, Speldhurst, Tunbridge Wells, Kent.
Typeset by Staples Printers Rochester Limited, Love Lane, Rochester, Kent.
Printed by Hartnolls, Bodmin, Cornwall

Contents

Contents

Colour Plates

Dedication

During the second week of November 1918, as the First World War came to its end, the Habsburg Emperor-King, Karl, withdrew from the government of the Austro-Hungarian Empire and, thereby, brought to a close the rule of the Imperial House over countries whose peoples made up a major part of the population of Central Europe.

The Empire then fragmented and has vanished almost without trace. The history and the manifold achievements of the army which had defended it have gone generally unrecognised. Yet that army was one of the major military forces of the world and, at one time, had been the paramount military power in Europe.

This record of the fighting troops of the Austro-Hungarian Empire will, it is hoped, keep alive the memory of that splendid army for there are very few people living today who can recall from personal experience the colour, the splendour—the uniqueness of that once-great force.

The book covers the years from just after the end of the war with Prussia to the opening months of the First World War. Those decades were the ones during which the tripartite army of Austria-Hungary was at its most colourful, just as, on a national level, it was the period during which the culture of Vienna was at its most influential.

Although written to commemorate all those soldiers who wore the Emperor's coloured coat, this work is dedicated in particular to the Imperial and Royal House of Habsburg, for whose honour and in whose service generations of men considered themselves privileged to offer their lives.

Acknowledgements

Over the many years that have been spent in the research and the writing of this book, I have been fortunate enough to enjoy the help and support of a great many people, not only from this country and from Austria but also from the United States of America. The assistance and encouragement so freely given I acknowledge with sincere and grateful thanks. It is not possible to name individually all those who gave their time and knowledge and I hope those who have been included only in this general expression of thanks do not feel that their contribution was any less valued or important.

The following Austrian officers, who served as Military Attachés in London—General Hubert Wingelbauer, General Lothar Brosch-Fohraheim and Brigadier Maximilian Trofaier—gave invaluable advice. In addition I must mention my father-in-law, the late Josef Anton Schranz, Lieutenant in kuk Regiment, Nr 88, and my very dear friend, the late Werner Auer, formerly of kuk Regiment, Nr 47.

To the Director and Staff of the Austrian Institute here in London as well as to the Director and Staff of the Heeresgeschichtliches Museum in Vienna go my special thanks, also to the officers of the Imperial War Museum and of the Army Historical Branch of the Ministry of Defence.

Among those friends here in England I must mention the late Mr Scherer, Mary Davies, née Harris, for her unfailing encouragement, Mr de Gebert and Matthew Cooper. My very special thanks go, as always, to my daughter, Barbara, who typed and retyped this manuscript, and, above all, to my beloved wife, Traude, through whom I first learned of the army of Austria-Hungary.

The illustrations for this book have been collected over the past forty years from such sources as the Imperial War Museum in London, the Heeresgeschichtliches Museum in Vienna and the personal albums of a great number of Austrian friends and relatives. The initials *IWM* indicate that the source is the Imperial War Museum and *HGM* that the copyright is held by the Heeregeschichtliches Museum. The provenance of other photographs is given where this has been positively established.

The uniform pieces and military badges were made available to be photographed by Diana Condell of the Department of Exhibits and Firearms in the Imperial War Museum. They were photographed by David Price, whose professional skill I gratefully acknowledge.

foreword

Our days are marked by basic changes in every run of life. That applies to sciences and technology, to politics, global relations and not less to what was in the past an important part of every young man's life: military service in the defence of the country.

The new weapons of mass destruction were at one time considered to mean the end of the armies. Experience since Hiroshima has shown that this is not the case. Selfless service remains indispensable. Military virtues are today as important as they were in the past, though their function has changed. Hence the interest increasingly shown everywhere for military questions and traditions.

It has often been said that uniforms and the pageantry of the soldiers no longer fitted our times. Still, people long for colour and inspiration in their otherwise drab lives. The interest in British military traditions, which today attracts thousands of tourists from overseas, proves this fact. It equally applies to other nations.

In this sense the present book—concerning the fighting troops of the Austro-Hungarian army—is a genuine achievement beyond scholarly research. This army was a multinational force which, in a crucial area of the European continent, was called upon to defend western civilisation. Today, when we endeavour to recreate a European Community, the lessons of the past are more valuable than ever. And military history is an integral part of that heritage.

In this sense I wish Mr Lucas and his work a well-deserved success.

OTTO von HABSBURG

Introduction

AUSTRIA-HUNGARY was a dual monarchy made up of the empire of Austria and the kingdom of Hungary. In the last fifty years of its life the army of that monarchy was unique among the military forces of the world's great powers because it was not a single force but three separate military bodies; Imperial, Austrian and Hungarian.

The Imperial Army was common to both partners in the dual monarchy and being 'common' recruited from both halves of the Empire. Units of the 'Common' army were titled Imperial and Royal (kaiserlich und koeniglich or kuk), from 1888 onwards. They had been titled, before that year, Imperial, Royal (kaiserlich, koeniglich, or kk). The national Army of Austria, the Landwehr, was recruited from the confederation of states and provinces which made up the Austrian half of the monarchy. Units and organisations from that part of the Empire were known as Imperial Royal. The national Army of the kingdom of Hungary drew the men for its regiments and battalions from that kingdom. This Hungarian force although called 'Landwehr' was more popularly known by the term 'Honved'. To avoid any possibility of confusion between the two forces and for ease of identification in this book, the Hungarian Landwehr will be called Landwehr (Honved). Regiments and institutions of the Landwehr (Honved) were known as Royal Hungarian (koeniglich ungarisch or ku).

The unique construction of the Army of the Dual Monarchy required the services of three separate Service Ministers. That for the Common Army was titled the Imperial Minister for War and his partners in the Landwehr and the Landwehr (Honved) were both known as Ministers of Defence. Three General Staffs were also required and each force had its own military budget which had to be voted annually by parliament.

It must be stressed that the two national forces were equal partners with the Common Army and were in no way inferior to it in status. It is absolutely wrong to equate the Landwehr or the Honved with the British Army's Territorial Force which is made up of part-time soldiers. The Austrian and the Hungarian military bodies were regular, full-time, military organisations, with the Common Army being *primus inter pares*.

At the head of the armed forces stood Franz Joseph I who, in addition to being Emperor of Austria, was also nine times a king, including among his crowns those of Hungary, Bohemia and Jerusalem. The greatest pride of Franz Joseph was, however, in the fact that he was the first soldier of the Empire. The link which connected the Emperor and his army was a firm, enduring, two-way process: from him to them and from each soldier of his armies to him and to the Imperial family. The army had always considered the Sovereign its feudal lord and within the Service the only loyalty was to the dynasty alone. Differences of class, religion or national allegiance had all been supressed in favour of this single loyalty. The army was, thus, a microcosm of that society which the Emperor and his statesmen hoped the whole Empire would become; a multi-national grouping, unified as one single whole, indissolubly linked to the Royal House, a supra-national State in which all races and peoples would work in harmony to attain the ideals of peace and prosperity.

The army, it can be said, was one of the three pillars upon which Habsburg power had rested and military service united the Empire in a way that neither the church nor the aristocracy—the other two great Estates of the Realm— could achieve. In the last fifty years of its life the army was the last of the

A motif which evokes the old Imperial Austria. A young Lieutenant in summer dress kissing the hand of a pretty girl.

institutions which had made Austria a great power and in those final decades of Empire, her glory began to dim, eclipsed in the German-speaking world by the rise of Prussia.

Austria's decline from power began as a result of the war which had been forced upon her by Prussia. On 3 July 1866 the decisive battle was fought at Koeniggraetz and by the evening of that day Prussia had demonstrated that power comes out of the muzzle of a gun and, in her case, the breech-loading, needle gun with which her infantry regiments were armed. The Austrian Army was forced to fight on two fronts; in the south against Italy and in the north against Prussia. Although the Austrian Army was considered to be the finest in Europe it was badly organised, had a weak staff system and its infantry regiments were still armed with the old-fashioned, slow, breech-loading musket. The attacks of the Habsburg infantry, although heroic, collapsed in the fire of the Prussian Army's faster firing weapon. Detlev von Liliencron, a German officer-poet, was moved to write of how the assaults of the Imperial infantry had 'flooded forward the whole day long . . . a sea of white, the enemy's wonderful Army'. Austria was able to achieve an outstanding victory on the southern front against Italy but the defeat of her armies facing Prussia forced Franz Joseph to sue for peace.

The military disaster of July 1866, following so closely upon that which Austria had suffered at the hands of a Franco-Italian coalition in 1859, proved to have consequences more far-reaching than the mere loss of a battle or the subsequent surrender of national territory to the victors. As a result of Koeniggraetz the House of Habsburg lost the primacy within the Confederation of German States while the influence of Prussia gew until, in 1870, her King was proclaimed Emperor of Germany. Henceforth, Austria, no longer the dominant German power and excluded from the Confederation, settled down to the husbandry of the vast Empire which alliances and battle had won for her. The Emperor had hoped to devote himself wholeheartedly, to restoring the Empire's position but was forced to deal with a succession of political crises, the most serious of which was the separatist demand of the Hungarians who were, after the German/Austrians, the largest political grouping in the Empire.

On 17 February 1867 the Emperor concluded a Settlement with the Magyars out of which was created the Dual Monarchy. Under the terms of that Settlement each partner was independent of the other. Only the person of the Monarch, the conduct of foreign affairs, matters of finance and the Imperial Army linked them.

The vast Empire, now no longer Austria but Austria-Hungary, had a population of forty-seven million people, made up of the main racial types of Europe. The people of the Empire spoke different tongues, had many religions and lived at varying levels of political and cultural development; but they were united under the Emperor-King. The kingdoms, duchies and provinces which formed Austria proper were known as Cisleithania and were governed from Vienna. Cisleithania embraced what is now Czechoslovakia, all of southern and much of eastern Poland and the major part of northern Italy as well as Slovenia in Jugoslavia. All units of the Common Army raised from Cisleithania were known as 'German' regiments irrespective of whether their national composition was German, Czech, Polish or Italian.

The provinces of Bosnia-Herzegovina which were formally annexed by Austria during 1908, were administered through a Bosnian Bureau since

His Imperial Majesty The Emperor Franz Joseph wearing the undress uniform of a General Officer. The collar of the tunic carries the rank device of a Field Marshal, c1908.

they did not form part of either Cisleithania or of Transleithania.

The other partner in the Dual Monarchy, Hungary, also known as Transleithania or the Land of St Stephan's crown, comprised the Magyar kingdom and also parts of present day Jugoslavia, particularly Croatia. It was administered from Budapest and Common Army regiments raised from that territory were known as 'Hungarian' even though some were Croat in composition.

The Settlement of 1867 was a political compromise and like most compromises did not meet with total approval. Many Austrians were of the opinion that the Settlement was nothing less than the recognition of Hungary as a completely separate State and that this would lead to a division of the army along nationalistic lines producing a rupture which might lead to civil war.

The Emperor sent General Beck, Chief of his Military Cabinet, to discuss the problem with the Hungarian Prime Minister. Beck returned from Hungary supporting the demand for a Hungarian national army which, in his opinion was the one concession which would prevent the break-up of the whole Imperial Service. Franz Joseph had also set up a committee whose terms of reference were to remodel and to modernise the Austrian Army. The chairman of the committee, The Archduke Albrecht, was appointed Inspector General of the Army and, armed with the wide-ranging powers of that office, he and his committee set to work.

The first priority was to increase the size of the army and the method chosen was universal male conscription. This was the first and the most radical of all the reforms, for by that decision Albrecht's committee broke the centuries-old Austrian tradition of a volunteer, professional army. Compulsory military service certainly increased the overall size of the Austro-Hungarian forces but, paradoxically, it also weakened them. The political concession which allowed the Magyars to raise and to maintain their own

The Heir to the Throne, Karl, and his wife The Archduchess Zita. He is wearing the undress uniform of a Colonel of Hussars. In undress the breeches and boots were replaced by slacks and light shoes. The shako is also the undress pattern.

The Archduke Albrecht, the initiator of the great reforms introduced after the 1866 war with Prussia, in the uniform of a Field Marshal.

Guests at the Coronation of The Emperor Karl in Budapest. The Ulan officer (left centre) is wearing the winter pattern ulanka and has the rank of Field Officer. The monocled officer is a Lieutenant of Ulans. Note the contrasting types of shapka. The Field Officer has the traditional pattern, while the junior one has the newer pattern which has a narrower neck and the square top is inclined at an angle.

national army, the Landwehr (Honved), required that Austria raise a parallel national force—the Landwehr. The setting up of those two national armies and the complications of their administration diminished the Common Army.

Albrecht's committee, with the assurance that conscription would ensure a regular flow of recruits, then set out to redesign the whole structure of the Imperial host along contemporary lines. The Prussian Army was chosen as the model to be followed. The traditional Austrian organisation was replaced by the all-arms infantry division and on the projection for manpower availability it was thought that a force of twenty-two Infantry and one cavalry division could be raised. There then followed a second series of reforms which included the phasing out of such obsolescent traditions as the Regiments Inhaber. It had been the custom for regiments in the combatant arms to be owned by a colonel who often exercised considerable, almost feudal, powers, including the right to promote or to demote officers as he chose. As a result of the Albrechtian reforms all formal executive and administrative powers were stripped from the colonels and their regiments were placed, henceforth, under the control of the Minister for War. The position of the Regiments Inhaber, or Colonel-in-Chief, then became an honorary one bestowed by the Sovereign upon native and foreign royalty or upon distinguished military commanders.

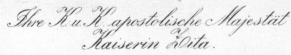

Ihre K.u.K. apostolische Majestät Kaiserin Zita.

Korpskommandant G.d.K. Eduard von Böhm-Ermolli.

The name of the colonel-in-chief was carried as part of the regimental title during the period of his command, but there was no provision to commemorate the service of past illustrious officers until Franz Joseph decreed, in 1888, that certain regiments should bear 'for all time' the name of a distinguished commander who had been associated with it. The tradition of the Austrian Service had been that no woman could hold the post. It was a title reserved for men. As a mark of singular respect and by special dispensation Franz Joseph allowed one woman, the long dead Empress Maria Theresia, to be named as Colonel-in-Chief of the 32nd Infantry Regiment and the rule was broken again when Karl succeeded to the throne and named his wife, the Empress Zita, Colonel of 16th Hussar Regiment.

Included among the traditions which were abolished by Albrecht's committee were cavalry bands and the carrying of guidons by all cavalry regiments except the 14th Dragoons. The number of Colours carried by infantry regiments was reduced to one. This was the standard carried by the regiment's first or senior battalion. From its background colour this was known as the 'White' to distinguish it from the 'Yellow' which had been the Colour carried by each of the two junior battalions. By an Imperial decree of 1888, certain regiments were permitted to carry a Yellow Colour instead

Left

Her Imperial Majesty The Empress Zita became only the second woman to be named as Colonel-in-Chief of a regiment, when she was appointed to the 16th Hussars.

Right

General of Cavalry, Eduard von Boehm-Ermolli, rose to become one of the most famous military commanders of the First World War. When colourful uniforms were replaced by grey service dress, Cavalry officers took to wearing specially commissioned regimental badges as marks of identification. These devices were not officially sanctioned, but the wearing of the unofficial badge of his old regiment by Boehm-Ermolli made it difficult to forbid the practice.

of the White, to commemorate the bravery of the junior battalions in some past battle.

The punishments of chaining up and flogging military criminals were done away with and in an Order, dated 14 October 1868, it was decreed that the rank and file were no longer to be addressed by the term Common Soldier. Instead they were to be called Rifleman, Dragoon, Gunner, etc. Nor would their superiors use the personal pronoun *du* when addressing them, but the formal pronoun *Sie*.

In matters of uniform, too, there was change and the most distinctive of those reforms was the abolition of the traditional white-coloured coat and the introduction of blue as the standard colour. Albrecht's committee tried hard to introduce new systems of identifying regiments but was forced to abandon its attempts in face of the army's united opposition to proposals for change. The regiments continued to wear on their tunics and headdress the facing colours by which they had been traditionally identified.

* * * * * * * *

The changes, carried out in the late 60s, marked the second of the three periods into which the military history of Austria is divided. The first of these began during the first decades of the 17th century when, as a result of a change in Imperial fortunes, Austria turned away from the New World of the Americas, in which the Spanish Habsburgs had created a vast Empire, and towards eastern and south-eastern Europe. Those regions and territories which she then wrested from the Turks in the wars of the 17th century were incorporated into the Empire of the Austrian Habsburgs.

In that first period, which lasted up to the defeat of Napoleon Bonaparte, sixty-two regiments of the infantry line were raised as were most of the light infantry formations (the various types of Jaeger) and the cavalry of the line. With the defeat of Bonaparte there were decades of peace in Europe until the wars of the 1850s and 60s.

A scene during the visit of The Emperor of Germany to Vienna for the ceremonies commemorating the Diamond Jubilee of the reign of The Emperor Franz Joseph, 1908. The Guard of Honour was drawn from one of the regiments of Kaiserjaeger.

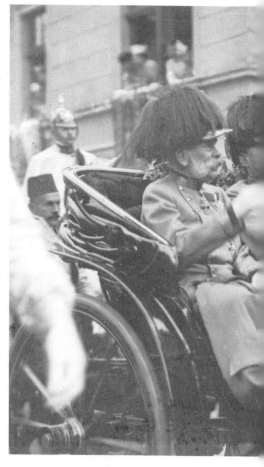

The second period of change in Austria's military history was that which came about after the war with Prussia in 1866. During that second period the number of infantry regiments was increased to eighty, a standardisation of the line cavalry was begun and the Landwehr and the Landwehr (Honved) were both formed. This period of change and expansion ended in 1882 and was followed by a third which began in 1883 and continued until the outbreak of war in 1914. In this third period the establishment of 102 Common Army infantry regiments was reached, four regiments of Kaiserjaeger and additional Feldjaeger battalions had been formed, four regiments of Bosnia-Herzegovinian infantry had been raised, a fifteenth Dragoon regiment added to the line and an expansion of the artillery arm and of the two Landwehr forces undertaken.

Above left
The visit of The Emperor Wilhelm of Germany to Vienna during the ceremonies commemorating the Diamond Jubilee of Franz Joseph's reign in 1908.

Above right
The Emperor Franz Joseph during a visit to Bosnia-Herzegovinia. With him in the carriage is General Potiorek, military governor of the province.

Left
The visit of The Emperor Wilhelm of Germany to Austria. The German Emperor is wearing the uniform of an Austrian Field Marshal and His Majesty The Emperor of Austria is wearing the uniform of a Field Marshal of the Prussian Army.

The growth of the infantry arm encouraged Beck, now Chief of the General Staff, to plan for a field force of forty-five infantry and ten cavalry divisions, to be found by the Common Army. These would be supported in the field by a second line, composed of the two Landwehr forces which would be organised into fifteen infantry and two cavalry divisions. It was intended that the Common Army would be employed wherever it was needed in the event of war, but that the Landwehr would only be used in the defence of their own national territory, except where abnormal political or military conditions required that they be employed extra-territorially. A third line of battle would be formed from the Landsturm, a militia of older men whose task would be to carry out guard and other security duties within their own unit areas.

It soon became clear that Beck's plan to raise fifty-five divisions could not be realised and that, because the Common Army was too small to wage a major war, the Landwehr and the Landwehr (Honved) should no longer be considered as second line troops, suitable only to be defenders of their own territories, but that they should become part of the first line of battle. From 20 March 1890, when the Order was published authorising those forces to be employed outside their own national borders, it was intended that the principal difference between the Common Army and the Landwehr forces would be in certain uniform details. A start was made to bring all the first line formations up to the same establishment in men, weapons and organisation, but this had not been achieved by 1914.

With the upgrading of Landwehr forces to first-line formations, the time had come for the Landsturm of both halves of the Empire to be modernised so that they could take over the role of territorial defence which had been formerly that of the two Landwehr.

When the Archduke Albrecht died on 18 February 1895, the army he had reformed was larger and better organised to meet the challenges of modern war, although many senior officers still considered that it was neither strong enough nor had the morale necessary to face those challenges. Those officers had anticipated massive increases in the army's establishments but the increases were very modest. The figures for those recruited by conscription in 1905 were 103,100 and were to have risen to 165,000 by 1914. It is surprising, despite the growth in population to 51,000,000 in 1910, that parliament should have kept the recruiting contingents so low. But this was a fact which the planners of the Austro-Hungarian Army had to accept.

During the late autumn of 1908, Austria-Hungary formally annexed Bosnia-Herzegovina, a small, politically superfluous act but one which played its part in laying the powder train to the First World War. Serbia which felt herself threatened by Austria's action drew closer to Russia. The division of Europe was widened by the Balkan Wars and, once again, because of Austria's partial mobilisation, Serbia moved more closely into Russia's camp. Alliances were made and remade. All that political activity heightened the prevailing tension.

During 1911 the Austrian parliament voted a military budget, which allowed for a larger recruiting contingent and for the requisition of waggons, telegraph communications and industrial undertakings in time of war. As a counter balance to those positive steps the politicians also voted to reduce the standard term of service with the Colours from three years to two.

Six years elapsed between the annexation of Bosnia-Herzegovina and the

Within half-an-hour of this photograph being taken on 28 June 1914 in Sarajevo, The Archduke Franz Ferdinand and his wife, The Duchess Sophie, had been murdered by terrorists. The assassination of the Heir to the Throne of Austria-Hungary led to a series of political crises out of which came the declaration of war against Serbia by Austria. Within weeks of that act a World War evolved.

The Archduke Karl in dark blue overcoat and undress shako, en route to the Front in 1914.

outbreak of the First World War. Years in which the military planners strove to modernise the army despite the overt and covert opposition of parliament. Years of haste towards, and of preparation for, a war which all knew would be destructive, but whose magnitude and violence none could have foreseen, nor foreseeing could have prevented. For it seemed, in 1914, as if all Europe was mad for war. On 28 June, while on a tour of duty in Bosnia, the Archduke Franz Ferdinand, heir to the throne, was murdered by a Serb nationalist. In Vienna, where the drift towards an eventual European war had been accepted with resignation bordering almost on fatalism, the murder of the Archduke and his Duchess was seen as the provocative act which would bring about that war. News that mobilisation had been ordered was greeted with enthusiasm by the peoples of the Empire and the streets of the cities soon presented a lively picture. Reservists and volunteers flooded into the barracks in such vast numbers that they swamped, albeit temporarily, the military administration. The thoroughfares were choked with carts as their owners brought the vehicles to designated collecting points. Then the infantry contingents marched out to active service, each headed by its band and regimental Colour. Flower bedecked trains, whose waggons were inscribed with patriotic slogans, conveyed the military to assembly areas in the eastern and south-eastern regions of the vast Empire. On a wave of patriotic fervour the polyglot army of nations which made up the military might of Austria-Hungary went forth to a war which its soldiers were to fight with great skill and amazing courage for four long and bitter years, against terrible odds, despite shortages, deprivation and even starvation.

The story of the Habsburg armies in the years of that terrible war lies outside the parameters of this book. Let it just be remembered that the Imperial Army which it had been fashionable to desribe as 'ramshackle' was, until only weeks before the armistice, a firm and aggressive force, faithful to the oath it had taken and loyal to that House which it had sworn to defend.

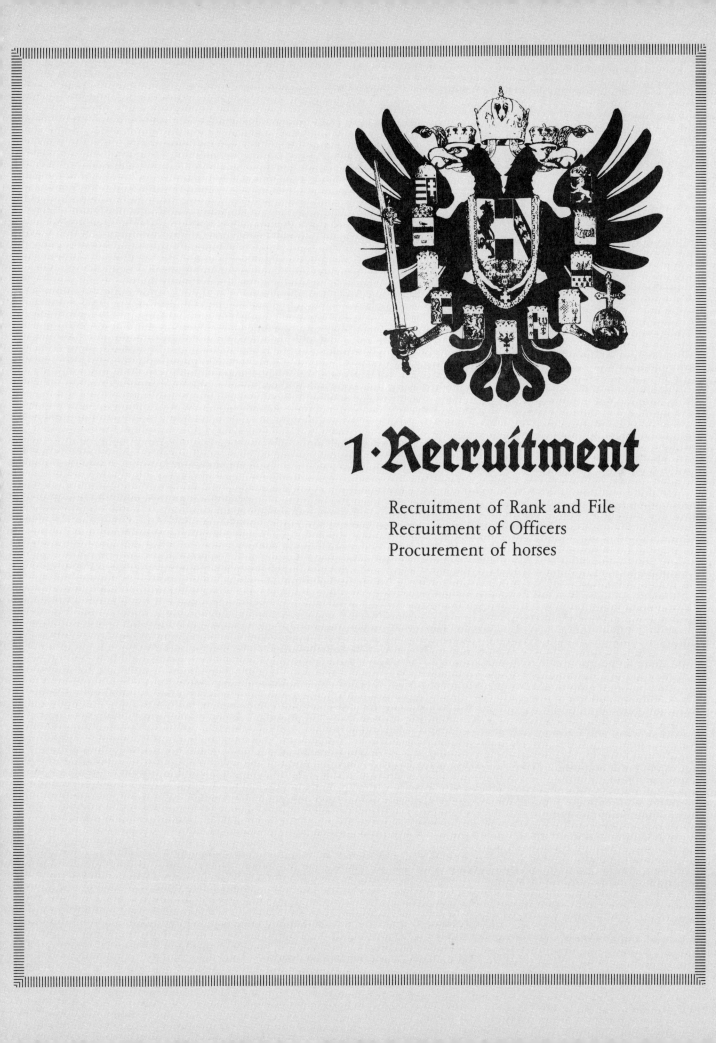

1·Recruitment

Recruitment of Rank and File
Recruitment of Officers
Procurement of horses

||||||||||||||||||||||||||||||||||||||||||||||||||||||||||||||||||||||||||||||||||

Recruitment of the Rank and File

||||||||||||||||||||||||||||||||||||||||||||||||||||||||||||||||||||||||||||||||||||||||||

The greatest number of men required to fill the regiments was obtained by conscription rendered in person by citizens of Austria, Hungary or Bosnia who fulfilled certain age and health qualifications. Entry into the Common Army could also be effected by voluntary enlistment, by graduation from a military school or, exceptionally, by voluntary transfer from the Landwehr/Landwehr (Honved). Each recruiting area of the monarchy had to supply a stated number of men. When the numbers obtained in a year fell below quota then the shortfall was added to the following year's contingent figures.

The whole term of military liability for which, in theory, every male citizen was subject, was known as 'Landsturm' service. This term included full-time Colour service as well as the years on the several types of Reserve. Landsturm duty began with the preparation of lists of all males who had reached the age of nineteen, but it was not until the spring of the year of his twenty-first birthday that a recruit was ordered to report to a selection centre. A medical inspection rejected those totally unfit for military duty and their names were deleted from the muster rolls. The remainder were graded according to the category of their fitness and at the end of the day the physically fit took the Oath of Allegiance. A Commission then decided which men were to be exempted from full-time military duty. These latter were placed on a General List known as the 'Ersatz Reserve', made up of men who, although in every respect fit for service, were surplus to immediate requirements. Certain categories of men were placed automatically in the Ersatz Reserve and these included the sole dependants of families, certain types of agricultural or forestry workers, seminary students and schoolmasters. In time of war the Ersatz Reserve could be drawn upon to bring the units of the Field Army up to establishment, and even in peacetime those in that category were liable to be called for service. Men placed on the Ersatz Reserve underwent only ten weeks' basic military training.

Whether a recruit served in the Common Army or the Landwehr was decided by lot: those with the lowest numbers being taken for the Imperial force and those drawing the next lowest numbers for the two national contingents.

In peacetime, full-time military service was generally for a period of three years with the infantry and four years for the cavalry and for the horse artillery. Once he had completed his service with the Colours the soldier then began a period of reserve service; ten years for the infantry—seven for the cavalry

Men of a Common Army German regiment marching through a village during the autumn manoeuvres at Gross-Meseritsch during 1909. The men are wearing the blue blouse which was later replaced by the grey service dress.

Infantry tactics of the Austro-Hungarian Army included a line of riflemen working ahead of the main infantry line, to pick off the enemy officers and commanders. The men seen in this line, during the manoeuvres at Gross-Meseritsch in 1909, form part of that forward line.

and the horse artillery. During those ten years he was liable for recall for short refresher courses of military training. He then spent a further five years as a First Landsturm Reservist before passing into the Second Landsturm Reserve. Men of that category were excused the refresher training and were only recalled to the Colours upon the proclamation of general mobilisation.

Thus it can be seen that the Empire had a reservoir of men of varying ages and degrees of military proficiency. The older and less well trained men of the Second Landsturm Reserve were not intended to be used as front-line soldiers in the Field Army, although many units did fight with distinction in both infantry and cavalry roles.

Bosnia-Herzegovina had no Landwehr or Landsturm organisation. In those provinces reservists of the youngest and most recently trained categories were classified as First Reserve. Two other categories, known as the Second and Third Reserve respectively, held the older men.

Volunteers for the army were accepted if they conformed to the nationality, age and health requirements laid down for conscripted soldiers. There was also the proviso that they were not criminals. Under-age recruits were accepted only with parental consent and foreigners could join the army only with the sanction of the Emperor and the permission of their own government. Voluntary enlistment was usually only possible into the Common Army, since such enlistment into either the Landwehr or the Landwehr (Honved) was limited to 5% of the whole. Terms of voluntary enlistment were for three years, both in the first instance and in subsequent re-enlistments, with Reserve obligations set at seven years after the first enlisted period. The privilege of selecting the arm of service in which one would serve was one of the advantages of voluntary enlistment.

In an effort to encourage the better educated classes to join the army, young men who reached certain standards of education and who undertook to clothe, feed and equip themselves—and in the mounted branches to provide their own horse and saddlery—served only one year with the Colours before passing into the reserve. These men were known as 'One Year Volunteers'. They were entitled to choose the year in which they would serve so long as it was completed before their twenty-fourth birthday. The object of this scheme was so that a man's study for a profession would not be damaged by a three-year term of conscripted service. It would also provide a reservoir of educated men of officer type.

Conscription not only produced an expansion of the military forces but also brought about improvements in conditions within the Service as a whole. In the middle decades of the 19th century there had been a rise in industrialism, advances in living standards and increased life expectancy. Politically it was a time of fresh ideas and social beliefs, of awareness of national identity, of radicalism and of class consciousness. The age of the masses had dawned and traditional institutions of the establishment were under pressure from political activists. The so called 'liberal' elements in the Empire despised the army's codes of honour and patriotism. There were many who rejoiced in the humiliation of their country's defeat by Prussia for they were confident that out of the chaos resulting from Koeniggraetz they would be able to wring political concessions.

Civilian attitudes towards the Imperial armed forces had always been unpredictable, covering at times any one of a variety of emotions ranging from wild enthusiasm to outright hatred. The casual acceptance of the

Josef Anton Schranz as a One Year Volunteer. The narrow band on the right sleeve of his blouse identifies his status.

Viennese of the defeat at Koeniggraetz was typical in that on the days following the battle the main topic of discussion was not the tragic outcome of the war but new waltzes which Johann Strauss had composed for a ball. Civilian opinions had to some extent been fostered by the army's own exclusiveness based on its special relationship with the Imperial House but now, in the final decades of the century, reformation was the order of the day with the implementing of the Archduke Albrecht's military reforms.

The most radical change was the introduction of conscripted service. Now there would be an annual regular influx of recruits and, also annually, a corresponding loss of trained soldiers. This revolutionary idea began a series of changes which brought about a wider based army; if not a people's army then at least an army of peoples who would send their sons for military service in a common cause.

It was clear that the military authorities would have to reappraise and adjust their attitudes so as to bring these into line with contemporary social ideas. Conscripts were not prepared to submit to the harsher military disciplines or to endure the primitive conditions which volunteer soldiers accepted. The army was forced to make concessions in order to make the military life more acceptable to the urban, civilian masses even though these were a minority in the Service. The men who were conscripted into the service of their Emperor were, for the most part, peasants drawn from rural communities and were to a high degree illiterate. Even in German/Austria

The Army of Austria-Hungary was the first to use motorcycles for its officer adjutants in a battlefield role. These two officers were used to carry despatches during the military manoeuvres in Reichstatt in 1899.

there were nineteen in every hundred who could neither read nor write and this figure rose to 42% in Hungary, 70% in Ruthenia and 78% in Dalmatia (all figures taken from the 1890 census). The unending toil in field or factory and poor wages had kept most of the rural population tied to their villages. Few had been as far as the nearest market town until they were called to the conscription board. Fewer still had ever travelled on a train, had seen buildings taller than two storeys high or could tell the time from a clock face.

The greatest number of these hardy, undemanding and unsophisticated peasants was drawn from the eleven nations which made up the Empire but it was the Slavs who supplied the most. More than 44% of the total strength of the army was supplied by that one race and Slavs constituted no less than 67% of the infantry. The German/Austrian percentage of the army's strength was 28% and that of the Magyars 18%.

The years spent in conscripted military service gave to the men of the Empire a shared experience. Through this common involvement, by the mixing within a regiment of national or social groups and through postings to every part of the Empire, the soldier was introduced to social and political attitudes outside his own familiar circles. Conscription was seen as a beneficial phenomenon and became accepted as such a normal fact of life that even Socialists who had served their time with the Colours looked down upon those of their own party who lacked this experience.

The conscripted army of the masses found to be unacceptable the living conditions which the old professional Army had tolerated. Until the early 1880s, when new barracks were being built to meet the demands created by the army's expansion, standards of accommodation were low and the infantry had been billeted either in old buildings or upon civilians. The cavalry regiments, having no permanent barracks, usually slept under canvas during the summer months and were billeted upon farmers or in rural communities during the cold weather. Military buildings put up in the 80s showed evidence of the better understanding by the army of the needs of its soldiers. Whereas in former days barracks had been fortress-like in design, having high outside walls and narrow windows, the new buildings were more open in construction, although by today's standards they would be considered unduly spartan. Despite the fact that the army had become a people's force, the maintenance of law and order as well as the needs of internal security demanded a high concentration of troops in towns for it was often the unpleasant task of the military to confront riots, demonstrations and strikes. In the wilder areas of the Empire, such as Bosnia, there was, until the first decades of the 20th century, an almost permanent state of guerrilla warfare with local bandits.

Not only was accommodation poor to begin with but food and pay were also very low. In 1874, taking this as a representative year, a soldier received only one hot meal per day and this consisted of soup, six ounces of beef, a similar amount of vegetables and bread. The only portion of the day's rations which could be retained for later consumption was the bread and this had to suffice the man for the evening meal and for breakfast. Although many men from the less well developed areas of the Empire found the amount and the type of food to be sufficient there were others, particularly from German/Austria, who had been used to a more substantial diet with more frequent meals. Nor did the low pay allow the soldier to supplement his rations by buying food outside the barracks since, after deductions for boot

His Imperial Highness The Archduke Franz Ferdinand at the autumn manoeuvres, 1910.

polish, barrack room damages and the like, almost nothing remained of his pay.

There had to be, and there were, improvements in the standard of messing and in the type of food provided. By 1905 an additional warm evening meal was being issued on five days of the week and dehydrated vegetables were used in the preparation of this supper: the first time that dried vegetables had been on general issue in any army. Despite the improvement in other conditions within the Service, it was not until 1903 that the military authorities conceded Sunday as a day of rest and thereby gave the soldier a six-day week. The army, once a conservative, exclusive, feudal society within society, had become pragmatic, common and modern.

||||||||||||||||||||||||||||||||||||||||||||||||||||||||||||||||||||||||||||||||||||||

Recruitment of Officers

||||||||||||||||||||||||||||||||||||||||||||||||||||||||||||||||||||||||||||||||||||||

It was during the last decades of Franz Joseph's long reign that bureaucrats and academics became more important than soldiers. From 1870 onwards there was peace among the major powers of Europe and in the case of Austria-Hungary only the troubles in Bosnia disturbed the Imperial calm. The sword which had created the Empire could now be sheathed and the army could stand down, leaving the Civil Service and other administrators to govern the Habsburg lands.

This social revolution, which diminished the military, was hastened when those aristocrats whose families had served the army for generations no longer enlisted into the Imperial regiments, but used their talents in the Diplomatic Corps or in the husbandry of their estates. This is not to say that the traditional leaders abandoned completely or immediately the military service.

Military manoeuvres were social occasions during which army wives could see their husbands in military actions, playing out the role they would be conducting in earnest in the event of war. These spectators, including one General Staff Officer, are at military manoeuvres at Klagenfurt during 1899.

Men of an infantry unit in defensive positions during the military manoeuvres in Galicia during 1900. The men kneeling down are from a Hungarian unit and, from the style of sash worn by the officers and the cuff decoration, it is clear that the unit is from the Landwehr (Honved). The officer in the light-coloured tunic in the right foreground is from a Hussar regiment.

There were still some to be found, although these were concentrated in certain crack regiments.

To ensure that there would be sufficient officers to command the army, commissions were offered to men from a far wider social circle than before. The former conditions of aristocracy and bravery were no longer sufficient to gain an officer's patent. Education was now the gateway and the sons of the petit bourgeoisie and, in certain cases of the artisan classes, were accepted—so long as they had the educational qualifications. Thus, within the span of a single lifetime the army's social tone changed completely from that of an aristocratic one to one that was essentially middle-class in origin and outlook. In addition to the aristocracy there was another group which had once supplied the Habsburg armies with officers but who, after 1870, no longer came forward. These were the men from the principalities and duchies of Germany who had enlisted with Habsburg in the past because battle experience and preferment came more easily in a major army, such as that of Austria, than in the smaller military forces of their own divided fatherland. With the proclamation of the German Empire in 1870, those keen and able officers no longer needed to serve Austria, but could use their skills and talents in the new German Army.

Those immediate shortages, coupled with the likelihood that when the army did expand to its full strength there might be an insufficient number of officers, caused concern that standard methods of officer recruiting would not produce the numbers of men who would be required. A regular and continuing flow of officer material could only be maintained by preparing

more candidates in a greater number of special schools. The number of preparatory and cadet institutions was increased. A pupil entered one of the junior preparatory schools at Koszeg, Fischau, Strass, Enns, St Poelten or Maros-Vasarhely, between his tenth and twelfth year. From thence he passed into one of the senior preparatory schools for Common Army candidates at Kassa, Cracow, Kismaron, Marburg, Maehrisch-Weisskirchen or Poszony. Pupils graduated from those institutions between the ages of fourteen and sixteen. At eighteen they entered a Military Academy: either the Maria Theresia for the non-technical arms of service or the Technical Academy at Moedling for artillery and engineer officers. Landwehr senior preparatory schools were located in Vienna or Sopron and the appropriate military academies were the Franz Joseph in Vienna and the Ludovice in Budapest.

Successful candidates graduated from one of those institutions and were gazetted, at the age of twenty-one, with the rank of second lieutenant.

Three-fifths of all army officer candidates were obtained from cadet schools, fourteen of which were reserved for Common Army pupils and three for the Landwehr. The graduates, having completed four years of study, entered the army as ensigns, a probationary grade which led to a second lieutenant's commission. Eleven of the fourteen Common Army cadet schools supplied ensigns for the non-technical arms of Service. Of the remaining three, Hainburg produced engineers; Traiskirchen the artillery ensigns; and Maehrisch-Weisskirchen those for the cavalry.

The newly commissioned officer was soon faced with a decision upon which his future career depended. He could either elect to remain with his regiment and very slowly ascend the ladder of military rank, or he could apply for a staff appointment. In a staff capacity he would never command men in the field, but he would certainly receive more rapid promotion than with the regiment. It was a difficult choice he had to make. Regimental officers could, in peacetime, expect to wait for years before promotion came. The general principle of promotion through seniority was followed for commissioned ranks up to that of a major. For lieutenant-colonels and up to the rank of major-general promotion was a combination of seniority and selection. The highest ranks of the military were filled entirely by selection. All promotions were the prerogative of the Emperor who could, but seldom did, promote officers out of turn.

As a general rule ensigns had a two-year probation to serve before promotion to commissioned rank, and second lieutenants then waited for a further four years to achieve full lieutenant status. The step up to captain rank was a further six or seven years away and captains had more than a decade to serve before promotion to major. There was then another five years' wait before achieving a lieutenant-colonelcy. In peacetime a regimental officer could not be promoted to the rank of captain until he had graduated from a course held at corps officers' school. To gain the rank of major he also had to pass an examination in tactical ability.

The grade of second lieutenant was eleventh in the twelve classes in the hierarchy of commissioned ranks. The twelfth grade was reserved for aspirant officers who were considered, until 1909, to be a form of superior non-commissioned officer. Officers were not only graded hierarchically but they were classified as being of either combatant or non-combatant status.

So now we have the freshly gazetted, peacetime officer, in a combatant arm of service, determined to serve in a regimental capacity and faced with the prospect of examinations preceding the promotions which would only come after years of service. Retirement and a pension waited either at the age of sixty or after the completion of forty years' service. Earlier retirement was permitted with the qualification that the officer made himself available for service in time of war. And what lay ahead for the new second lieutenant?

If he had no private means there would be years in which he would be the unwilling subject of the dreary virtues of poverty, chastity and obedience. Army pay was very low and left nothing over to pay for luxuries. The only financial enterprise in which an officer might engage was the sale of horses to his brother officers. Chastity would be enforced by the fact that the number of married officers on the strength of a regiment was severely limited and marriage, while still a junior officer, required that either the officer was rich

Below

The Colour of the Maria Theresia Military Academy being paraded during a passing out ceremony. The NCO cadet, who is serving here as the Ensign, is wearing Infantry pattern parade dress. The officer on the right is a Field Officer of a Hussar regiment of the Common Army. The Field Officer nearest the camera is from an Infantry unit. Note the difference between the Infantry and the Cavalry methods of holding their swords.

The Emperor Franz Joseph at the Imperial manoeuvres in Bohemia, 1912.

enough or that the parents put up a very large marriage bond—a sort of male dowry.

The tasks facing the newly commissioned officer were daunting. He was expected to be the ambassador of his country, a standard bearer of its culture, an example of soldierly virtues to his men and a credit to the service. An officer serving in a regiment made up of his own countrymen encountered only the usual problems, but if he had been posted to a unit whose language he did not understand, he would have to master the new tongue if he was to communicate with his men, for it was part of Austrian military law that every soldier had the right to have his problems dealt with by a superior officer who spoke his language. Regimental officers had to learn the language of the men in their companies within three years and as an example of how difficult this might be, the 29th Infantry Regiment of the Common Army was made up of 35% Serbs, 30% German/Austrians, 20% Magyars and 15% Roumanians.

In each regiment there was an official regimental language. That was the language spoken by the greatest number of its soldiers. Units which had a high proportion of other national groupings, as for example the 29th Regiment, had a second or even a third official regimental language. It has been calculated that from all the units on the Common Army establishment only 142 had a single regimental language; 163 had two; twenty-four units had three languages; and in a few there were four, or even five, spoken. In the Landwehr only nineteen units had one regimental language. Forty-two had two and one had three regimental languages. Such a problem did not arise in the Landwehr (Honved) where either Magyar or Croat were spoken as the official and also as the regimental languages.

Newly commissioned officers swearing the oath of allegiance before proceeding on active service, Vienna 1914.

The language of command in the Common Army and in the Austrian Landwehr was German. In the Common Army each non-German recruit was taught a basic vocabulary of eighty German words which covered the commands used in drill, in musketry and on manoeuvres.

It does not need to be stressed that an army composed of men of so many races and speaking so many different tongues is harder to train and to lead than an homogenous force. It follows, then, that the officers of such a polyglot army have to be more than usually able if they are to produce efficient, potent regiments and the officers of Franz Joseph's were very, very able.

Officers at a race meeting in Vienna, 1910.

Newly commissioned officers of a military academy at the passing out parade. Among the uniforms can be seen those of Hussars, Dragoons, Jaeger and Line Infantry, 1913.

Regimental officers dining out in the Prater, Vienna c1900.

Procurement of horses for the Army

Austria-Hungary, in common with the military forces of the world, was tied to horse power when on active service. Austria's geographical position in Central Europe, coupled with the Empire's extensive efficient railway network, allowed whole armies to be moved rapidly within the homeland. Once at the front, however, the movement of guns, waggons and supplies depended almost completely upon horses and mules.

In order to ensure that the service had sufficient cattle for its needs, a ten-yearly census was made and the findings of the one completed just before the outbreak of the First World War showed that there were over four million horses in the Empire. One million six hundred thousand of those met the high standards demanded by the military.

Efforts which had begun as early as 1867 to improve the quality and breeding of horses for the service resulted in the setting up of ten stud farms in Austria, Bosnia and Hungary, together with thirteen stallion depots and a number of foal stations.

In peacetime each of the three army administrations procured the cattle it required: the Common Army through a General Remount Inspectorate; and the Landwehr and Landwehr (Honved) through local purchasing commissions. Those several organisations obtained approximately 40% of the beasts required, the balance being made up from horse fairs or by direct purchase by the regiments.

The height standards were:

Riding horses	..	..	158-165cms
Artillery riding horses		..	155-160cms
Mountain units	..	..	142-155cms
Draught horses	..	..	161-170cms
Foals ..	..	..	155-166cms
Pack Animals	..	..	148-153cms

Usually, foals were bought in the spring and fully grown horses in the autumn. The latter were purchased between 4½ and 7 years of age and entered regimental service immediately, but foals, generally bought when 3 years old, were held until the age of 4 to 4½ before joining a unit. A riding horse was expected to give a maximum of eight years' service and a draught animal ten years. To maintain the level in trained animals, regiments were allowed to cast off, annually, 10% of their riding horses and

Mountain artillery gun broken down into loads for pack animals.

12% of their draught cattle. There was, therefore, a flow of beasts entering and leaving the Service.

Chargers were issued at public expense to certain junior officers of the cavalry, artillery and train. Other officers bought their own mounts. In peacetime a government-issue horse became the personal property of its officer after six years' service.

Horses which were cast off when their period of service with the regiment had been completed, were sold to civilians who were legally required to return the beasts for certain short periods of training. In peacetime horses which had been ex-regimental for more than six years stayed in civilian ownership but on general mobilisation all animals were returned to the army.

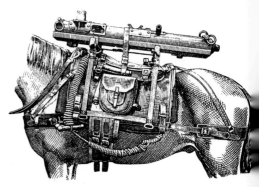

The military authorities soon appreciated that a large reserve would be required in time of war. The estimated establishment of 300,000 beasts was considered inadequate to meet all the demands that war would make upon the service. A law passed in 1912 ordered the registration of all horses for military use. Civilian owners of conscripted beasts were offered a price, set at 10% above the calculated value of the animal. Owners of horses passed fit for service were given a docket which bore the animal's description, its price, medical category and the place to which it was to be brought in time of war.

Common Army horses were branded on the left side of the body: the neck with the purchase number; at the saddle with the number of the military Commission and on the left buttock with the regimental brand. The latter was a capital letter set above the regiment's Army List number. Thus the capital letter D set above the number 15, indicated a beast on the strength of the 15th Regiment of Dragoons. The branding of reversed crowns on the right buttock and neck of Common Army beasts indicated a cast-off animal.

Landwehr and Landwehr (Honved) beasts bore all their brand marks on the left side of the body: the purchase number and regimental brand on the neck and the cast-off brand on the buttock.

During the war a critical shortage of animal feeding stuffs brought about a severe reduction in the number of horses on the army establishment. The stabilisation of the combat zone into trench warfare and the consequent change in the role of cavalry enabled the military planners, initially, to lower the establishments in mounted regiments and, finally, to dismount most of the remainder. Surplus horses were then dispersed to areas where there was sufficient grazing for their needs or were returned to farms for agricultural purposes. The best cattle were handed over to the artillery army which was undergoing a considerable expansion.

Laws regulating waggons, saddlery and pack animal equipment had also been passed in 1912, under which carts and beasts were liable for compulsory purchase in time of war. Lists of available carts were drawn up by local authorities and in many cases the locally purchased vehicles were accompanied by their civilian drivers. These were paid on a daily rate and were not conscripted for any form of military service.

2·Supreme Command and the Staff

|||||||||||||||||||||||||||||||||||||||||||||||||||||||||||||||||||||||||||||||||||||||||||||||||

Supreme Command and the Staff

|||||||||||||||||||||||||||||||||||||||||||||||||||||||||||||||||||||||||||||||||||||||||||||||||||||

In the late decades of the 19th century it became clear that a revolution had occurred in battlefield control. In future wars masses of men would be involved and battles would be fought over vast areas. Direct control of military operations would then no longer be exercised, as it had been in former days, by a Supreme Commander viewing the battle from a hilltop and issuing orders through relays of mounted couriers. The scale of war would no longer be restricted to battles fought in daylight hours and lasting only a few days. Wars had become long and complex struggles.

As a result of its own sad experiences in 1866, the Austrian Army changed its attitude towards the staff, its officers and the qualifications which were required to serve on it. Those who elected to serve, or who were called to serve, in a staff capacity were expected to achieve a high standard of professionalism and those who could not meet the challenge were rejected. The fruits of those changes can best be seen in the military performance of General Conrad von Hoetzendorff, Chief of the General Staff of the Austro-Hungarian Army. He was considered by many to be the finest strategist of the First World War. Two other Austrian officers; Hoffmann and Krauss were held to be the most competent corps commanders in the armies of the central powers. The officers of the Imperial General Staff demonstrated their fluency and ability when, in the first weeks of the First World War, they changed the thrust line of a quarter of the entire field force from south-eastwards towards Serbia to eastwards against Russia.

The task of a General Staff is to plan, train, organise and supply the national army so that it is always ready to fight and win a war. The Chief of the General Staff, who directs the operations which he has planned, does so through teams of executive officers who control various staffs and Arms of Service. But he, himself, although Chief of the General Staff, is also a subordinate.

By tradition, the Emperor of Austria, as the first soldier of the Empire, led his armies in person in the field but at the outbreak of war in 1914, Franz Joseph felt himself too old to shoulder the burden. He delegated that authority to the Archduke Friedrich who carried it until Karl became Emperor in 1916 and took upon himself the power of the highest war lord.

In peacetime the Monarch was advised on military affairs by the Chief of the General Staff, just as in wartime his approval was needed for the strategic plans which that officer laid before him. The chain of command flowed from the Sovereign through a military chancellery which, although

The Archduke Louis Salvator (dark overcoat), and General Conrad von Hoetzendorff, Chief of the General Staff.

Field Marshal The Archduke Friedrich, who took over command of the Armies in the Field in 1914, wearing the grey field service dress.

it had neither power nor authority, acted and legislated as the Emperor directed. The Chief of the General Staff was a member of that military chancellery and was directly responsible to the Emperor and not to any political body.

The tripartite military organisation of the Habsburg forces required a triple staff system and, therefore, a greater than usual number of liaison officers, committees and advisory boards. Although the three forces, Common Army, Landwehr and Landwehr (Honved), became a single body in time of war, the Austrian and Hungarian Defence Ministers were active in the interest of their own respective forces and, in the case of the Magyars, often obstructive to the demands of the Supreme Command.

The Chief of the General Staff exercised direct control over a body made up of four parallel sections or departments. These were sub-divided. The first of the main departments, for example, contained eight sub-sections, the most important of which was the small secretariat which controlled the working of the whole General Staff. A second sub-section dealt with planning and operations. A third was the cadre around which, in wartime, the Quarter Master General's Department would be formed. There were other sub-sections in that first department which dealt with training, military cartography, Intelligence, railways and telegraphs.

The second of the four parallel sections was made up of members of the

Monarch's personal staff and officers who liaised with the several army inspectors, the Imperial War Ministry, with the two national Army Ministries (the Landwehr and the Landwehr (Honved) and with other senior command groups.

The third parallel was the Training Section, while the fourth dealt with officers' postings and with the staffs of military academies.

In addition to the General Staff which dealt with the army generally, there were other specialist, technical artillery, engineer and adjutant staffs. The first two are self-evident but the third group needs to be explained. The adjutants' branch was large and hierarchical, for there were such officers at every level of command. Due to its tripartite structure the Imperial Service needed a greater than usual number of liaison officers, aides and adjutants. The group was divided into general adjutants, senior (flugel) adjutants, personal aides-de-camp and orderly officers. The Sovereign had a number of general adjutants on his staff. Certain senior (flugel) adjutants served with the higher command groups. Other flugel adjutants were on the staff of the heir to the throne, on the staff of the Minister for War, the Chief of the General Staff, with the army inspectors general and, in time of war, with the individual army commanders and/or the army group commanders.

Personal aides-de-camp or adjutants liaised with the Common Army, the Landwehr and the Landwehr (Honved), with the Chief of the General Staff, the army inspectors and the corps commanders. Orderly officers, the final category of the special staffs, served with the Landwehr High Command, the Landwehr (Honved) Defence Minister and at senior command levels in time of war.

The command structures of the two Landwehr organisations were, of course, less extensive than that of the Common Army, but did include staff officers with the tasks of ensuring that their respective forces were trained and equipped ready for war.

Mention has been made that the military organisation of the Austro-

The Archduke Karl and members of his staff at Divine Service. One of the standard features of life in the Imperial Army was open air Mass.

Opposite page
Above
Major General Franz Ritter von Hofer-Feldsturm, Deputy Chief of the General Staff, 1914.

Below
Field Marshal Josef Radetz von Radetzky.

Hungarian Army was based on corps. There was no peacetime establishment for any superior group *ie,* an army or army group structure. Regulations did exist and cadre staffs were held around which armies could be formed in time of war. The General Staff plan of battle foresaw a field force of six armies, whose commanders would be the inspectors general, five of whom were stationed in Vienna and the sixth in Sarajevo. This latter officer also headed the provincial government as well as holding the post of General Officer Commanding troops in Bosnia, Hergezovina and Dalmatia.

Upon general mobilisation those army cadres would be activated, each army headquarters coming to full strength and becoming a miniature of the Supreme Command structure. The headquarters of those six armies were located in Vienna (1st Army), Budapest (2nd Army), Pozsony (3rd Army), Vienna (4th Army), Agram (5th Army) and Sarajevo (6th Army).

From a strength of six armies made up of sixteen corps, controlling forty-nine infantry and eleven cavalry divisions, the Austro-Hungarian Army was to expand, during the First World War, to a mighty force of nine armies with twenty-six corps, controlling seventy-one divisions. What this represented was the equivalent of raising, organising, training and equipping an almost completely new field army, each major unit of which required its own staff structure. Thanks to the excellence of peacetime training, whereby a staff officer was always qualified to take over the next senior post, even though he might never attain it, the commanders and staffs which were required were always found. There were occasional temporary shortages and these were aggravated by the fact that many young staff officers volunteered for front-line service. The longer the war lasted so much greater did the need become for trained and efficient staff officers to control the huge field armies, and that need was always met.

The personality of a commander shapes the army which he leads. It reflects his attitudes, decisiveness and devotion to duty. The history of the Habsburg Army contains the names of many famous soldiers who had once led it to resounding successes in war or who, in defeat, had reorganised the shattered hosts. Commanders such as Eugene of Savoy, Schwarzenberg, The Archduke John, Radetzky and the Archduke Albrecht are familiar, but the military ability of, perhaps, the greatest Chief of Staff, Conrad von Hoetzendorff, is less well-known. Yet, in the greatest war in Austria's long history it was his strategic plans which directed, his military genius which guided the Austro-Hungarian Army for the greatest part of that war.

As commander of 8th Infantry Division, Conrad demonstrated new tactical ideas on operations in alpine regions; a branch of study which had been almost totally neglected and his handling of that Division in the pre-war Imperial manoeuvres had brought him to the attention of Franz Ferdinand, the Inspector General of the Army. In November 1906, Conrad was promoted Chief of Staff and became aware that the army was totally unprepared for that war which in his opinion was inevitable. He set about making good past neglect and demanded a field army of seventy divisions, backed by a reserve force similar to that of the German Army. The money which would have raised twenty-two divisions and fourteen mountain brigades could not be made available to the army. It had been allocated to the navy and Conrad saw the funds, which might have created major units for the defence of the whole Empire, used to build a single squadron of naval dreadnoughts.

There were, however, steps that could be taken without the expenditure of vast sums of money. Conrad determined to improve the physical condition of the soldiers so that they would be able to bear the rigours of war and he introduced battle realism into manoeuvres. These mock battles were fought as closely as possible to actual combat conditions and Conrad made demands upon the men, their officers and the staff similar to those strains that active service would impose. He went on to improve battlefield tactics by stressing the importance of close support between the infantry and the artillery. In the field of alpine warfare he was personally responsible for the fact that Austria-Hungary had the best mountain troop organisation of any army.

Conrad's political realism made him see Austria as being surrounded by an enemy ring which might be broken by a pre-emptive blow. During 1911, Italy was engaged in a war in Tripoli and he proposed striking at the troublesome Latin neighbour. In those proposals for a pre-emptive war Franz Joseph saw a threat to his own prerogative as a maker of policy and removed Conrad from office. But those views were not his alone and his successor, Schema, had no hesitation in telling the Emperor that the monarchy was already at war and that only the formal declaration was lacking. Slav victories in the Balkan Wars then revived the menace of Serbia and during the new European crisis of 1912, the Emperor reinstated Conrad as Chief of Staff.

While working on his war plans Conrad was aware that the army was not strong enough to fight a two-front war and concluded that of the potential Slav enemies, Serbia would be the easier to defeat. He planned to destroy the Balkan enemy before Russia could fully mobilise. Then, relying upon Austria's interior lines he would switch eastwards those forces which had gained victory over the Serbs. On the Eastern front they, together with the remainder of the Imperial army, would strike the Russian colossus.

In 1914, two major power blocs confronted each other in Europe. One was made up of the Entente: France, Russia and Britain together with those small nations with whom the major powers had treaty obligations. The second bloc was that of the central powers: Austria-Hungary, Germany, Italy and Roumania. The background to war, the paths which led to the outbreak of hostilities cannot be developed here, nor can we delineate those intrigues by which Italy and Roumania ceased to be the allies of Austria and Germany and became instead their active enemies. Let it be enough to say that the assassination in Sarajevo on 28 June 1914 of the Archduke Franz Ferdinand provided the pretext for war. Austria issued an ultimatum to which Serbia gave no satisfactory reply. A partial mobilisation by Austria was followed by the order for general mobilisation. Only days later Europe was at war.

Under the order for general mobilisation those troops who were to undertake the campaign against Russia moved forward to their concentration areas, but a new political crisis then developed. Roumania refused to support Austria against Russia and would not deploy her army. There was now a gap on the right flank of the Austrian armies on the Eastern Front and to block this Conrad was forced to switch 2nd Army away from Serbia and towards the Russian Front. It was a brilliantly successful piece of staff work, unparalleled in the history of modern warfare.

The Russian battle plan was for a descent by the southern wing upon the heartlands of the Austrian Empire through the passes in the Carpathian mountains together with a simultaneous assault by the northern wing upon East Prussia. As a reserve to those Russian field armies in the north and in the south, there were two other forces grouped, centrally, near Warsaw, whose

Conrad von Hoetzendorff, Chief of the General Staff, in conversation with The Archduke Franz Ferdinand, Tirol 1912.

task it was to exploit any breakthrough by either of the attacking army groups.

Conrad, who anticipated the Russian strategy, planned to counter it by advancing eastwards into enemy territory as fast and as far as he could. He intended to smash the Russian armies during their approach to battle operation, that is before they had been deployed for battle. Together with Moltke, the German Commander-in-Chief, Conrad drew up a plan of campaign for the Eastern Front, in which both Austrian and German forces would be used. He was aware that the demands of the Schlieffen plan, the all-out attack upon France, would commit the greatest part of the German Army to fight in the west, but was assured by Moltke that the defeat of France was a matter of weeks. Perhaps six weeks was the German Commander-in-Chief's optimistic assessment of how long the campaign against France and Britain would last. Once France was defeated the German Army would turn around and the combined forces of Germany and Austria-Hungary would then go on to defeat the Russian masses.

The Eastern Front battle plan was scrapped by Moltke when the Schlieffen Plan failed to achieve its objectives. France was not defeated. The help promised by Moltke to Conrad was reduced to a single corps and that of German Landwehr. Undeterred by this betrayal, Conrad thrust his 1st and 4th Armies between the Bug and the Vistula rivers, while 3rd and 2nd Armies protected the flank of the advance. The Austro-Hungarian offensive struck two Russian armies and shattered them, but a Russian counter-attack then drove back Conrad's flank armies. A series of vast and bitter battles was fought and although the Imperial forces had to withdraw into western Galicia, the Russian plan to drive into Austria's eastern regions had been thwarted. But the cost of that effort was high. The Austro-Hungarian Army had been sacrificed.

To refill the depleted ranks there was a frantic expansion of the army, but this was carried out on an ad hoc basis and not according to the plans which had been made. One positive aspect was that the armed forces were released from the financial restraints imposed by civilians and there were no longer any restrictions on conscription for the forces.

There were, however, new problems to meet and to overcome. There was as much need for men in the factories and on the farms as there was to man the battle line. The efficient use of the available manpower and the organisation of the Empire's industrial potential was not begun until very late in the war, by which time the effects of the allied blockade had brought about shortages and deprivation. Even the use of soldiers to gather in the harvest and the capture of the grain-producing regions of the Ukraine could not maintain adequate food supplies to the civil population and to the army. Starvation brought about revolution. But all those dark events lay in the future. The end of 1914 saw the Imperial Army coiling itself in Galicia ready to spring forward again as soon as campaigning weather allowed it to resume the offensive against the Russian enemy.

3·Major Formations of the Army

Corps and Divisions
Infantry and Cavalry

Order of Battle 1905

Corps and Divisions

For recruiting purposes the Empire was divided into sixteen territorial military districts each of which raised an Army Corps consisting principally of troops raised within that district. The XV Corps was the exception to that rule for its area held troops furnished from the district of other Corps.

Eight of the military Corps areas were in Austria, six of them were in Hungary, one in Bosnia-Herzegovina and one in Dalmatia.

Corps	Headquarters	Recruited in
I	Cracow	Western Galicia, Silesia and northern Moravia
II	Vienna	Lower Austria and southern Moravia
III	Graz	Styria, Carinthia, Carniola, Istria, Goerz.
IV	Budapest	Central and south-western Hungary
V	Pozsony	Western Hungary
VI	Kassa	North-eastern Hungary
VII	Temesvar	Central and southern Hungary
VIII	Prague	South-western Bohemia
IX	Leitmeritz	North-eastern Bohemia
X	Przemysl	Central Galicia
XI	Lemberg	Eastern Galicia and the Bukovina
XII	Nagyszeben	South-eastern Hungary
XIII	Agram	Croatia, Slavonia and Fiume
XIV	Innsbruck	Tirol, Vorarlberg, Upper Austria, Salzburg
XV	Sarajevo	Bosnia and Herzegovina
XVI	Ragusa	Dalmatia

Listed below are the infantry and cavalry divisions which were on the peacetime establishment or which were raised during 1914.

INFANTRY

1st Common Army	Sarajevo	7th Common Army	Esseg
2nd Common Army	Jaroslau	8th Common Army	Bozen
3rd Common Army	Linz	9th Common Army	Prague
4th Common Army	Bruenn	10th Common Army	Josephstadt
5th Common Army	Olmuetz	11th Common Army	Lemberg
6th Common Army	Graz	12th Common Army	Cracow

13th Landwehr	Vienna
14th Common Army	Pozsony
15th Common Army	Miskolcz
16th Common Army	Nagyszeben
17th Common Army	Nagy Varad
18th Common Army	Mostar
19th Common Army	Pilsen
20th Landwehr (Honved)	Nagy Varad
21st Landwehr	Prague
22nd Landwehr	Graz
23rd Landwehr (Honved)	Szeged
24th Common Army	Przemysl
25th Common Army	Vienna
26th Landwehr	Leitmeritz
27th Common Army	Kassa
28th Common Army	Laibach
29th Common Army	Theresienstadt
30th Common Army	Lemberg
31st Common Army	Budapest
32nd Common Army	Budapest
33rd Common Army	Kormaron
34th Common Army	Temesvar
35th Common Army	Kolozsvar
36th Common Army	Agram
37th Landwehr (Honved)	Pozsony
38th Landwehr (Honved)	Kolozsvar
39th Landwehr (Honved)	Kassa
40th Landwehr (Honved)	Budapest
41st Landwehr (Honved)	Budapest
42nd Landwehr (Honved)	Agram
43rd Landwehr	Czernowitz
44th Landwehr	Innsbruck
45th Landwehr	Przemysl
46th Landwehr	Cracow
47th Common Army	Castelnuovo
48th Common Army	Sarajevo
49th Common Army	Broken up at the outbreak of war.
50th Common Army	Raised October 1914
51st Landwehr (Honved)	Raised October 1914
52nd Common Army	Raised October 1914
53rd Common Army	Raised October 1914
54th Common Army	Raised October 1914

55th Common Army	Raised October 1914
56th Common Army	Raised October 1914
95th Landsturm	Raised August 1914
106th Landsturm	Raised August 1914

CAVALRY

1st Common Army	Temesvar
2nd Common Army	Pozsony
3rd Common Army	Vienna
4th Common Army	Lemberg
5th Landwehr (Honved)	Budapest
6th Common Army	Jaroslau
7th Common Army	Cracow
8th Common Army	Stanislau
9th Common Army	Prague
10th Common Army	Budapest
11th Landwehr (Honved)	Debreczen

Lieutenant General Josef Roth, one of the finest Corps commanders.

Order of Battle of the Army 1905

COMMON ARMY DIVISIONS

I CORPS (Cracow)

5th Infantry Division

9th Infantry Brigade (Olmutz)
54th, 93rd Infantry Regts
5th Feldjaeger Bn

10th Infantry Brigade (Troppau)
1st, 18th Infantry Regts
16th Feldjaeger Bn

12th Infantry Division

23rd Infantry Brigade (Cracow)
13th, 56th Infantry Regts
13th Feldjaeger Bn

24th Infantry Brigade (Cracow)
20th, 57th, 100th Infantry Regts

Cracow Cavalry Division

11th Cavalry Brigade (Tarnow)
12th Dragoon Regt
2nd Ulan Regt

20th Cavalry Brigade (Cracow)
3rd, 10th Dragoon Regts

1st Artillery Brigade (Cracow)
I Corps Artillery Regt
1st, 2nd, 3rd Divisional Artillery Regts

II CORPS (Vienna)

4th Infantry Division

7th Infantry Brigade (Znaim)
81st, 99th Infantry Regts

8th Infantry Brigade (Brunn)
8th, 49th Infantry Regts
4th Bn 3rd Infantry Regt

25th Infantry Division

49th Infantry Brigade (Vienna)
84th Infantry Regt
Three battalions of 1st Bosnia-Herzegovinian Infantry Regt
Bosnia-Herzegovinian Feldjaeger Bn

50th Infantry Brigade (Vienna)
4th Infantry Regt
4th Bosnia-Herzegovinian Infantry Regt
21st Feldjaeger Bn

47th Infantry Division

93rd Infantry Brigade (Vienna)
60th, 72nd Infantry Regts
17th Feldjaeger Bn

94th Infantry Brigade (Vienna)
6th, 51st, 101st Infantry Regts

Vienna Cavalry Division

8th Cavalry Brigade (Brunn)
11th, 15th Dragoon Regts

10th Cavalry Brigade (Vienna)
5th Dragoon Regt
3rd Ulan Regt

17th Cavalry Brigade (Vienna)
6th Dragoon Regt (detached to XIV Corps)
4th Hussar Regt

2nd Artillery Brigade (Vienna)
II Corps Artillery Regt

4th, 5th, 6th Divisional Artillery Regts
1st Fortress Artillery Regt (2nd and 3rd Bns only)

14th Artillery Brigade (Vienna)
XIV Corps Artillery Regt
40th Divisional Artillery Regt (on temporary attachment to II Corps)
41st and 42nd Divisional Artillery Regts

III CORPS (Graz)

6th Infantry Division

11th Infantry Brigade (Graz)
7th Infantry Regt
2nd Bosnia-Herzegovinian Regt

12th Infantry Brigade (Klagenfurt)
17th Infantry Regt
7th, 8th, 9th, 20th Feldjaeger Bns

28th Infantry Division

55th Infantry Brigade (Trieste)
87th, 97th Infantry Regts

56th Infantry Brigade (Laibach)
27th, 47th Infantry Regts

3rd Cavalry Brigade (Marburg)
4th Dragoon Regt
6th Hussar Regt
5th Ulan Regt
(on temporary attachment to XIII Corps)

3rd Artillery Brigade (Graz)
III Corps Artillery Regt
7th, 8th, 9th Divisional Artillery Regts

IV CORPS (Budapest)

31st Infantry Division

61st Infantry Brigade (Budapest)
44th, 52nd Infantry Regts

62nd Infantry Brigade (Budapest)
69th Infantry Regt
3rd Bosnia-Herzegovinian Infantry Regt
24th Feldjaeger Bn

32nd Infantry Division

63rd Infantry Brigade (Budapest)
23rd, 38th Infantry Regts
2nd Bn of 6th Infantry Regt

64th Infantry Brigade (Budapest)
32nd, 86th Infantry Regts
1st Bn of 68th Infantry Regt

4th Cavalry Brigade (Budapest)
8th, 16th Hussar Regts
12th Ulan Regt

4th Artillery Brigade (Budapest)
IV Corps Artillery Regt
10th, 11th, 12th Divisional Artillery Regts
2nd Bn 6th Fortress Artillery Regt

V CORPS (Pozsony)

14th Infantry Division

27th Infantry Brigade (Pozsony)
71st Infantry Regt
2nd Bn of 72nd Infantry Regt

28th Infantry Brigade (Sopron)
48th, 76th Infantry Regts

33rd Infantry Division

65th Infantry Brigade (Gyor)
19th, 26th Infantry Regts
19th Feldjaeger Bn

66th Infantry Brigade (Komarom)
83rd Infantry Regt
4th Bn of 12th Infantry Regt
11th Feldjaeger Bn

16th Cavalry Brigade (Pozsony)
5th, 9th, 11th Hussar Regts

5th Artillery Brigade (Pozsony)
V Corps Artillery Regt
13th, 14th, 15th Divisional Artillery Regts
Headquarters and 1st Bn No 6 Fortress Artillery Regt

VI CORPS (Kassa)

15th Infantry Division

29th Infantry Brigade (Ungvar)
5th, 66th Infantry Regts

30th Infantry Brigade (Miskolcz)
65th Infantry Regt
3rd Bn of 60th Infantry Regt

27th Infantry Division

53rd Infantry Brigade (Kassa)
25th, 34th Infantry Regts
32nd Feldjaeger Bn

54th Infantry Brigade (Eperjes)
67th, 85th Infantry Regts

6th Cavalry Brigade (Miskolcz)
14th, 15th Hussar Regts

6th Artillery Brigade (Kassa)
VI Corps Artillery Regt
16th, 17th, 18th Divisional Artillery Regts

VII CORPS (Temesvar)

17th Infantry Division

33rd Infantry Brigade (Nagyvarad)
37th, 39th Infantry Regts

34th Infantry Brigade (Arad)
33rd Infantry Regt
1st Bn of 61st Infantry Regt

34th Infantry Division

67th Infantry Brigade (Temesvar)
29th Infantry Regt
3rd Bn of 101 Infantry Regt

68th Infantry Brigade (Fehertemplon)
43rd, 46th Infantry Regts

7th Cavalry Brigade (Temesvar)
7th, 12th Hussar Regts

7th Artillery Brigade (Temesvar)
VII Corps Artillery Regt
19th, 20th, 21st Divisional Artillery Regts

VIII CORPS (Prague)

9th Infantry Division

17th Infantry Brigade (Prague)
91st, 102nd Infantry Regts

18th Infantry Brigade (Prague)
11th, 73rd Infantry Regts

19th Infantry Division

37th Infantry Brigade (Pilsen)
35th Infantry Regt

4th Bn of 88th Infantry Regt
6th, 22nd Feldjaeger Bns

38th Infantry Brigade (Budweis)
28th, 75th Infantry Regts
13th Dragoons Regt (on temporary detachment from IX Corps Cavalry Brigade)

8th Artillery Brigade (Prague)
VIII Corps Artillery Regt
22nd, 23rd, 24th Divisional Artillery Regts

IX CORPS (Leitheritz)

10th Infantry Division

19th Infantry Brigade (Leitheritz)
36th, 98th Infantry Regts

20th Infantry Brigade (Koeniggratz)
21st, 42nd Infantry Regts
2nd Feldjaeger Bn

29th Infantry Division

57th Infantry Brigade (Theresienstadt)
92nd, 94th Infantry Regts

58th Infantry Brigade (Reichenberg)
74th Infantry Regt
2nd Bn of 18th Infantry Regt
12th Feldjaeger Bn

9th Cavalry Brigade (Pardubitz)
7th Dragoon Regt
13th Dragoon Regt (temporarily attached to VIII Corps)

9th Artillery Brigade (Leitheritz)
IX Corps Artillery Regt
25th, 26th, 27th Divisional Artillery Regts

X CORPS (Przemysl)

2nd Infantry Division

3rd Infantry Brigade (Rzeszow)
40th, 90th Infantry Regts
4th Feldjaeger Bn

4th Infantry Brigade (Jaroslau)
10th, 89th Infantry Regts

24th Infantry Division

47th Infantry Brigade (Przemysl)
9th, 45th Infantry Regts

48th Infantry Brigade (Przemysl)
58th, 77th Infantry Regts

Jaroslau Cavalry Division

5th Cavalry Brigade (Jaroslau)
8th Dragoon Regt
3rd, 13th Hussar Regts

14th Cavalry Brigade (Rzeszow)
1st Dragoon Regt
6th Ulan Regt

10th Artillery Brigade (Przemysl)
X Corps Artillery Regt
28th, 29th, 30th Divisional Artillery Regts

XI CORPS (Lemberg)

11th Infantry Division

21st Infantry Brigade (Lemberg)
15th, 80th Infantry Regts

22nd Infantry Brigade (Lemberg)
30th Infantry Regt
1st, 25th, 30th Feldjaeger Bns

30th Infantry Division

59th Infantry Brigade (Lemberg)
24th, 41st Infantry Regts
1st Bn of 58th Infantry Regt
29th Feldjaeger Bn

60th Infantry Brigade
55th, 95th Infantry Regts
23rd Feldjaeger Bn

Lemberg Cavalry Division

18th Cavalry Brigade (Zloczow)
9th Dragoon Regt
13 Ulan Regt

21st Cavalry Brigade (Lemberg)
4th, 7th Ulan Regts

Stanislau Cavalry Division

13th Cavalry Brigade (Stanislau)
14th Dragoon Regt
10th Hussar Regt
1st Ulan Regt

15th Cavalry Brigade (Tarnopol)
2nd Dragoon Regt
8th Ulan Regt

11th Artillery Brigade (Lemberg)
XI Corps Artillery Regt
31st, 32nd, 33rd Divisional Artillery Regts

XII CORPS (Nagyszeben)

16th Infantry Division

31st Infantry Brigade (Brasso)
50th Infantry Regt
4th Bn of 51st Infantry Regt

33rd Infantry Brigade (Nagyszeben)
2nd Infantry Regt
1st Bn of 63rd Infantry Regt
28th Feldjaeger Bn

35th Infantry Division

69th Infantry Brigade (Gyulafehervar)
31st, 64th Infantry Regts

70th Infantry Brigade (Kolozsvar)
62nd, 82nd Infantry Regts

12th Cavalry Brigade (Nagyszeben)
1st, 2nd Hussar Regt

12th Artillery Brigade (Nagyszeben)
XII Corps Artillery Regt
34th, 35th, 36th Divisional Artillery Regts

XIII CORPS (Agram)

7th Infantry Division

13th Infantry Brigade (Esseg)
53rd, 78th Infantry Regts

14th Infantry Brigade (Peterwardein)
61st, 70th Infantry Regts

36th Infantry Division

71st Infantry Brigade (Fiume)
79th, 96th Infantry Regts

72nd Infantry Brigade (Agram)
16th Infantry Regt
31st Feldjaeger Bn
5th Ulan Regt (on detachment from III Corps Cavalry Brigade)

13th Artillery Brigade (Agram)
XIII Corps Artillery Regt
37th, 38th, 39th Divisional Artillery Regts

XIV CORPS (Innsbruck)

3rd Infantry Division

5th Infantry Brigade (Linz)
59th Infantry Reft
1st Bn of 14th Infantry Regt

6th Infantry Brigade (Salzburg)
4th Regt Tiroler Kaiserjaeger
10th Feldjaeger Bn

8th Infantry Division

15th Infantry Brigade (Innsbruck)
14th Infantry Regt
1st Regt Tiroler Kaiserjaeger

16th Infantry Brigade (Trient)
88th Infantry Regt
2nd, 3rd Regts Tiroler Kaiserjaeger
6th Dragoon Regt (on detachment from II Corps)
40th, 41st Divisional Artillery Regts (on detachment from II Corps)

Artillery Command (Innsbruck)
Mountain Battery Half Regt
Headquarters and No 2 Company of 1st Fortress Artillery Bn

XV CORPS (Sarajevo)

1st Infantry Division

7th Mountain Brigade (Sarajevo)
2nd Bn of 11th Infantry Regt
4th Bn of 21st Infantry Regt
3rd Bn of 1st Bosnia-Herzegovinian Infantry Regt

8th Mountain Brigade (Foca)
2nd Bn of 25th Infantry Regt
1st Bn of 26th Infantry Regt
2nd Bn of 78th Infantry Regt

9th Mountain Brigade (Plevlje)
63rd Infantry Regt
1st Bn of 5th Infantry Regt
4th Bn of 86th Infantry Regt

10th Mountain Brigade (Sarajevo)

68th Infantry Regt
1st Squadron 12th Ulan, Regt

11th Mountain Brigade (Dolnja Tuzla)
2nd Bn of 23rd Infantry Regt
1st Bn of 66th Infantry Regt
3rd Bn of 3rd Bosnia-Herzegovinian Infantry Regt
1st Squadron 11th Dragoon Regt

12th Mountain Brigade (Banja Luka)
2nd Bn of 53rd Infantry Regt
4th Bn of 82nd Infantry Regt
3rd Bn of 2nd Bosnia-Herzegovinian Infantry Regt

18th Infantry Division

1st Mountain Brigade (Mostar)
3rd Infantry Regt
2nd Bn of 64th Infantry Regt
3rd Bn of 4th Bosnia-Herzegovinian Infantry Regt

2nd Mountain Brigade (Trebinje)
12th Infantry Regt

3rd Mountain Brigade (Nevesinje)
3rd Bn of 29th Infantry Regt
1st Bn of 36th Infantry Regt
3rd Bn of 96th Infantry Regt

6th Mountain Brigade (Bilek)
2nd Bn of 32nd Infantry Regt
2nd Bn of 52nd Infantry Regt
1st Bn of 69th Infantry Regt

Artillery Command (Sarajevo)
No 1 Command (four mountain batteries)
No 2 Command (three mountain batteries)
No 3 Command (four mountain batteries)
No 4 Command (four mountain batteries)

XVI CORPS (Ragusa)
At that time known as Territorial District Zara

4th Mountain Brigade (Cattaro)
3rd Bn of 22nd Infantry Regt
2nd Bn of 42nd Infantry Regt
4th Bn of 71st Infantry Regt
1st Bn of 73rd Infantry Regt

5th Mountain Brigade (Zara)
22nd Infantry Regt

LANDWEHR DIVISIONS

The recruiting districts of the Landwehr parallelled those of the Common Army and from them eight Landwehr Infantry Divisions were raised.

These are listed below, together with their constituent Brigades and Regiments.

I CORPS (Cracow)

46th Landwehr Infantry Division

91st Landwehr Infantry Brigade (Cracow)
16th, 31st, 32nd Landwehr Infantry Regts

92nd Landwehr Infantry Brigade (Olmütz)
13th, 15th Landwehr Infantry Regts
4th Ulan Regt

II CORPS (Vienna)

13th Landwehr Infantry Division

25th Landwehr Infantry Brigade (Vienna)
1st, 24th, Landwehr Infantry Regts

26th Landwehr Infantry Brigade (Brünn)
14th, 25th Landwehr Infantry Regts
5th Ulan Regt

III CORPS (Graz)

22nd Landwehr Infantry Division

43rd Landwehr Infantry Brigade (Graz)
3rd, 26th Landwehr Infantry Regts

44th Landwehr Infantry Brigade (Laibach)
4th, 5th, 27th Landwehr Infantry Regts

VIII CORPS (Prague)

21st Landwehr Infantry Division

41st Landwehr Infantry Brigade (Pilsen)
7th, 29th Landwehr Infantry Regts

42nd Landwehr Infantry Brigade (Prague)
6th, 8th, 28th Landwehr Infantry Regts

IX CORPS (Josephstadt)

26th Landwehr Infantry Division

51st Landwehr Infantry Brigade (Josephstadt)
11th, 12th, 30th Landwehr Infantry Regts

52nd Landwehr Infantry Brigade (Leitmeritz)
9th, 10th Landwehr Infantry Regts
2nd Ulan Regt

X CORPS (Przemysl)

45th Landwehr Infantry Division

89th Landwehr Infantry Brigade (Przemysl)
18th, 33rd Landwehr Infantry Regts

90th Landwehr Infantry Brigade (Jaroslau)
17th, 34th Landwehr Infantry Regts
3rd Ulan Regt

XI CORPS (Lemberg)

43rd Landwehr Infantry Division

85th Landwehr Infantry Brigade (Lemberg)
19th, 20th, 35th Landwehr Infantry Regts

86th Landwehr Infantry Brigade (Czernowitz)
22nd, 36th Landwehr Infantry Regts
1st Ulan Regt

XIV CORPS (Innsbruck)

44th Landwehr Infantry Division

87th Landwehr Infantry Brigade (Linz)
2nd, 21st Landwehr Infantry Regts

88th Landwehr Rifle Brigade (Innsbruck)
I and II Landwehr Rifle Regt (Landesschüetzen)
6th Ulan Regt
Half Regt Tirolean Mounted Rifles

General Freiherr von Georgi, the Austrian Defence Minister, in the undress uniform of a General Officer, 1914.

||||||||||||||||||||||||||||||||||||||||||||||||||||||||||||||||||||||||||||||||||||||||||||

LANDWEHR (HONVED) DIVISIONS

The Landwehr (Honved) recruited from seven districts. Their sub-division covered forty-seven of the forty-eight Common Army regimental areas. From those areas thirty-two Landwehr (Honved) regiments were raised. Fiume, the forty-eighth area, recruited for the Navy.

LANDWEHR (HONVED) DISTRICT No 1 (Budapest)

79th Landwehr (Honved) Infantry Brigade (Budapest)
1st and 2nd Landwehr (Honved) Infantry Regts

80th Landwehr (Honved) Infantry Brigade (Debreczen)
3rd and 4th Landwehr (Honved) Infantry Regts
1st and 2nd Landwehr (Honved) Hussar Regts

LANDWEHR (HONVED) DISTRICT No 2 (Szeged)

45th Landwehr (Honved) Infantry Brigade (Szeged)
5th and 6th Landwehr (Honved) Infantry Regts

46th Landwehr (Honved) Infantry Brigade (Lugos)
7th and 8th Landwehr (Honved) Infantry Regts
3rd and 4th Landwehr (Honved) Hussar Regts

LANDWEHR (HONVED) DISTRICT No 3 (Kassa)

77th Landwehr (Honved) Infantry Brigade (Kassa)
9th and 10th Landwehr (Honved) Infantry Regts

78th Landwehr (Honved) Infantry Brigade (Szatmar Nemeti)
11th and 12th Landwehr (Honved) Infantry Regts
5th Landwehr (Honved) Hussar Regt

LANDWEHR (HONVED) DISTRICT No 4 (Pozsony)

73rd Landwehr (Honved) Infantry Brigade (Pozsony)
13th and 15th Landwehr (Honved) Infantry Regts

74th Landwehr (Honved) Infantry Brigade (Nyitra)
14th and 16th Landwehr (Honved) Infantry Regts
6th Landwehr (Honved) Hussar Regt

LANDWEHR (HONVED) DISTRICT No 5 (Szekesfehervar)

81st Landwehr (Honved) Infantry Brigade (Szekesfehervar)
17th and 18th Landwehr (Honved) Infantry Regts

82nd Landwehr (Honved) Infantry Brigade (Pecs)
19th and 20th Landwehr (Honved) Infantry Regts
7th and 8th Landwehr (Honved) Hussar Regts

LANDWEHR (HONVED) DISTRICT No 6 (Kolozsvar)

75th Landwehr (Honved) Infantry Brigade (Kolozsvar)
21st and 22nd Landwehr (Honved) Infantry Regts

76th Landwehr (Honved) Infantry Brigade (Nagyszeben)
23rd and 24th Landwehr (Honved) Infantry Regts
9th Landwehr (Honved) Hussar Regt

LANDWEHR (HONVED) DISTRICT No 7 (Agram)

83rd Landwehr (Honved) Infantry Brigade (Agram)
25th and 26th Landwehr (Honved) Infantry Regts

84th Landwehr (Honved) Infantry Brigade (Esseg)
27th and 28th Landwehr (Honved) Infantry Regts
10th Landwehr (Honved) Hussar Regt

4·Infantry Arm of Service

||||||||||||||||||||||||||||||||||||||||||||||||||||||||||||||||||||||||||||||||||||||||||||||||||||||||||||||||

Infantry Arm of Service

||||||||||||||||||||||||||||||||||||||||||||||||||||||||||||||||||||||||||||||||||||||||||||||||||||||||||||||||

In the Austro-Hungarian Service the infantry was the paramount arm. It alone won battles. Daring charges by cavalry and destructive bombardments by artillery were mere auxiliaries to the foot soldier, for it was he and only he who could wrest ground from the enemy and hold it. Only the infantry: Queen of Battles, unaffected by conditions of climate, terrain or supplies could face, close with and defeat the foe.

Army manuals had always acknowledged the superior position of the Foot and the 1911 regulations reaffirmed this superiority by asserting that '. . . the infantry is the main arm . . . it decides the outcome of battle . . . it can bring any battle to a successful conclusion . . .' The experiences of the First World War were to demonstrate that co-operation between the Foot and the Guns was the key to military success, but the supreme position of the infantry in that partnership was never challenged.

The infantry line of battle in 1866, eighty regiments strong, was increased on 1 January 1883, when a further twenty-two came onto establishment. Between 1883 and the outbreak of war in 1914 there were no further expansions and thus it was with 102 serially-numbered line regiments that Austria-Hungary took the field.

Each of those regiments was designated 'Imperial and Royal' (kaiserlich und koeniglich); in abbreviation, kuk. That prefix was followed by the name of the Colonel of the Regiment, the so-called Regiments Inhaber. The regimental title closed with the unit's Army List number, shown in Arabic numerals.

For example:

> The Imperial and Royal Infantry Regiment, Alexander I, Emperor
> of Russia, No 2.

When a new colonel-in-chief was appointed the name was changed except for those regiments which were authorised to carry, as a permanent distinction, the name of a long deceased Monarch or General Officer. Examples of those will be found in the following pages.

The infantry line contained not only standard regiments but also Jaeger or rifle units of which the most famous were the four, serially-numbered Tiroler Kaiserjaeger regiments which were titled: 'Imperial and Royal Tiroler Kaiserjaeger Regiment, No . . .' with the number displayed in roman numerals. There were also on the Jaeger establishment thirty-three battalions of Feldjaeger; light, mobile reconnaissance formations, one of which was usually attached to each infantry division. Feldjaeger battalions had no

Group of NCOs of the Kaiserjaeger, c1902. Each of them has the marksman's distinction: a cord running towards the left shoulder from which are suspended woollen balls. The two NCOs on the left have the golden cord of a first class marksman.

The Archduke Joseph Ferdinand talking with some of the Kaiserjaeger after he had presented the 2nd Regiment with a new Colour.

colonels-in-chief and were titled simply as 'Imperial and Royal Feldjaeger Battalion No . . .' with the number shown in roman numerals.

To complete the muster of Common Army infantry units there were four Bosnia-Herzegovinian regiments which were not included in the line or Jaeger establishment. Neither were they classified Imperial and Royal, but were designated 'Bosnia-Herzegovinian Infantry Regiment, No . . .' with the number given in roman numerals.

Each infantry unit of the Common Army had within its recruiting area a depot which served as a recruit training centre, a staging post; as the regiment's administration centre and as a holding unit for those cadres around which field units would be formed upon general mobilisation. Consequent upon the proclamation of mobilisation the regiment battle and ration train were formed around their respective cadres. The regiment's fourth, or reserve, machine-gun company cadre, was filled out and sent on active service. A specially raised company from each regiment was despatched from depot to form part of the divisional headquarters defence battalion and, finally, the first replacement or 'Marsch' units were formed. Upon the outbreak of a war it was the task of Depot to maintain the flow of men, animals and supplies to the parent unit in the field.

On the following pages are listed the 102 regiments of the infantry line together with brief details of their history, facing colour, button colour, whether they were German or Hungarian, and their recruiting areas.

The Austrian Landwehr

Under the statute setting up the Austrian Landwehr, seventy-nine battalions were to be raised from the whole of Cisleithania, except the provinces of Tyrol and Vorarlberg, which had their own organisation. The battalions were numbered serially and were classified as being either infantry or Jaeger. The establishment was then increased to eighty-two infantry and ten Jaeger battalions; those latter being known as Landesschuetzen. During 1889 the infantry battalions were grouped regimentally but those of the Landesschuetzen did not undergo this reorganisation until 1893. In 1901 the Landwehr establishment was raised to thirty-six regiments and a thirty-seventh was formed during 1906. By that year restructuring of the force had produced regiments each with a three-battalion establishment. All those regiments, save one, were grouped into Landwehr brigades and divisions.

The Archduke Rudolph, Heir to the Throne of Austria, in the uniform of a Colonel of Infantry. The Archduke was Colonel-in-Chief of kuk 19th Infantry Regiment. The 'bear's paw' device shown on the cuffs identifies this as a Hungarian regiment.

Lieutenant Josef Anton Schranz, of the kuk 88th Regiment, wearing the blue blouse, salonhosen and new pattern undress shako.

The Landwehr raised machine-gun units and pioneer teams within the regimental establishments along the lines of the Common Army.

In most respects, particularly in those of organisation, armament and equipment, the battalions classified as infantry were equated with Common Army infantry battalions, while the Landesschuetzen were considered the equivalents of Feldjaeger battalions of the Common Army. All differences between the two types of Landwehr were abolished in 1889 and the whole force was formed on the infantry pattern.

There was then a further reorganisation as a result of which the force was made up of standard infantry regiments and two sorts of Jaeger. These were, firstly, the three regiments of Landesschuetzen and, secondly, the 4th and 27th Landwehr regiments, which were organised, outfitted and named as Gebirgsschuetzen, or alpine troops.

The Landwehr came under the administration of the Austrian Minister of Defence and the prefix to the regimental name was 'Imperial, Royal', (kaiserlich, koeniglich, or kk). Landwehr units were not allocated a regimental colonel-in-chief but were given instead the name of their Depot town. *For example:*

The Imperial Royal Landwehr Infantry Regiment, Vienna, No 1.

The organisation of the Depot for both Landwehr and Landwehr (Honved) units differed from that of the Common Army. As both national bodies recruited over a far wider area than a Common Army infantry regiment, it was usual for them to have a Depot-in-miniature for each of the battalions making up the regiment. A regimental Depot cadre did exist but was not activated until general mobilisation had been ordered.

The life of the Landwehr force was marked by several minor changes. In 1884 the term 'Landwehrmann' was abolished and, thereafter, a soldier was called either Infantryman or Rifleman. White Colours, which had been issued to each regiment, were withdrawn from them and never reissued although plans were made for their reintroduction during the early years of the war. Another unusual feature of the Landwehr organisation was that there were no military bands on establishment although regimental trumpeters could be grouped under a bandmaster.

Details of Landwehr dress are given in the uniform section of this book, but it is worth noting that the Austrian force adopted Jaeger type uniform. The parade headdress of a Jaeger cap with feather plume was authorised for Other Ranks during 1894. Landesschuetzen officers had worn that pattern headdress since 1869 and by 1886 it had become standard for all officers of the Austrian Landwehr.

The Austrian Landsturm

The traditional Landsturm was a badly armed and unwieldy mass of men put into the field to increase an army's numbers. Such a body had, therefore, very little military value. This concept lasted until a re-evaluation of the problems of Imperial defence showed how essential it was to upgrade the Landwehr to a first-line force. It followed, then, that the Landsturm should inherit the original Landwehr tasks and become the Empire's second line of battle. This it did, after 1887, but the conversion from a *levée en masse* to a properly organised second-line force took so long that it had not been completed by 1914.

In the first battles of the First World War and in those areas of the Empire which suffered invasion, the Landsturm fought as front-line troops although they were without modern weapons and often had no uniform other than an armband.

From 1867 the Landsturm came within the competence of the Austrian Defence Minister and its units were entitled 'Imperial Royal' (kaiserlich, koeniglich, or kk). The organisation was eventually regimentally structured and although the Landsturm was the successor to the Landwehr, their regimental districts did not always match and often the respective Depots were in different towns. Cisleithania was divided into forty-one Landsturm Districts, from one or more of which each of the seventeen regiments on the peacetime establishment was raised. The regiment was a purely administrative term for there was no cadre around which it could be formed but merely a District Headquarters whose task it was to form the regiment upon mobilisation. Two or three Landsturm infantry regiments were grouped to form a Landsturm Infantry Brigade for, in Austria, only infantry was raised. There was no Landsturm cavalry establishment.

The Landwehr (Honved)

The enthusiasm with which the Hungarian people welcomed the setting up of the national Landwehr force, called by them the Honved, was evident from the first. By the spring of 1869 cadres had been formed and training programmes prepared for the first recruits to the eighty-two battalions of infantry which were to be raised.

Of that proposed establishment only four battalions were Croatian for most Croats were serving with the so-called Grenzer or Frontier units. Such regiments had held the peace along Austria's southern frontier since the time of the Turkish wars and there were, thus, only a small number of Croats available for service with the Landwehr (Honved). To increase its recruiting contingent the Magyar authorities demanded and obtained the abolition of Grenzer units. There were then more Croats available for service with the Landwehr (Honved).

As early as 1874, plans were drawn up to form regiments. Half-brigades were created in 1886, followed in 1890 by a reorganisation to a regimental level. The title showed the administration under which the regiment served, *ie* the Royal Hungarian (koeniglich ungarisch, or ku). Then came the name of the Depot town and, finally, the regiment's number in the Army List. *For example:*

The Royal Hungarian Budapest Landwehr Infantry Regiment, No 1.

The Armed Forces Law of 1912 doubled the number of men available for service with the Landwehr (Honved) and as a result of that increase and of several reorganisations the Landwehr (Honved) had a strength of thirty-two regiments of infantry. Like the Common Army and the Austrian Landwehr, the Landwehr (Honved) formed machine-gun detachments. Indeed, it is true to say that throughout most of its life, and particularly in the last decades before the First World War, the standard of equipment and armament of the Landwehr (Honved) kept pace with those of the Common Army.

Company of Landwehr (Honved) Infantry on parade, c1912. The rank and file are wearing the pattern of Honved Infantry uniform which became full dress once the grey service dress was on general issue. (Kalman collection)

The Hungarian Landsturm

The Hungarian Landsturm, like the Landwehr (Honved), came under the administration of the Magyar Defence Minister and its units were thus, 'Royal Hungarian'.

Unlike the Austrian Landsturm, the Hungarian administration raised both infantry and cavalry units.

Several Hungarian Landsturm units served in the line on the Eastern Front but the greatest number were on lines-of-communications duties and other important but non-combatant tasks.

The areas from which the Landsturm units were raised parallelled those of the Landwehr (Honved).

||||||||||||||||||||||||||||||||||||||||||||||||||||||||||||||||||||||||||||

INFANTRY · COMMON ARMY

1 · Regiments of the Common Army

||||||||||||||||||||||||||||||||||||||||||||||||||||||||||||||||||||||||||||

The Corps districts into which the Empire was divided were sub-divided into 112 sub-districts, sixty of which were Austrian, forty-eight Hungarian and four Bosnian-Herzegovinian. 102 of those sub-districts each raised a Common Army regiment. Three districts were the recruiting preserves of the Kaiserjaeger and a further four were set aside for the Bosnian regiments. The remaining three districts: Trieste, Sabenico and Fiume recruited for the Navy.

No.	Recruited	Corps
1	Troppau	Cracow
2	Brasso	Nagyszeben
3	Kremsier	Vienna
4	Vienna	Vienna
5	Szatmar-Nemeti	Kassa
6	Ujvidek	Budapest
7	Klagenfurt	Graz
8	Bruenn	Vienna
9	Stryj	Przemysl
10	Przemysl	Przemysl
11	Pisek	Prague
12	Komaron	Pozsony
13	Cracow	Cracow
14	Linz	Innsbruck
15	Tarnopol	Lemberg
16	Belovar	Agram
17	Laibach	Graz
18	Koeniggraetz	Leitmeritz
19	Gyoer	Pozsony
20	Neusandez	Cracow
21	Caslau	Leitmeritz
22	Sinj	Zara
23	Zombor	Budapest
24	Kolomea	Lemberg
25	Losoncz	Kassa
26	Esztergom	Pozosny
27	Graz	Graz
28	Prague	Prague
29	Nagybecskerek	Temesvar
30	Lemberg	Lemberg
31	Nagyszeben	Nagyszeben
32	Budapest	Budapest
33	Arad	Temesvar
34	Kassa	Kassa
35	Pilsen	Prague
36	Jungbunzlau	Leitmeritz
37	Nagy-Varad	Temesvar
38	Kecskemet	Budapest
39	Debreczen	Temesvar
40	Rzeszow	Przemysl
41	Czernowitz	Lemberg
42	Theresienstadt	Leitmeritz
43	Karansebes	Temesvar
44	Kaposvar	Budapest
45	Sanok	Przemysl
46	Szeged	Temesvar
47	Marburg	Graz
48	Nagykanizsa	Pozsony
49	St Poelten	Vienna
50	Gyulefehervar	Nagyszeben
51	Kolozsvar	Nagyszeben
52	Pecs	Budapest
53	Agram	Agram
54	Olmuetz	Cracow
55	Brzezany	Lemberg
56	Wadowice	Cracow
57	Tranow	Cracow
58	Stanislau	Lemberg
59	Salzburg	Innsbruck
60	Eger	Kassa
61	Temesvar	Temesvar
62	Maros-Vasarhely	Nagyszeben
63	Besztercza	Nagyszeben
64	Szaszvaros	Nagyszeben
65	Munkacs	Kassa
66	Ungvar	Kassa
67	Eperjes	Kassa
68	Szolnok	Budapest
69	Szekesfehervar	Budapest
70	Peterwardein	Agram
71	Trencsen	Pozsony
72	Pozsony	Pozsony
73	Eger	Prague
74	Jicin	Leitmeritz
75	Neuhaus	Prague
76	Sopron	Pozsony
77	Sambor	Przemysl
78	Esseg	Agram
79	Otocan	Agram
80	Zleczow	Lemberg
81	Iglau	Vienna
82	Szekelyndvarhely	Nagyszeben
83	Szombathely	Pozsony
84	Vienna	Vienna
85	Maramarosziget	Kassa
86	Szabadka	Budapest
87	Cilli	Graz
88	Beraun	Prague
89	Grodek	Przemysl
90	Jaroslau	Przemsyl
91	Budweis	Prague
92	Komotau	Leitmeritz
93	Maehrisch-Schoenberg	Cracow
94	Turnau	Leitmeritz
95	Czortkow	Lemberg
96	Carlstadt	Agram
97	Trieste	Graz
98	Hohenmauth	Leitmeritz
99	Znaim	Vienna
100	Teschen	Cracow
101	Bekescaba	Temesvar
102	Beneschau	Prague

Tiroler Kaiserjäger Regiments recruited in the following districts:

Innsbruck	Innsbruck
Brixen	Innsbruck
Trient	Graz

Bosnia-Herzegovinian Infantry Regiments recruited in the following districts:

Sarajevo	Sarajevo
Banjaluka	Sarajevo
Donja Tuzla	Sarajevo
Mostar	Sarajevo

2 · Histories of the Regiments and Battalions

Kaiser Franz Joseph No 1

A German regiment
Recruiting area: *Troppau*
Facing colour: *dark red*
Button colour: *yellow metal*

The regiment was raised during 1715 as the Courtrai Regiment by Carl Ignas, Duke of Lorraine and Bar. One year later it passed into Imperial Service as the Old Lorraine Regiment and had Leopold Clement, Prince of Lorraine, as its Colonel. Ten years later Franz Stephan of Lorraine assumed the colonelcy and in 1745 Franz I, the Holy Roman Emperor, took over the regiment beginning the custom whereby the reigning Monarch was Colonel-in-Chief of the premier infantry regiment of the army. Twenty years later he was succeeded by Joseph II and in 1792 Leopold II assumed the title. Franz, the last Holy Roman Emperor, attained the colonelcy and then, in 1835, the Emperor Ferdinand gained it. From 1848 the Emperor Franz Joseph was the Colonel-in-Chief.

The medal commemorating the Golden Jubilee of the Emperor Franz Joseph was bestowed upon the 1st Regiment in 1898 and was carried pinned to the Regimental Colour.

The *Trautenauer Battle March,* composed by J. Preis, was adopted as the regimental march by the 1st Regiment. It was chosen to commemorate the storming of the Kapellenberg at Trautenau during 1866, throughout which that march was played.

Alexander I, Kaiser von Russland No 2

A Hungarian regiment
Recruiting area: *Brasso*
Facing colour:
Imperial yellow
Button colour: *yellow metal*

Raised in 1741 as the Ujuary Regiment after its first Colonel. In 1749 the Archduke Charles assumed the colonelcy and in 1761 the Archduke Ferdinand held the post. He was succeeded by Johann von Hiller in 1806. In 1825 General Franz von Koller took up the post and two years later it

passed to General Adam Retsey de Retse. In 1852 he was succeeded by General Ferdinand von Schirnding who held it until 1866 when General Anton von Ruckstuhl assumed command. From 1873 to 1881 Alexander II, Tsar of Russia, was the Regimental Colonel.

In memory of the Tsar Alexander, who died in 1825, the regiment was authorised to retain his name as a permanent distinction.

The regiment was further honoured by being allowed to parade the Yellow Colour of 3rd Battalion in place of the regulation White Colour. This distinction was granted to acknowledge the bravery of the 2nd and 3rd Battalions.

In addition to the *Trautenauer March,* which it shared with both 1st and 3rd Infantry Regiment, the 2nd also played a march composed for it by von Persius and entitled *Alexander March.*

Carl, Erzherzog Generalissimus und Feldmarschall No 3

A German regiment
Recruiting area: *Kremsier*
Facing colour: *sky blue*
Button colour: *white metal*

The regiment was raised in 1715 as the Courtrai Regiment, Lorraine and Bar by Charles Duke of Lorraine. Taken into Imperial Service in 1716 as the Young Lorraine Regiment and commanded by Prince Franz Stefan of Lorraine.

When he relinquished the colonelcy in 1726 it passed to Leopold, Count de Ligneville. Eight years later the regiment had as its Colonel-in-Chief General Gottfried von Wuttgenau and two years later, in 1736, Lukas, Count of Pallavicini succeeded him. The colonelcy passed back during the same year to the Lorraine family when Field Marshal, Charles, Duke of Lorraine assumed the post. From 1780 to 1791 it was held by General Damien von Dreschel when General Joseph Staader took command. He held it until 1808 when it passed to General Count Nicholas Weissenwolf. In 1827 General Rudolf Salis-Zizers took over the post and held it until 1840 when it passed to General Anton von Puchner. General Joseph von Fiedlier held the appointment from 1853 to 1876.

To mark the association of the regiment with the Archduke Carl, it was permitted to carry his name, in perpetuity, as the regimental title. The Archduke died in Vienna in 1847.

The 3rd Regiment played the same march as the 1st and 2nd Infantry Regiments.

Hoch und Deutschmeister No 4

A German Regiment
Recruiting area: *Vienna*
Facing colour: *sky blue*
Button colour: *yellow metal.*

From the date of its raising in 1696 the regiment carried the title and was closely associated with the Grand Master of the Order of the Teutonic Knights (the Hoch und Deutschmeister). Its many Colonels-in-Chief were drawn from the most noble families and included, Clement, Princely Count of Cologne; Charles, the Archduke of Lorraine; Field Marshal the Archduke Charles and General The Archduke Anton Victor. In 1835 General The Archduke Maximilian Joseph D'Este assumed the colonelcy and he was followed by General The Archduke William who held the post from 1863 to 1894. He was succeeded by General The Archduke Eugene, who held the appointment until the regiment was disbanded at the end of the First World War.

As a result of an 1868 Army Order the Hoch und Deutschmeister Regiment carried as its Colour the yellow Standard of 3rd Battalion to commemorate the heroic deeds which the 2nd and 3rd Battalions had carried out.

In 1896 J. N. Fuchs wrote the *Pfalz-Neuburg Teutschmeister March*, using motives from the 12th and 17th centuries, to commemorate the 200th anniversary of the raising of the regiment.

General Wilhelm Klobucar No 5

A Hungarian regiment   Facing colour: *rose red*
Recruiting area: *Szatmar*   Button colour: *yellow metal*
         -Nemeti

Raised in 1762 as the 1st Szekler Frontier Regiment, the unit was reorganised in 1764 and converted to a Line Infantry status in 1851. The first Colonel-in-Chief was Edward, Prince of Liechtenstein, who was succeeded in 1864 by Ludwig II, King of Bavaria. In 1888, after a two-year gap, during which there was no Colonel-in-Chief, the regiment was commanded by Ludwig, King of Portugal. A year later he was succeeded by General Theodor Braumuller von Tannbruck and in 1904 General Klobucar assumed command.

The 5th Regiment had as its regimental march the *Monte Croce*, composed by H. Grimm to commemorate the battle of Custozza in 1866.

Carl I, König von Rumänien No 6

A Hungarian regiment   Facing colour: *rose red*
Recruiting area: *Ujvidek*   Button colour: *white metal*

Raised in 1762 as the 2nd Szekler Frontier Regiment, the unit was reorganised in 1764 before conversion to Line Infantry status in 1851. The first Colonel-in-Chief was General The Count Johann Coronini-Cromberg. He was succeeded in 1881 by the King of Rumania.

Feldmarschall Graf Ludwig Khevenhuller von Aichelburg auf Frankenburg No 7

A German regiment   Facing colour: *dark brown*
Recruiting area: Button colour: *white metal*
Klagenfurt

The regiment was raised in 1691 and commanded by William, Count of Oettingen-Baldern. He was succeeded in the same year by General Johann Ferdinand von Pfeffershofen. In 1700 Field Marshal The Count Eberhard von Neipperg took up the appointment and seventeen years later Reinhard von Neipperg became the Colonel-in-Chief. In 1774 General The Count Franz-Xavier Harrach assumed the command and in 1783 General Charles von Schroder. Sixteen years later Ferdinand Grand Duke of Wuerzburg took over the colonelcy and in 1814 this passed to Field Marshal The Grand Duke of Tuscany. In 1824 Field Marshal Christopher von Lattermann held the appointment and in 1835 it passed to General Franz von Guelphenburg. In 1862 the colonelcy was held by General Joseph von Maroicic di Madonna del Monte, before passing to General Dahlen von Orlaburg in 1857.

The name Field Marshal The Count Ludwig Khevenhuller was bestowed upon the regiment to be carried in perpetuity. The Field Marshal, who died in 1744, was one of the most celebrated commanders of the old Austrian Army.

Erzherzog Karl Stephan No 8

A German regiment   Facing colour: *grass green*
Recruiting area: *Bruenn*   Button colour: *yellow metal*

The regiment was raised in 1642 by Colonel Alexander von Schifer and command passed to Colonel Johann von Knoering in 1646. One year later and the colonelcy had passed to General The Count Johann von Starhemberg who held it until 1661, when he was succeeded by General The Marquis Pio of Savoy. In 1676 General The Count Prosper von Arco assumed command and in 1679 this passed to Field Marshal Maximilian von Starhemberg. He was succeeded in 1700 by Field Marshal The Count Palffy, and thirty-two years later Prince Joseph von Sachsen-Heldburghause took command. In 1747 the colonelcy was taken up by General Count Pallavicini and in 1790 by General Charles von Huff. The Archduke Joseph took over command of the regiment in 1801. In 1865 General Joseph von Gersten took over the position and in 1870 this passed to General Friedrich Jacobs von Kantstein. He held the post for seven years and then it passed to General Vinzenz von Abele, who was then succeeded by The Archduke Carl Stephan in 1890.

Feldmarschall Graf Carl Clerfayt de Croix No 9

A German regiment
Recruiting area: *Stryj*

Facing colour: *apple green*
Button colour: *yellow metal*

A number of Dutch national regiments which had served with the Austrian Army were grouped together and taken into the Imperial Service during 1725. The first Colonel-in-Chief was Field Marshal Franz Marquis von Los-Rios and he was succeeded in 1775 by Franz Count Clerfayt de Croix. In 1802 the colonelcy passed to Field Marshal Prince Adam Czartoryski-Sangusco. Twenty-three years later the appointment was taken up by General Prince Wilhelm Bentheim-Steinfurt. In 1839 it passed to General The Count Prokop von Hartmann-Klarstein and he was succeeded in 1869 by General Charles von Mertens. From 1874 to 1888 the post was held by General Friedrich Packenj von Kilstadten.

The name Field Marshal Clerfayt de Croix was bestowed upon the regiment to be carried as a permanent distinction and in commemoration of the Field Marshal, who died in 1798.

Gustav V, König von Schweden No 10

A German regiment
Recruiting area: *Przemysl*

Facing colour: *parrot green*
Button colour: *white metal*

The regiment was raised in 1715 by Prince Heinrich von Wurttemberg and command passed in 1717 to Prince Ludwig von Wurttemberg. In 1734 General George Lindemann von Lindesheimb assumed the colonelcy and in 1740 this passed to Field Marshal Prince Ernst von Braunschweig-Wolfenbuettel. In 1790 General Charles von Kheul took over command and he was succeeded by General The Count Christian von Auspach und Bayreuth in 1802. Four years later General Anton von Mittrovsky became the Colonel-in-Chief, and three years later General Franz Reisky von Dubnitz. In 1817 General The Count Alois Mazzuchelli took over the colonelcy and held it until 1869 when it passed to General Heinrich von Handel. He relinquished the post in 1887 and was succeeded by Oscar II, King of Sweden, upon whose death the appointment passed to Gustav V.

Johann Georg Prinz von Sachsen No 11

A German regiment
Recruiting area: *Pisek*

Facing colour: *ash grey*
Button colour: *yellow metal*

Formed in 1629 from five companies of a Regiment of Foot raised by Albrecht von Waldstein (Wallenstein). The first Colonel of the Regiment was Julius Count Herdegg. There was a reorganisation in 1630 when ten companies were formed. In 1636 Colonel Franz von Mers assumed command and he held it until 1667 when General Ludwig von Monteverques took over the post. Two years later Colonel Albert von Tasso had become the Colonel of the Regiment. In the same year a new Colonel was appointed. He was General Jobst von Knigge and he was succeeded in 1683 by General The Count Philip von Metternich-Winneburg. In 1698 Field Marshal Heinrich von Hasslingen assumed the command and in 1739 it passed to Field Marshal Count Franz von Wallis. In 1801 General The Archduke Rainer assumed the responsibility and he held it until 1853 when Albert, Crown Prince of Saxony, assumed command. In 1873 George, Prince of Saxony, took up the post and he held it until 1901 when he was succeeded by Johann George, Prince of Saxony.

General Oskar Parmann No 12

A Hungarian regiment
Recruiting area: *Komarom*

Facing colour: *dark brown*
Button colour: *yellow metal*

In 1702 the regiment was taken into the Imperial Service and was known as the Wolfenbuettel Regiment. It was first commanded by Adolf August, Duke of Holstein-Ploen. In 1704 Field Marshal Hubert du Saix d'Arnan assumed the colonelcy and in 1728 this passed to General Christophe von Kettler. Six years later General The Count von Rumpf became the Colonel-in-Chief and in 1736 General Gottfried von Wuttgenau. One year later General Friedrich von Reitzenstein was Colonel. His two-year period of command ended with the appointment of Field Marshal The Marquis Anton Botta d'Adorno. In 1775 General Count Joseph Khevenhuller-Metsch assumed command and he held it until 1792 when it passed to General the Marquis Manfredini. Alois, Prince of Liechtenstein, then became Colonel in 1809 and in 1834 General Count Leonhard von Rothkirk und Panthen. The Archduke Wilhelm held the appointment from 1842 to 1884 and he was succeeded by General George von Kovacs who held the post for seven years. In 1901 General Moritz Schmidt became Colonel and three years later General Parmann took up the post.

Feldmarschall Graf Guidobald Starhemberg No 13 (Jung Starhemberg)

A German regiment
Recruiting area: *Cracow*

Facing colour: *rose red*
Button colour: *yellow metal*

Raised in 1814 around a nucleus of Italian units which were in the Imperial Service. The new regiment was first commanded by Field Marshal Maximilian von Wimpffen from whom the colonelcy passed in 1855 to General Prince Gustav Hohenlohe-Langenburg. In 1861 General Joseph von Bamberg assumed command and was succeeded ten years later by General Carl von Baltin. From 1873 to 1889 General Count Johann Huyn held the post of Colonel-in-Chief.

An earlier infantry regiment carrying the number 13 was raised in 1642 and disbanded in 1809.

The regimental name and number were retained as permanent distinctions to commemorate Graf Guidobald Starhemberg who died in 1737.

Ernst Ludwig, Grossherzog von Hessen und bei Rhein No 14

A German regiment Facing colour: *black*
Recruiting area: *Linz* Button colour: *yellow*

Raised in 1733 and first commanded by the Rheingraf Leopold von Salm-Salm. In 1770 the Colonel-in-Chief was General Count Joseph Ferraris. Within five years command had passed to General Joseph von Tillier who held it until 1788 when he was succeeded by General Wilhelm von Klebek. In 1811 the Archduke Rudolph was appointed to command the regiment and he was succeeded in 1832 by General Franz Xavier von Binnenthal. General Johann Hrabovsky von Hrabova came to the post in 1840 and held it until 1849 when General Ludwig von Wohlgemuth took over the command. The appointment of Ludwig III, Grand Duke of Hesse, in 1851 led to the command of the regiment being invested in the rulers of that House, with Ludwig IV from 1877 to 1892 and Ernst Ludwig in 1893.

General von Georgi No 15

A German regiment Facing colour: *madder red*
Recruiting area: *Tarnopol* Button colour: *yellow metal*

Taken into the Imperial Service as the Osnabruck Life Guard Regiment in 1701 and commanded by Duke Carl von Lorraine and Bar, Bishop of Osnabruck, who was succeeded in 1716 by Carl, Prince of Lorraine. Twenty years later Field Marshal Count Giovanni Lukas Pallavicini became the Colonel-in-Chief and in 1773 General Comote Dominic Fabris took over the post.

There was a succession of princely commanders including Dom Pedro Emperor of Brazil in 1827, and from 1846 to 1890 Adolph, Duke of Nassau.

General von Giesl No 16 (The Varasdin Regiment)

A Hungarian regiment Facing colour: *sulphur yellow*
Recruiting area: *Belovar* Button colour: *yellow metal*

Raised in 1703 by General Count Damien von Virmond who was succeeded in 1722 by General Count Alano Livingstein. In 1741 Field Marshal Count Christian von Konigsegg-Rothenfels assumed command and held the post for four years when General Franz, Marquise of Lusignan was appointed Colonel-in-Chief of the 16th Regiment.

General Count Christian Kinski took up the post in 1833 and in 1835 the regiment had two Colonels-in-Chief in one year. General Peter Zanini, who became Colonel in 1848, was succeeded in 1855 by General Stephan von Wernhardt. Between the years 1870 and 1881 General Gustav Wetzlar von Plankenstern commanded the regiment which then passed to General Heinrich Giesl von Gieslingen.

General Hugo von Milde No 17

A German regiment Facing colour: *red brown*
Recruiting area: *Laibach* Button colour: *white metal*

The regiment was raised in 1674 by Heinrich von Reuss-Plauen from whom it passed during the following year to Colonel Ferdinand von Stadl. During the period of his command, which lasted until 1679, the regiment was reformed. General Carl Prince von Furstenberg-Moeskirch took command of the regiment and his period in office lasted until 1703. During that year there were two other Colonels-in-Chief, the latter of whom, Alexander Prince of Wurttemberg held the appointment until 1737 when he was succeeded by Field Marshal Count Kajetan Kolowrat-Krakovsky. In 1773 General Johann von Koch took up the appointment and seven years later command was assumed by General Prince Friedrich William of Hohenlohe-Kirchberg. He was succeeded in 1801 by Field Marshal Prince Heinrich von Reuss-Plauenberg. A second member of the Hohenlohe-Kirchberg family, General Gustav, was appointed to lead the 17th Regiment in 1826 and held the post for forty years. In 1866 he was succeeded by General Franz Kuhn von Kuhnenfeld, whose period of command lasted until 1896 when he was succeeded by General von Milde.

Erzherzog Leopold Salvator No 18

A German Regiment Facing colour: *dark red*
Recruiting Area: Button colour: *white metal*
 Koeniggratz

The regiment was raised in 1682 by Colonel Leopold, Duke of Lorraine, who was succeeded in the command by Joseph, Duke of Lorraine. In 1705 General Johann von Wetzel was appointed to the colonelcy and this passed in 1706 to

1 The Archduke Franz Ferdinand
Colonel-in-Chief of the 6th Artillery Regiment

Schach! Schach!

Soll nimmer diefen ftolzen Kreis en
welhen!
Theodor Friedrich

Opposite page above:
2 Conrad von Hoetzendorff and von
Hindenburg checkmating the war
plans of the Allies.

Opposite page below:
3 Men of the 29th Feldjaeger
Battalion in an attack. Note the
cowhide pack, the mess tin on top of
the pack, the water bottle on the left
hip, the entrenching tool below that,
and the bayonet knot.

Above:
4 This card issued in 1914 shows the
senior commanders of the German
and Austro-Hungarian Armies.
Included in the group are The Archduke Friedrich, Conrad von
Hoetzendorff, Ludendorff and von
Hindenburg.

Right:
5 The Emperor Franz Joseph in the
uniform of a Hungarian General of
the Imperial Army, wearing the rank
badges of a Field Marshal.

A series of five watercolours by the famous military artist Alexander Pock.

Left:
6 Brigade Commander escorted by his Aides-de-Camp, a Dragoon and a Lieutenant of the Artillery. *(HGM)*

Below:
7 Trooper of a Common Army regiment of Ulans.
(Private collection)

Right:
8 The Kaiserjaeger during a march past, 1914.
The green cord and balls worn by some of the rank and file are for proficiency in marksmanship. When
(HGM)

SERJAEGER

Alexander

Left:
9 Hussar of the Imperial Army
(HGM)

Right:
10 A Dragoon. *(HGM)*

The following three paintings are by the artist Johann Karger.

Below:
11 Mountain units of the Austrian Landwehr; Landesschuetzen regiments and 4th Landwehr Infantry Regiment.
From left to right: Private soldiers of the Landwehr in parade dress and field service dress, and Captain in field service dress. Field Officer in parade dress, Sergeant in parade dress and two Landesschuetzen figures; Other Rank in field service dress and Officer in parade dress.

Above: 12 Men of Landwehr (Honved) units. In the left foreground can be seen infantry in winter and summer field service dress; Officer and NCO together with Standard bearer, all in parade dress. The mounted figures in the rear of the picture show Hussars: one of the rank and file on the left, and an Officer on the right. The standing figures in the right foreground are military officials, a medical officer and a man of the Veterinary Corps.

Below: 13 Troops of the Austrian Landwehr. *In the foreground, from left to right:* Sergeant of the Dalmatian Rifles in field service order. Private of the Landwehr Infantry in parade dress. NCO in drill dress. Officer in undress uniform. Officer in parade dress. Other Rank of the Landwehr Infantry in winter field service dress. Long serving NCO in field service dress and Officer wearing a cloak. *Left:* (mounted) Tirolean Rifleman in field service order. *Right:* (mounted) Field Officer in field service order.

The following ten illustrations of uniforms of Arms of Service form
part of a series of thirty-four paintings held in the
Heeresgeschichtliches Museum in Vienna.
These finely executed works of art were produced by Oskar Bruech,
sometime Lieutenant in the Imperial and Royal Army.

14 GERMAN INFANTRY

Pioneer of an Infantry regiment in winter marching order.
Lieutenant in parade dress.
Captain (mounted) in marching order.
Officer in marching order.
Standard bearer in parade dress.
Infantryman in parade order.
Field Officer (mounted) in parade order.
Corporal in winter parade dress.
Company bugler in marching order.

Above:

15 HUNGARIAN INFANTRY

Cadet Officer in marching order.
Corporal in parade dress. Captain
(mounted) in marching order.
Infantry pioneer in marching order.
Drummer in winter parade dress.
Standard bearer in parade dress.
Major (mounted) in parade order.
Lieutenant in parade dress.
Officer in winter marching order.
Infantryman in winter marching
order.

Left:

16 DRAGOONS

Officer in winter parade order.
Colonel (mounted) in parade order.
Trumpeter in winter parade dress.
Officer in winter walking out dress.
Officer in marching order. Dragoon
(mounted) in marching order.
Dragoon in marching order.
NCO in marching order.

Above:

17 JAEGER TROOPS

Private soldier in marching order. Battalion trumpeter (mounted) in parade order. Pioneer of a Jaeger unit in winter marching order. Lieutenant in walking out dress. Lieutenant in parade order. Captain in marching order. Colonel (mounted) in parade dress. Private soldier in parade dress. Long service Sergeant in winter marching order.

Right:

18 BOSNIA-HERZEGOVINIAN INFANTRY

Captain (mounted) in marching order. Lieutenant in marching order. Infantry pioneer in marching order. Infantryman in parade order. Major (mounted) in parade order.

19 HUSSARS

Trumpeter in winter parade dress.
Hussar (mounted) in parade dress.
NCO in parade dress.
Officer in winter walking out dress.
Officer in marching order.
Officer in winter parade dress.
Field Officer (mounted) in parade dress.
Hussar in winter marching order.
Corporal in service dress.

20 ULANS

Ulan in marching order.
Ulan (mounted) in marching order.
Lieutenant in walking out dress.
Captain in marching order.
Officer in winter parade dress.
Major (mounted) in parade dress.
NCO in winter marching order.
Corporal in marching order.
Ulan in winter marching order.

21 FIELD ARTILLERY

Sergeant in parade dress.
Sergeant in winter marching order.
Major (mounted) in parade dress.
Officer in winter service dress.
Lieutenant in walking out dress.
Captain in marching order.
Gunner (mounted) in marching order.
Trumpeter of a half regiment in parade dress.
Gunner in marching order.

22 GENERALS

General in winter walking out dress.
Lieutenant General in German service dress.
Lieutenant General (mounted) in German parade dress.
General of Cavalry or of the Artillery in German gala dress.
General (mounted) in Hungarian winter parade dress.
Cavalry General in Hungarian gala dress.
Major General in Hungarian service dress.

23 AIDES-DE-CAMP AND GENERAL STAFF

Lieutenant Colonel as a Senior Adjutant of the Emperor.
Major as a Senior Adjutant of a General Officer.
Captain (mounted) of the General Staff in marching order.
Lieutenant of Infantry, seconded to the General Staff, in marching order.
Lieutenant of the Field Artillery, seconded to the General Staff, in parade dress.
General Staff officer in winter walking out dress.
Lieutenant of Ulans as an Adjutant,(mounted) in service dress.
Colonel of the General Staff in parade dress.

Colonel Johann von Hoffman. Within a year command had changed again and this time to General Count Johann Sonnenberg von Heindl, who held the appointment for seven years until he was succeeded by General Damien von Sickingen. The colonelcy passed very quickly through a number of commanders until in 1742 General Count Ernst of Marshcall auf Burgholhausen was appointed and commanded the regiment for twenty-nine years. General Jakob von Brinken who succeeded him led the 18th Regiment for eighteen years. In 1791 General Count Patrick Stuart held the colonelcy which passed to General Konstantin d'Aspre in 1809. There was another quick succession of commanders until in 1848 the regiment was bestowed upon Constantin, Grand Prince of Russia, who led it until 1892.

Erzherzog Franz Ferdinand von Österreich-Este No 19

A Hungarian regiment   Facing colour: *sky blue*
Recruiting area: *Gyor*   Button colour: *white metal*

The regiment was raised in 1734 by Field Marshal Count Leopold Palffy, who held the appointment until 1773 when he was succeeded by General Count Richard D'Alton. In 1786 Field Marshal Joseph Alvintzi de Berberek was given the colonelcy and passed it in 1812 to Field Marshal Prince Phillip von Hessen-Homburg. General Prince Carl Schwarzenberg held the post from 1847 until 1858 when General The Archduke and Crown Prince Rudolf of Austria was appointed. Upon his death in 1889 command of the 19th Regiment passed to the Heir Apparent to the Throne, the Archduke Franz Ferdinand.

Heinrich, Prinz von Preussen No 20

A German regiment   Facing colour: *lobster red*
Recruiting area: Button colour: *white metal*
  Neu Sandez

The regiment was raised in 1681 by Colonel Ludwig the Pfalzgraf zu Neuburg who commanded it until 1694 when Field Marshal Count Hans Thungen took up the post. In 1709 Field Marshal Prince Friedrich Wilhelm von Holstein-Beck became the Colonel-in-Chief and he was succeeded ten years later by General Count Johann Diesbach. In 1744 Field Marshal Count Anton von Colloredo-Waldsee was appointed to lead the regiment which he did until 1785 when command was invested in General Count Wenzel von Kaunitz-Rietberg. Count Friedrich von Hochenegg took up the appointment in 1826 and in 1849 he was succeeded by General Ludwig von Welden. In 1853 there began the association of the Prussian Royal

Family with the 20th Regiment when Prince Friedrich Wilhelm became the Colonel-in-Chief, and upon his death Friedrich, German Emperor and King of Prussia succeeded him.

Feldmarschall Ferdinand von Abensberg und Traun No 21

A German regiment   Facing colour: *sea green*
Recruiting area: *Caslau*   Button colour: *yellow metal*

The regiment was raised in 1733 by General Count Franz Colmenero, from whom command passed a year later when General Count Ludwig Schulenburg-Oeynhausen became Colonel-in-Chief. In 1754 Field Marshal Duke Carl Arenberg assumed command and it passed in 1778 to General Sigismund von Gemmingen auf Hornberg. The colonelcy of the 21st Regiment then passed, in 1808, to General Prince Roman and he was succeeded as Colonel of the Regiment by General Count Albert Gyulai von Maros Nemeth in 1810. After a period in office of twenty-five years he was succeeded by General Johann von Paumgarten who was succeeded in 1849 by General Felix Prince Schwarzenberg. Three years later Count Christian Leiningen-Westerburg became the Colonel-in-Chief and in 1857 General Sigismund Reischach succeeded him. From 1878 to 1886 the post of Colonel was held by Friedrich von Mondel and in 1887 General Count Zeno Welsersheimb assumed command.

The name and number of the regiment were held in perpetuity to commemorate Field Marshal von Abensberg who died in 1748.

Graf Moritz von Lacy No 22

A German regiment   Facing colour: *Imperial yellow*
Recruiting area: *Sinj*   Button colour: *white metal*

The regiment was raised in 1709 by General Engelhard von Plischau. It was bestowed upon General Franz Laimpruch zu Epurz in 1718 and command passed to General Prince Adalberg Brandenberg-Culmbach in 1723. General August von Suckow succeeded him in 1734 and held the appointment until 1741 when he was succeeded by General Wilhelm von Roth. The colonelcy passed in 1748 to General Jakob von Hagenbach and from him to General Salomon Sprecher von Bernegg in 1757. After only a year in office he was succeeded by Field Marshal Count Lacy who commanded the 22nd Regiment until 1802. In that year Friedrich, Prince of Sachse-Coburg-Saalfeld had the regiment bestowed upon him and held the post until 1815 when Friedrich, Duke of Nassau-Usingen, was appointed. He held the appointment for only one year and was succeeded by Leopold, Prince of the Two Sicilies. Between 1851 and 1870 General Count Franz Wimpffen held the colonelcy and in 1871 General Joseph von Weber took up the post.

The regimental name and number were retained as permanent distinctions to commemorate the Field Marshal, who died in 1801.

Feldmarschall Ludwig Wilhelm I, Markgraf von Baden-Baden No 23

A Hungarian regiment   Facing colour: *cherry*
Recruiting area: *Zambor*   Button colour: *white metal*

The regiment was formed in 1814 from Italian regiments which were in Imperial Service. General Franz von Mauroy de Merville assumed command during 1815 and within two years the colonelcy had passed to General Carl Greth. During 1827 General Joseph Soeldner von Soeldenhofen assumed command of the regiment and this passed in 1837 to General Count Ferdinand Ceccopieri. He was succeeded in 1850 by General Paul von Ajroldi and he, in turn, by General Joseph von Doepfner in 1883. General von Doepfner held the colonelcy until 1891.

A former 23rd Regiment was raised in 1672 and was disbanded in 1807.

The regimental name and number were retained as permanent distinctions to commemorate the Field Marshal who had commanded the former 23rd Regiment from 1676 until his death in 1707.

General von Kummer No 24

A German regiment   Facing colour: *ash grey*
Recruiting area: *Kolomea* Button colour: *white metal*

The regiment was raised in 1662 around seven companies of the Infantry Regiment Mers and three newly recruited companies. It was commanded by Lukas Spitch von Uibergau von Langenau. Three years later General Count Jakob Leslie assumed command and held it until 1675 when General Prince Mansfeld zu Fondi had the colonelcy bestowed upon him. He was succeeded by General Count Maximilian Starhemberg in 1703 and he held the post thirty-eight years. In 1741 General Emmanuel von Stark became Colonel-in-Chief and after another three-year incumbency General Johann von Preiss succeeded to the command. In 1801 General Count Carl von Auersperg became the Colonel-in-Chief and he was succeeded in 1808 by General Count Gottfried von Strauch. In 1836 Carl Ludwig, Duke of Lucca, was appointed to the post and he was succeeded in 1848 by Carl Ludwig, Duke of Parma,

who held the appointment until 1883. After two years without a Colonel, General Wilhelm von Reinlander was appointed.

General Hermann von Pokorny No 25

A Hungarian regiment   Facing colour: *sea green*
Recruiting area: *Losoncz* Button colour: *white metal*

The regiment was raised in 1672 by General Count Johann Serenti and in 1691 command passed to General Franz von Amenzager. Two years later General Count Scipio Bagni took over the colonelcy and held it until 1721 when he was succeeded by General Philip von Langlet. In 1731 General Count Wachtendonk assumed command and held it for ten years when General Prince Piccolomini was appointed to command the 25th Regiment. In 1757 Field Marshal Count Franz Thurheim became the Colonel-in-Chief and in 1801 command passed to General Count Johann Spork.

After a period in office of only eight years he passed the colonelcy to General Count Zedtwitz. In 1823 this passed to General Werner von Trapp and in 1842 to General Gustav von Wocher, who relinquished the command in 1858 in favour of General Count Heinrich Salis-Zizers. From 1878 to 1901 the 25th Regiment was commanded by General Vinzenz Purker von Purkhein.

General Schreiber No 26

A Hungarian regiment   Facing colour: *black*
Recruiting area: *Esztergom* Button colour: *yellow metal*

The regiment was raised in 1717 as the Anspach Regiment and was taken into Imperial Service during that year. Its first Commander was General Carl Prince of Brandenburg-Anspach. He was succeeded in 1724 by General Heinrich von Mueffling and he, in turn, by General Count Nicholas Gruenne during 1737. In 1751 General The Conde de Puebla assumed command and held it until 1776 when General Carl von Riesse took over. During 1786 there were two Colonels, the first of whom was General Joseph de Beberek von Alvinizi, and the second General Richard Count D'Alton.

Four years later, in 1790, General Wilhelm von Schroeder became Colonel-in-Chief and held the post until 1803 when General Prince Ludwig Hohenlohe-Bartenstein took over the position. In 1814 he was succeeded by General Prince Wilhelm von Oranien and, only one year later, by Field Marshal Wilhelm I, King of the Netherlands. General The Archduke Ferdinand von Este took up the appointment in 1844 and in 1852 Michael, Grand Prince of Russia, became Colonel of the Regiment.

Albert I, König von Belgien No 27

A German regiment
Recruiting area: *Graz*

Facing colour: *Imperial yellow*
Button colour: *yellow metal*

The regiment was raised in 1682 by General Count Ottavio Negretti from whom the command passed in 1706 to Field Marshal Johann von und zum Jungen. He held the post until 1732 when Field Marshal Prince Maximilian von Hessen-Cassel took up the appointment. In 1753 Field Marshal Prince Christian zu Baden-Durlach became the Colonel-in-Chief and held the post until 1791 when General Count Leopold Strassoldo held the colonelcy. In 1809 General The Marquise Chatteller de Courcelles was appointed to command the 27th and he was succeeded in 1826 by General Jakob von Lurem. General Ludwig von Piret de Binain took up the colonelcy in 1841 and passed it, in 1853, to the first of the Belgian Kings to command the regiment. This was Leopold I who had the 27th bestowed upon him. He was succeeded in 1865 by Leopold II and he, in turn, by Albert, who became Colonel-in-Chief in 1908.

Viktor Emmanuel III, König von Italien No 28

A German Regiment
Recruiting area: *Prague*

Facing colour: *grass green*
Button colour: *white metal*

The regiment was raised in 1698 from six companies of Infantry Regiment 'Metternich' (which became Infantry Regiment No 11) and six newly recruited companies. General Count Franz Sebastian Thurheim raised and commanded the regiment until 1713. In that year General Philip von der Lanckhen became the Regimental Colonel and was succeeded in 1716 by Field Marshal Duke Leopold Arhemberg.

In 1754 there were two Colonels. The first of these was General Leopold von Scherzer and the second, Field Marshal Count Georg Wied-Runkel. General Count Wilhelm Wartensleben took up post in 1779 and held it for twenty years. General Michael von Frelich succeeded him and he, in turn, was succeeded by General von Kutschera in 1815. Seventeen years later General Count Theodor Baillei von Latour was appointed to command the 28th and handed over the command to General Ludwig von Benedek in 1849.

In 1881 Humbert I, King of Italy, had the regiment bestowed on him and at his death command passed to Victor Emmanuel III.

Feldmarschall Gideon Ernst Loudon No 29

A Hungarian regiment
Recruiting area:
  Nagybecskerek

Facing colour: *light blue*
Button colour: *white*

The regiment was raised in 1709 by Prince Ferdinand of Braunschweig-Wolfenbuttel-Bevern by the amalgamation of thirteen companies of a disbanded regiment. In 1736 the colonelcy passed to Prince Carl of Braunschweig-Wolfenbuttel-Bevern and from him to Field Marshal Gideon Loudon in 1760. He held the post for thirty-one years and command of the 29th was bestowed upon General Count Olivier Wallis. In 1803 General Carl von Lindenau took over command and held it until 1818 when Wilhelm, Duke of Nassau, became the Colonel-in-Chief. General Joseph von Foelseis assumed command in 1840 but his incumbency was brief and during the following year General Anton Hartmann von Hartenthal took over command. In 1844 General Carl von Schmeling became Colonel and was succeeded in 1847 by General Carl von Schoenhals. He held command for ten years and in 1857 General Count Carl Thun-Hohenstein took over the position of Colonel to be succeeded in 1876 by General Anton von Scudier.

The regimental name and number were retained as permanent distinctions to commemorate the Field Marshal who had commanded the regiment from 1760 to 1791.

General Schoedler No 30

A German regiment
Recruiting area: *Lemberg*

Facing colour: *pike grey*
Button colour: *yellow metal*

The regiment was raised from Dutch national regiments which were already in Imperial Service in 1725 and was first commanded by General Johann Prince Turinetti, Marchese de Pancaliere. He was succeeded in 1753 by General Prince Wilhelm of Sachse-Gotha and he, in 1771, by Field Marshal Prince Carl de Ligne. In 1815 Field Marshal Count Laval Nugent von Westmeath became the Colonel-in-Chief and command passed from him to General Joseph Martin von Nossed in 1862. Seven years later General Joseph von Jablonski del Monte Berico assumed command. Between the years 1876 and 1893 General Joseph von Ringelsheim held the post and when, in 1895, General Joseph von Watteck took over the command his tenure of office was of only one year's duration. His successor, General Count Hans von der Schulenburg also held the post for only a year before it passed to General Franz Fiedler who was succeeded by General Shoedler in 1905.

General Eduard Pucherna No 31

A Hungarian regiment   Facing colour: *Imperial yellow*
Recruiting area: *Tarnow*   Button colour: *white metal*

The 31st Regiment of the Infantry Line was raised by Colonel Haller in 1741 and was first known as the Haller Regiment. In 1747 General Samuel Haller von Hallerstein was in command and thirty years later he was succeeded by Major General Count Anton Esterhazy von Galantha. His three-year term of office ended and in 1780 General Count Joseph Orosz took over the colonelcy. In 1792 General Johann Peter von Beaulieu became Colonel of the Regiment and was succeeded in 1794 by General Johann Benjovszky von Benjow.

Maximilian Joseph I, King of Bavaria, had the regiment bestowed upon him in 1817 and in 1825 the colonelcy had passed to General Franz Splenyi von Milhady. In 1829 General Count August Leiningen-Westerburg took up the post and held it for twenty years. General Carl von Coloz succeeded him and laid down the appointment in 1863. He was followed by Field Marshal The Grand Duke of Mecklenburg-Strelitz who held the appointment until 1904.

Kaiserin und Königin Maria Theresia No 32

A Hungarian regiment   Facing colour: *light blue*
Recruiting area: *Budapest*   Button colour: *yellow metal*

The regiment was raised by Colonel Count Forgach and named the Forgach Regiment. The Colonel, later General, held the command for thirty-two years and was succeeded by Samuel Count Gyula von Maros-Nemeth. He held the regimental command until 1802 and was succeeded by Prince Nicholas Esterhazy von Galantha. From 1834 until 1875 Franz Duke of Modena held the post.

In 1888 as a result of an Imperial proclamation, colonelcies 'for all time' were bestowed upon certain regiments and the 32nd received the distinction of being the only formation in the army to carry the name of the famous Empress who had died in 1780.

Kaiser Leopold II No 33

A Hungarian regiment   Facing colour: *ash grey*
Recruiting area: *Arad*   Button colour: *white metal*

The 33rd Regiment was raised in 1741 by, and named after, Count Adrassy. He held the colonelcy until 1753 when he was succeeded by Prince Nicholas Esterhazy von Galantha. General Count Sztaray von Nagy-Minaly assumed command in 1791 and held it until 1809 when he was succeeded by General Count Hieronimus Colloredo-Mansfeld. In 1823 General Emmerich von Bakonyi came to the command and held the appointment for twenty-two years. General Count Franz Gyulai von Maros-Nemeth, who then took over the appointment, held it until 1869. His successor, General Emil von Kussevitch von Szamober, commanded until 1887.

The regimental name and number were retained as permanent distinctions to commemorate the Emperor Leopold II who died in 1792.

Wilhelm I, Deutscher Kaiser und König von Preussen No 34

A Hungarian regiment   Facing colour: *madder red*
Recruiting area: *Kassa*   Button colour: *white metal*

The regiment was raised in 1733 by General Laidslaus von Kokenyesdy from whom the command passed in 1756 to General Count Adam Batthyani. In 1780 General Prince Anton Esterhazy von Galantha took over the colonelcy and ten years later General Paul von Kray de Krayova became the Colonel-in-Chief. He was succeeded in 1804 by General Paul von Davidovitch who held the command until 1815. In that year General Prince Friedrich von Wied-Runkel was given command of the regiment. General Josef von Benczur took up the appointment in 1827 and this passed in 1841 to Wilhelm Prince of Prussia who, in 1871, became Wilhelm I, King of Prussia and Emperor of Germany.

The regimental name and number were retained as permanent distinctions to commemorate the former Colonel-in-Chief, who died in 1888.

General Moritz Daublensky von Sterneck No 35

A German regiment   Facing colour: *lobster red*
Recruiting area: *Pilsen.*   Button colour: *yellow metal*

The regiment was raised in 1683 by General Duke George of Wurttemberg from whom it passed two years later to Colonel The Marquise John Spinola. A year later Guido von Starhemberg had assumed command and within two years General Count Ludwig Archiente Conte de Tayna took command.

The command of 35th Regiment passed through nine different Colonels by 1788 and a further nine by 1842. General Count Franz Khevenhuller, who took up the post in 1842, held it until 1867 when he was succeeded by General Joseph von Philipovic und Philipsberg. In 1890 he passed the command to General Moritz Daublensky von Sterneck.

Reichsgraf Browne von Mountany No 36

A German regiment
Recruiting area: *Jungbunzlau*

Facing colour: *pale red*
Button colour: *white metal*

The regiment was raised in 1683 by Field Marshal Count Jakob Leslie from whom command passed in 1692 to Phillip, Prince of Luxembourg. He was succeeded in 1704 by General Count Maximilian Ludwig Wallis and he, in turn, by Field Marshal Browne von Mountany in 1737. In 1757 General Count Joseph Browne de Camus became Colonel-in-Chief but his tenure of office was brief as was that of his two successors. In 1761 Field Marshal Prince Kinsky took up the post and thirty-six years later General Prince Furstenberg. There were five Colonels between 1797 and 1876 when General Ziemiecki von Ziemiecin was appointed. The regiment held the title in perpetuity.

Erzherzog Joseph No 37

A Hungarian regiment
Recruiting area: *Nagy Varad*

Facing colour: *scarlet*
Button colour: *white metal*

The regiment was raised in 1741 by Colonel Thomas Szirmay and named after him. Three years later the regiment was commanded by General Count Joseph Esterhazy and named the Esterhazy Regiment. General Count Joseph Siskovics assumed command in 1762 and he was succeeded in 1784 by General Joseph von de Vins.

General Franz von Auffenberg took up post in 1803 and five years later General Count Franz Auersperg succeeded him. During the same year the colonelcy passed to General von Weidenfeld and six years later General Andreas Mariassy von Markus took over the appointment. He held it until 1846 when Michael, Grand Prince of Russia had the regiment appointed to him. In 1850 Ivan Fedorovitch Paskievitch, Prince of Warsaw, took over the colonelcy and in 1856 he was succeeded by General The Archduke Joseph. The regimental name and number were retained as permanent distinctions to commemorate the Archduke, who died in 1905.

Alfonso XIII, König von Spanien No 38

A Hungarian regiment
Recruiting area: *Kecskemet*

Facing colour: *black*
Button colour: *white metal*

The regiment was raised in 1814 from Italian regiments which were already in the Imperial Service. The first Colonel-in-Chief was General Johann von Prochaska and he was succeeded in 1824 by General Count Eugene Maugwitz. He held the appointment for forty-three years and was succeeded by General Anton Molinary von Monte Pastello who handed over the colonelcy in 1905 when Alfonso XIII, King of Spain, had the regiment bestowed upon him.

There had been a former regiment with the number 38 in the Imperial Service. This had been raised in 1725 and was disbanded in 1800.

General von Conrad No 39

A Hungarian regiment
Recruiting area: *Debreczen*

Facing colour: *scarlet*
Button colour: *white metal*

The regiment was raised in 1756 by Colonel Count Johann Palffy ab Erdoed from whom command passed, in 1758, to General Jakob von Prysach. General Count Thomas Nadasdy took over the colonelcy in 1787 and held it until 1803 when General Peter von Duka took up the appointment.

From 1827 to 1866 the post of Colonel-in-Chief of the 39th Regiment was invested in Dom Miguel, Infant of Portugal. He was succeeded in 1866 by General Josef von Habermann von Habersfeld who commanded until 1872. Alexis, Grand Prince of Russia, assumed command in 1872 and held it until 1908.

The 39th Regiment was one of those which carried a Yellow Colour instead of the 1st Battalion White Colour. This privilege was granted to commemorate the bravery of the junior battalions in former battles.

General Pino von Friedenthal No 40

A German regiment
Recruiting area: *Rzeszov*

Facing colour: *light blue*
Button colour: *yellow metal*

The regiment was raised in 1733 by Field Marshal Wolfgang von Damnitz who held the post until 1754 when General Count Carl Colloredo succeeded him. General Count Joseph Mittrowsky took over the appointment in 1786 and in 1809 the colonelcy passed to Field Marshal Ferdinand, Duke of Wurttemberg.

General Joseph von Koudelka assumed command of the 40th Regiment in 1834 and held the appointment until 1850 when General Heinrich von Rossbach took up post. Seventeen years later General Henry Rupprecht-Virtsolog became the Colonel-in-Chief. In 1878 General Count Gottfried Auersperg was appointed Colonel and held the post until 1893. There was a two-year period with no Colonel and then in 1895 General Eduard von Handel-Mazzetti held the post. General Prince Wilhelm von Schaumburg-Lippe, who was then appointed to the command, held it until 1906 in which year General Pino von Friedenthal took up post.

Erzherzog Eugen No 41

A German regiment
Recruiting area:
 Czernowitz

Facing colour: *sulphur yellow*
Button colour: *white metal*

A regiment from the Bukovina, raised in 1701 from six existing Bayreuth companies and ten newly raised ones. The regiment was taken into the Imperial Service in the same year.

The first Colonel-in-Chief was Christian Markgraf von Bayreuth who handed over command in 1704 to Georg Wilhelm, Prince of Bayreuth. The family connection was maintained when Wilhelm Ernst took up the appointment in 1727 and again in 1734 when Friedrich assumed command.

With the appointment of General Thomas von Plunkett in 1763 the connection of the Markgraf of Bayreuth with the regiment ended. In 1770 Prince Joseph of Furstenberg took over the colonelcy and held it for seven years. He was succeeded by General Count Ludwig Barbiane di Belgiogi. Within a year command had passed to Field Marshal Blasius von Bender who handed over the appointment, in 1803, to Wilhelm Friedrich Prince of Wurttemberg. He was succeeded in 1815 by General Prince Ludwig Hohenlohe-Bartenstein and he, in turn, only two years later by General Ignaz Marschall von Perclat.

In 1823 General Wenzel von Watlet took over the colonelcy and held it until 1841 when General Johann von Sivkovitch was appointed. Command was held by him for sixteen years and then General Friedrich Kellner von Koellenstein became the Colonel-in-Chief. From 1883 to 1890 General Joseph von Vecsey de Vecse was in command of the regiment.

The 41st had the privilege of carrying a Yellow Battalion Colour and not the White Regimental Colour.

Ernst August, Herzog von Cumberland No 42

A German regiment
Recruiting area:
 Theresienstadt

Facing colour: *orange yellow*
Button colour: *white metal*

The regiment was raised in 1685 and was taken into Imperial Service in the same year as the Wurttemberg Regiment. It was commanded by General Hans Carl Thungen. In 1694 there were two Colonels in one year. The first of these was Colonel Leopold von Thavonat and the second General Count Wenzel Guttenstein. In 1707 General Johann von Wetzel took over command and held it until he was succeeded by General Philip von Bettendorf in 1720. General Count Johnann O'Neill became Colonel-in-Chief in 1734 and in 1743 General Count Sigmund Gaisruck took up post.

His period in office was twenty-six years and he was succeeded by General Reinhard von Genningen auf Hornberg who held the colonelcy until 1775 when General Andreas von Matheson was appointed. In 1793 General Count Carl Ernbach-Schoenberg was appointed to the post and he was succeeded in 1818 by Field Marshal Arthur, Duke of Wellington. George, King of Hannover was appointed to command the regiment in 1852 and he handed over the colonelcy to Duke Ernst August of Cumberland in 1879.

As a reward for special bravery shown during the battle of Deutsch-Wagram in 1809 the 42nd was permitted to play the *Grenadier March* on ceremonial occasions.

Rupprecht, Kronprinz von Bayern No 43

A Hungarian regiment
Recruiting area:
 Karansebes

Facing colour: *cherry red*
Button colour: *yellow metal*

The regiment was raised in 1814 around a cadre of Italian regiments already in Imperial Service. In 1815 General Prince Johann Paar took over the colonelcy and passed this to General Menrad von Geppert in 1821. He held it until 1855 when it passed to General Wilhelm von Aleman and he was succeeded by General Stephan von Jovanovic in 1883. In 1895 Jovanovic laid down the office and this then passed to General Count Phillip Gruenne in 1897 who held it until 1902.

A former regiment carrying the number 43 had been raised in 1715. It was disbanded in 1809.

Erzherzog Albrecht No 44

A Hungarian regiment
Recruiting area: *Kaposvar*

Facing colour: *madder red*
Button colour: *yellow metal*

The regiment was raised in 1744 by General Anton The Marquise Clerici who was succeeded in 1769 by General Count Rudolf Gaisruck. In 1778 General Count Belgiojoso Barbiano assumed command and held it until 1801. In that year General Count Friedrich Bellegarde became the Colonel-in-Chief and twenty-nine years later Field Marshal The Archduke Albrecht was appointed to the command and held it until his death in 1895.

The regimental name and number were retained as permanent distinctions to commemorate the great reformer of the army.

Erzherzog Joseph Ferdinand No 45

A German regiment
Recruiting area: *Sanok*

Facing colour: *scarlet*
Button colour: *yellow metal*

The regiment was formed in 1816 around a cadre from

four disbanded Light Infantry battalions and in 1817 was commanded by General Anton von Mayer von Heldensfeld. He was succeeded in 1842 by General Heinrich Herbert von Rathkeal. After a period in office of only five years he was succeeded by General The Duke Sigismund who held the post until 1891. In the following year the regiment was bestowed upon Crown Prince, later King, Friedrich August of Saxony who held the colonelcy until 1905.

A former regiment with the number 45 had been raised in 1682. It was disbanded in 1809.

(Title vacant) No 46

A Hungarian regiment Facing colour: *parrot green*
Recruiting area: *Szeged* Button colour: *yellow metal*

The regiment was raised in 1762 as the 1st Siegenburg Walschen Frontier Infantry Regiment. Three years later it was reorganised and in 1849 became the 1st Romanen Frontier Infantry Regiment. Not until 1851 did it become a regiment of the Infantry Line. It was then commanded by General Count Joseph Hellavic de Butzim. His eight-year period in office ended in 1859 and he was succeeded by General Prince Alexander of Hessen. Bernard, Duke of Sachsen-Meiningen became Colonel-in-Chief during 1862 and held the appointment for nineteen years. He was succeeded in office by General Count Ladislaus Szapary. In 1887 General Count Geza Fejevary de Komlos Keresztos was appointed Colonel.

There had been a former regiment with the number 46. This had been raised in 1745 as the Tirol Field and County Regiment, but was disbanded in 1809.

General Friedrich von Beck-Rzikovsky No 47

A German regiment Facing colour: *steel green*
Recruiting area: *Marburg* Button colour: *white metal*

The regiment was raised in 1682 and was first commanded by General George von Wallis. During 1689 command passed to General Count Franz Jorger de Tollet and from him to General Count Wilhelm Oettingen-Baldern in 1691. By 1694 there had been two changes of colonelcy but with the incumbency of General Count Joseph Harrach the regiment enjoyed a long period with only one commander. Count Harrach remained as Colonel of the Regiment from 1704 until 1764, when General Friedrich The Markgraf of Bayreuth assumed the command. His period was brief and that of his successor, Carl von Ellrichshausen, not much longer for by 1779 General Count Franz Kinsky had become the Colonel-in-Chief. Two other Colonels came to the post and in 1827 General Count

Anton Kinsky assumed command. His period of office lasted until 1864 when General Ernst von Hartung succeeded him. Fifteen years later General Edward von Litzelhofen took up the post and held it until 1883 when General Count Friedrich Beck was appointed to command the 47th Regiment.

General Rohr No 48

A Hungarian regiment Facing colour: *steel green*
Recruiting area: *Nagykanisza* Button colour: *yellow metal*

The regiment was raised in 1798 and during the following year General Philip von Vukassovitch took up the post of Colonel. He was succeeded in 1809 by General Joseph von Simbschen and he, in turn, during 1815, by General Paul von Radivojevitch. At the end of his period of office he was succeeded by General Alois Gollner von Goldenfels in 1820. In 1845 the regiment was bestowed upon General The Archduke Ernst and in 1899 command passed to another member of the Imperial family: General The Archduke Ferdinand.

There had been a former regiment carrying the number 48. This unit had been raised in 1721 from Spanish national regiments which were in the Imperial Service. It was disbanded in 1796.

Feldmarschall Heinrich Hess No 49

A German regiment Facing colour: *pike grey*
Recruiting area: *St Poelten* Button colour: *white metal*

The 49th Regiment was raised in 1715 as the Baden Regiment and was commanded, from 1716 to 1724, by Field Marshal the Markgraf of Baden Durlach. He was succeeded by General Count Otto Walsegg who held the post for nineteen years. In 1743 General Johann von Baernklau took over the post and held it for four years. Field Marshal Count Carl Keuhl was Colonel of the Regiment until 1758 when General Ludwig von Angern succeeded him. He, in turn, was succeeded by Field Marshal Count Clement Pellegrini in 1767 and in 1797 General Wilhelm von Kerpen assumed the command. In 1824 General Friedrich von Langenau was made Colonel and was followed by General Michael Schoen von Treuenwerth in 1840. In 1844 Field Marshal Heinrich Hess was appointed to command the 49th Regiment and he died during his period in office.

The regimental name and number were retained as permanent distinctions to commemorate his service.

Friedrich Wilhelm, Grossherzog von Baden No 50

A Hungarian regiment   Facing colour: *parrot green*
Recruiting area: Button colour: *white metal*
   Gyulafehervar

The regiment was raised in 1762 as the 2nd Siebenburg-Walschen Frontier Infantry. It was reorganised during the following year. In 1849 the name of the regiment was changed to 2nd Romanen Frontier Infantry Regiment and during 1851 the unit was converted to line regiment status.

The first of its three Colonels-in-Chief was General Prince Hanibal von Thurn und Taxis who held the post from 1851. His successor was Friedrich Wilhelm The Grand Duke of Baden who held the post until 1907 and who was followed by Friedrich The Grand Duke of Baden.

The regiment had the special distinction of wearing on the 1st Battalion Colour a golden medal which had been bestowed by the Emperor as recognition for the faithful service of the 50th Regiment in 1848.

There had been a former 50th Regiment on the Imperial establishment. This unit had been raised in 1629 and was disbanded in 1809.

General von Boroevic No 51

A Hungarian regiment   Facing colour: *ash grey*
Recruiting area: *Koloszvar* Button colour: *yellow metal*

The regiment was raised in 1702 by Colonel Paul Bagosy who held command until 1707 when he was succeeded by General Count Franz Gyulai. His period in office lasted until 1729 when General Count Franz Palffy ab Erdoed was appointed to command. A second member of the Gyulai family assumed the colonelcy in 1736 and Stephan Gyulai was succeeded in 1759 by Franz.

In 1788 General Gabriel von Splenyi von Minaldy was appointed to the post and was succeeded in 1822 by General Johann Mecsery de Tsoor. Eleven years later General The Archduke Carl Ferdinand had the 51st bestowed upon him and he commanded it until 1875 when General The Archduke Heinrich succeeded him. General Anton von Bils held the appointment from 1891 to 1894 and in 1897 General Emil Probszt von Obstorff became the Colonel-in-Chief.

Erzherzog Friedrich No 52

A Hungarian regiment   Facing colour: *dark red*
Recruiting area: *Pecs*   Button colour: *yellow metal*

The regiment was raised in 1741 and was first commanded by Colonel Count Bethlen after whom it was named. In 1747 General Wolfgang Bethlen assumed command and he was succeeded in 1763 by General Count Franz Karolyi von Nagy-Karoly.

From 1791 the 52nd Regiment had members of the royal family as Colonels-in-Chief. General The Archduke Anton Viktor held the post until 1804 when Archduke Franz Carl succeeded him. His incumbency extended over a period of many years and in 1879 The Archduke Friedrich had the regiment bestowed upon him.

General Dankl No 53

A Hungarian regiment   Facing colour: *dark red*
Recruiting area: *Agram*   Button colour: *white metal*

This regiment was raised in 1741 as the Pandur Corps and was commanded by Colonel Franz von der Trenk. Four years later there was a change of name and the unit was known as the Trenk Pandur Regiment. Three years later, as the result of reorganisations, the regiment was reduced to battalion strength and renamed the Slavonic Battalion. In 1753 Colonel Carl von Simbschen took over command from Colonel Adam von Buday, and during Simbschen's period in office the battalion was reformed into a regiment, converted to line status and numbered 53.

In 1763 General Philip von Beck became Colonel-in-Chief and he was succeeded in 1768 by General Count Johann Palffy ab Erdoed. General Johann Jellacic de Buzim assumed command in 1791 and was succeeded in 1814 by General Johann von Hiller. General Demeter von Radossevich von Rados became Colonel in 1825 and held the post for twenty-eight years. His successor was General The Archduke Leopold. From 1898 to 1904 General Joseph Latour von Thurnburg held the colonelcy and he was succeeded in 1905 by General Gustav Pletzner von Scharneck.

Feldmarschall Ernst Starhemberg No 54 (Alt Starhemberg)

A German regiment   Facing colour: *apple green*
Recruiting area: *Oelmutz* Button colour: *white metal*

The regiment was raised in 1661 and taken into service as the Kur Brandenburg Regiment. The first Colonel-in-Chief was General Count Ladislav Sparr who held the post for eight years. In 1669 he was succeeded by Field Marshal Count Ernst Starhemberg who, after thirty-two years in office passed the command to General von Kriechbaum. From him it passed to General Bertrand von Wachtendonck in 1710 and in 1720 it was held by General Count Lothar Konigsegg-Rothenfels. He was succeeded in 1751 by General Klaudius von Sincere and he, in turn, by General

Count Carl Callenberg in 1769. His long period in office ended in 1802 when General Count Ferdinand Mortin took up the post. He held the colonelcy for only three years and it then passed to General Count Josef Lamezan-Salius. In 1831 General Prince Emil von Hessen und bei Rhein assumed command and held the post for twenty-six years, being relieved in command by General Wilhelm von Graeber in 1857. He, too, held office for a long period (twenty years) and was succeeded in 1877 by General Count Franz Thun-Hohenstein.

The regimental name and number were retained as permanent distinctions to commemorate the 'Old Starhemberg' who died in 1701.

Nikolaus I, König von Montenegro No 55

A German regiment   Facing colour: *red brown*
Recruiting area: *Brzezany*   Button colour: *yellow metal*

Formed in 1799 around a nucleus of battalions drawn from five Walloon regiments and commanded by the Archduke Franz Josef. General Count Ludwig Baillot-Merlemont, who took over command in 1807, held it for four years after which it passed to General Toussaint Bourgeois. General The Duke of Casa Lanza was appointed in 1855 and held the colonelcy for ten years. The next officer to command the regiment, General Count Leopold Gondrecourt, led the regiment for twenty-three years.

A former 55th Regiment was raised in 1742 as a Dutch national infantry regiment and was disbanded in 1809.

Fürst Leopold Joseph Maria Daun von Thiano No 56

A German regiment   Facing colour: *steel green*
Recruiting area: *Cracow*   Button colour: *yellow metal*

The regiment was raised in 1684 by General Paul von Houchin. He was succeeded by Field Marshal Count Wirisch Daun, Prince of Thiano, in 1699. Field Marshal Count Anton Mercy-Argenteau was appointed in 1741 and held the post until 1767 when General Count Jakob Nugent was given the post. In 1784 Field Marshal Count Colloredo-Waldsee assumed command and held it until 1825 when General Carl von Furstenwurther succeeded him. General Franz von Gorizutti then led the 56th Infantry until he was replaced by General Alois von Baumgartner, who held the post from 1875 to 1895.

The regimental name and number were retained as permanent distinctions to commemorate Fuerst Leopold Daun who died in 1766.

Prinz Josias zu Sachsen-Coburg-Saalfeld No 57

A German regiment   Facing colour: *pale red*
Recruiting area: *Tarnow*   Button colour: *yellow metal*

The regiment was raised in 1689 by General Duke Albrecht III, of Sachse-Coburg who led it for ten years. In 1699 General Carl von Kratz became Colonel-in-Chief and held the post until 1704, when General Damian von Sickingen replaced him. General Johann von Wellenstein was appointed in 1713 but within two years the post had passed to General Browne de Camus. From 1731 to 1734 General Franz von O'Neillan led the regiment and after incumbency of General Adam von Thungen it passed to General Joseph von Andlau. General Count Joseph Colloredo-Waldsee was appointed in 1869 and held the post until 1823 when Joseph Friedrich von Minutillo replaced him. There were other Colonels-in-Chief before Prince Phillip von Sachse-Coburg-Gotha was appointed to lead the regiment in 1902.

The regimental name and number were retained as permanent distinctions to commemorate Prinz Josias who died in 1815.

Erzherzog Ludwig Salvator No 58

A German regiment   Facing colour: *black*
Recruiting area: *Stanislau*   Button colour: *white metal*

In 1763 this French regiment was taken into the Imperial Service under the command of General Charles Albert de St Omer Vierset. General Johann Peter von Beaulieu succeeded him in 1794 and he, in turn, was succeeded by General Count Joseph L'Espine. In 1827 General Carly Veyden von Malberg became the Colonel-in-Chief and held the post until he was succeeded by General The Archduke Stephan in 1830. Colonel The Archduke Ludwig Salvator was appointed to command the regiment in 1867.

Erzherzog Rainer No 59

A German regiment   Facing colour: *orange yellow*
Recruiting area: *Salzburg*   Button colour: *yellow metal*

This regiment, the Salzburg 'House' regiment, was raised in 1682 by General Melchior von der Beckiy who was succeeded in 1693 by General Count Ludwig Marsiglia. In 1704 General Count Jorger de Tollet was appointed to command the regiment and twelve years later General Count Ottokar Starhemberg took up the appointment. General Count Franz Wallis assumed command in 1731 and in 1740 Count Leopold Daun became Colonel-in-Chief. A second member of the Daun family, Colonel Count Franz Carl, took up the post in 1766 but held it for only five years and was succeeded by General Peter Langlois who commanded the 59th for eighteen years. In 1815 began the association of the regiment with the Ducal family of Baden when three Grand Dukes in succession held the colonelcy. In 1852 the regiment was bestowed upon General The Archduke Rainer.

General von Ziegler No 60

A Hungarian regiment   Facing colour: *steel green*
Recruiting area: *Eger*   Button colour: *white metal*

The regiment was raised in 1798 and was commanded from 1801 by General Count Ignatius Gyulia von Maros-Nemeth. He was succeeded in 1831 by General Prince Gustav Wasa and he, in turn, by General Alexander Benedek. The colonelcy was then bestowed upon General Carl Nagy von Toeboer-Ethe in 1878 from whom it passed to General Johann von Appel in 1883. From 1905 General von Ziegler held the appointment.

General von Frank No 61

A Hungarian regiment   Facing colour: *grass green*
Recruiting area: *Temesvar* Button colour: *yellow metal*

Raised in 1798. In 1802 General Count Franz Saint-Julien took over command of the regiment and held that post for thirty-four years. He was succeeded by General George Rukavina von Vidovgrad from whom command passed in 1848 to General Count Julius Strassoldo-Graffemberg.

In 1855 General Zobel von Gibelstadt was appointed to command the regiment and held that post until 1859, when the Tsarevitch Nicholas took over the post. That appointment began a close association between the Ruling House of Russia and the 61st Regiment. Alexander the Tsarevitch was appointed to command the regiment in 1865 and held the post until 1894 during which period he ascended the Russian throne. The post of Colonel-in-Chief passed out of the hands of the Romanovs in 1897 when General Hold von Ferneck became the new commander and he was succeeded by General Otto Morawetz von Klienfeld in 1902. From 1905 General von Frank held the post.

Ludwig III, König von Bayern No 62

A Hungarian regiment   Facing colour: *grass green*
Recruiting area: Button colour: *white metal*
    Maros-Vasarhely

Raised in 1798 and commanded by General Franz Jellacic de Buzim from 1802 to 1810 when General Theodor Wacquant Geozelles assumed the colonelcy. He was succeeded by General Johann von Turszky in 1844. His twelve-year period of command ended in 1856 when General The Archduke Heinrich became the Colonel-in-Chief. The regiment was bestowed upon Ludwig, Prince of Bavaria, in 1868 and changed when he became Ludwig III, King of that State.

|||||||||||||||||||||||||||||||||||||||||||||||||||||||||||||||||||||||||||||||||||||

The next wave of expansion to the infantry arm raised the establishment to eighty regiments of the line.

General Heinrich von Pitreich No 63

A Hungarian regiment   Facing colour: *orange yellow*
Recruiting area: *Besztercze* Button colour: *white metal*

Formed on 1 February 1860 from two battalions of the 62nd Regiment and one battalion of the 41st Regiment.

Wilhelm III, King of the Netherlands, was the first Colonel-in-Chief and held the appointment for thirty years. He was succeeded by Paul Alexandrovitch, Grand Prince of Russia.

A former regiment which had held the number 63 was renumbered 55 on 1 November 1852.

General von Auffenberg No 64

A Hungarian regiment   Facing colour: *orange yellow*
Recruiting area: Button colour: *yellow metal*
    Szaszavaros

The regiment was formed by an amalgamation of a battalion from 31st Regiment and one each from the 50th and 51st Regiments.

From the time of its raising the Colonel-in-Chief was Carl Alexander Grand Duke of Sachse-Weimar-Eisenach. He was succeeded in 1890 by General Carl von Mertens who laid down the office in 1903 and was followed by General von Auffenberg.

A former regiment with the number 64 was raised in 1801 as the Tirol Jaeger Regiment and was converted into a standard Jaeger regiment during 1806. That regiment was disbanded in 1808 and then split up to form nine independent Jaeger units, these then forming the cadre of Feldjaeger Battalions 1-9.

Erzherzog Ludwig Viktor No 65

A Hungarian regiment   Facing colour: *pale red*
Recruiting area: *Munkacs* Button colour: *yellow metal*

The regiment was raised on 1 February 1860 from two battalions of 5th Regiment and one battalion from 58th Regiment.

Erzherzog Peter Ferdinand No 66

A Hungarian regiment
Recruiting area: *Ungvar*

Facing colour: *pale red*
Button colour: *white metal*

Raised on 1 February 1860 from one battalion each of 34th, 40th and 57th Regiments.

The first Colonel-in-Chief was Ferdinand IV, Grand Duke of Tuscany.

General Paul Kray de Karjova et Topolya No 67

A Hungarian regiment
Recruiting area: *Eperjes*

Facing colour: *lobster red*
Button colour: *white metal*

Formed on 1 February 1860 from the amalgamation of two battalions of 20th Regiment and one battalion of the 60th Regiment.

From 1860 to 1884 the regiment had as its Colonel-in-Chief General von Schmerling. In 1885 General Count Edward Graef von Libloy took over the post and held it until 1892.

The regiment was authorised to carry the title and number as a permanent distinction in commemoration of General Kray de Krajova who died in 1804.

General Josepf von Reicher No 68

A Hungarian regiment
Recruiting area: *Szolnok*

Facing colour: *red brown*
Button colour: *yellow metal*

Formed on 1 February 1860 from one battalion each of 33rd, 37th and 46th Regiments.

The Colonel-in-Chief of the regiment from 1860 to 1866 was General Carl von Steininger, and from 1867 to 1890 General Gabriel von Rodich.

(Title vacant) No 69

A Hungarian regiment
Recruiting area: *Szekesfehervar*

Facing colour: *pike grey*
Button colour: *white metal*

Raised on 1 February 1860 from an amalgamation of two battalions of the 19th Regiment and one battalion of 27th Regiment.

The Colonel-in-Chief of the 69th Regiment was General Count George Jellacic de Buzim, who commanded it from its raising until 1901. He was succeeded by General Aton von Pitreich in that year.

General von Appel No 70

A Hungarian regiment

Facing colour: *sea green*

Recruiting area:
Beszterczbanya
to 1875 and then
Peterwardein

Button colour: *yellow metal*

This regiment was raised on 1 February 1860 from one battalion each of 1st, 3rd and 25th Regiments.

This Hungarian regiment recruited in Slavonia and in the Beszterczbanya until 1 October 1875, when the recruiting area was changed to Peterwardein. That area had supplied men for the 9th Frontier Infantry Regiment and when that formation was disbanded the 70th Regiment received the auxiliary title of the Peterwardein Regiment.

From 1860 until 1872 the regiment had as its Colonel-in-Chief General Laidslaus Nagy von Also-Szopor, and from 1873 until 1903 General Franz Philipovic von Phillipsberg.

General Anton Galgotzy No 71

A Hungarian regiment
Recruiting area: *Trencsen*

Facing colour: *lobster red*
Button colour: *yellow metal*

Formed on 1 February 1860 from one battalion each of 8th, 12th and 54th Regiments.

The first Colonel-in-Chief was Leopold II, Grand Duke of Tuscany, who held the post from the time that the regiment was raised until 1870. He was succeeded by General Rudolf von Rossbacher who held the appointment until 1886, when Field Marshal Helmuth Moltke assumed command.

General Emil David von Rhofeld No 72

A Hungarian regiment
Recruiting area: *Poszony*

Facing colour: *light blue*
Button colour: *yellow metal*

Raised on 1 February 1860 from two battalions of the 4th and one battalion of the 23rd Regiment.

The first Colonel-in-Chief of the regiment was General Wilhelm Ramming von Riedkirchen who held the appointment until 1876. He was succeeded in that year by General Joseph Dormus von Kilianshausen. In 1890 General von Rhonfeld assumed command of the regiment.

Albrecht, Herzog von Württemberg No 73

A German regiment
Recruiting area: *Eger*

Facing colour: *cherry red*
Button colour: *yellow metal*

When the regiment was raised on 1 February 1860 its first Colonel-in-Chief was General Alexander Mensdorff-Poully. He held the appointment for five years and was succeeded by General, The Duke Wilhelm of Wurttemberg. The Duke Albrecht succeeded to the post in 1898.

The battalion was created from one battalion each of 35th, 42nd and 55th Regiments.

General Franz von Schönaich No 74

A German regiment   Facing colour: *madder red*
Recruiting area: *Jicin*   Button colour: *white metal*

Formed on 1 February 1860 from one battalion each of 28th, 36th and 55th Regiments.

From 1860 to 1884 the post of Colonel-in-Chief of the regiment was held by General Count Nobili. In 1886 General Friedrich von Bouvard was appointed and in 1903 was succeeded by General Franz von Schoenaich.

(Title vacant) No 75

A German regiment   Facing colour: *light blue*
Recruiting area: *Neuhaus*   Button colour: *white metal*

The regiment was raised on 1 February 1860 by an amalgamation of one battalion each from 11th, 18th and 21st Regiments.

For the first eight years of its life the regiment had as its Colonel-in-Chief General Count Franz Folliot de Crenneville-Poutet and he was succeeded in 1888 by Christian IX, King of Denmark.

General Daniel von Salis-Soglio No 76

A Hungarian regiment   Facing colour: *pike grey*
Recruiting area: *Sopron*   Button colour: *yellow metal*

Raised on 1 February 1860, the regiment was made up of two battalions from 49th Regiment and one battalion of the 43rd.

The first Colonel-in-Chief, General Franz von Paumgarten, held the post for six years and was then succeeded by General Franz von John. In 1876 General Albert Knebel von Treuenschwert was appointed and held the post until 1890. One year later, General Salis-Soglio became the Colonel-in-Chief.

Phillip, Herzog von Württemberg No 77

A German regiment   Facing colour: *cherry red*
Recruiting area: *Sambor*   Button colour: *white metal*

Formed on 1 February 1860 from two battalions of the 9th Regiment and one battalion of the 10th, the regiment was commanded by General The Archduke Carl Salvator and in 1892 he was succeeded by Philip von Wurttemberg.

General Gerba No 78

A Hungarian regiment   Facing colour: *red brown*
Recruiting area: *Esseg*   Button colour: *white metal*

The regiment was formed on 1 February 1860 from one battalion each of 17th, 47th and 53rd Regiments.

From the date of its founding the regiment was commanded by General Joseph von Sokcevic and in 1897 he was succeeded by General Wilhelm von Gradl.

Count Joseph Jellacic No 79

A Hungarian regiment   Facing colour: *apple green*
Recruiting area: *Otocac*   Button colour: *white*

A Hungarian regiment, raised in Croatia, was formed on 1 February 1860 from two battalions of the 26th Regiment and one battalion of the 22nd.

On 1 October 1873 the former recruiting area in Hungary was given up and a new area, in Croatia, was taken over.

The regiment was first commanded by General Charles von Franck and he was succeeded in 1867 by General The Count Huyn. The name of Count Joseph Jellacic was bestowed upon the regiment to be carried in perpetuity. The Count, who died in 1859, was one of the great Croat commanders of the old army.

The 79th also had an additional title, the Otocan Regiment, to commemorate one of the recruiting areas which it had surrendered in 1873.

Wilhelm Ernst, Gross Herzog von Sachsen-Weimar-Eisenach No 80

A German regiment   Facing colour: *scarlet*
Recruiting area: *Zloczow*   Button colour: *white*

The regiment was raised on 1 February 1860 from two battalions of the 16th Regiment and one battalion from the 13th Regiment.

From 1860 to 1893 Wilhelm, Prince of Schleswig-Holstein-Glucksburg, served as Colonel-in-Chief and he was succeeded by Arnulf, Prince of Bavaria. The appointment was then taken up by Wilhel Ernst of Sachse-Weimar-Eisenach.

In 1883 there was an increase in the number of regiments forming the Infantry Line and Regiments 81 to 102 were raised.

General Johann von Waldstätten No 81

A German regiment Facing colour: *carmine*
Recruiting area: *Iglau* Button colour: *white metal*

Raised on 1 January 1883 from battalions taken from the 1st, 3rd, 8th and 54th Regiments.

The first Colonel of the Regiment was General Franz von Vlasits who was succeeded in 1887 by General von Waldstaetten.

General Schwitzer von Bayersheim No 82

A Hungarian regiment Facing colour: *carmine*
Recruiting area: Button colour: *white metal*
Szekelyudvarhely

Formed on 1 January 1883 from battalions taken from 2nd, 31st, 62nd and 63rd Regiments.

General Anton von Schonfeld was Colonel of the Regiment from the date of its raising until 1898, in which year he was succeeded by General von Bayersheim.

General von Schikofsky No 83

A Hungarian regiment Facing colour: *dark brown*
Recruiting area: Button colour: *white metal*
Szombathely

The regiment was raised on 1 January 1883 from battalions taken from 29th, 33rd, 43rd and 61st Regiments.

The first Colonel of the Regiment was General Christopher Graf von Degenfeld-Schonfeld. He was succeeded in 1909 by General von Schikofsky.

General Artur von Bolfras No 84

A German regiment Facing colour: *carmine*
Recruiting area: *Vienna* Button colour: *yellow metal*

Raised on 1 January 1883 from battalions drawn from 4th, 14th, 40th and 59th Regiments. The first Colonel was General Ferdinand von Bauer, who was succeeded by Alfred, Duke of Sachse-Coburg-Gotha, in 1894. He, in turn, was succeeded by General von Bolfras in 1900.

General Gaudernack von Kis-Demeter No 85

A Hungarian regiment Facing colour: *apple green*
Recruiting area: Button colour: *yellow metal*
Maramorosziget

The regiment was formed by the amalgamation of one battalion each of the 5th, 34th, 60th and 65th Regiments. It was commanded from the date of its raising in 1883 until 1906 by General Georg von Kees, and thereafter by General von Kis-Demeter.

General Carl von Steininger No 86

A Hungarian regiment Facing colour: *amarin red*
Recruiting area: *Szabadka* Button colour: *yellow metal*

The regiment was formed by the amalgamation of one battalion each from the 6th, 23rd, 32nd and 38th Regiments on 1 January 1883.

From 1883 until 1886 the regiment was commanded by General Georg Stubenrauch von Tannenburg and he was succeeded by General Anton Szveteney de Nagy-Ohay who held the colonelcy until 1883. In 1894 a new Colonel-in-Chief was appointed—General Julius Forinyak—and he commanded until 1905. During 1906 command of the regiment was bestowed upon General Carl von Steininger.

General Succovaty von Vezza No 87

A German regiment Facing colour: *sea green*
Recruiting area: *Cilli* Button colour: *white metal*

Raised on 1 January 1883 from battalions of 7th, 27th, and 47th Regiments as well as from the Feldjaeger Battalion No 35.

The first Colonel was General, Prince Hohenlohe-Schillingfurst who held the appointment from 1883 to 1896 and was succeeded by General Julian von Roszkowski in that year. One year later, General von Vezza had taken over the post.

(Title vacant) No 88

A German regiment Facing colour: *wine red*
Recruiting area: *Beraun* Button colour: *white metal*

The first Colonel was General Friedrich von Trautsteinberg but when he laid down the appointment no other Colonel was appointed.

General Eugene von Albori No 89

A German regiment Facing colour: *wine red*
Recruiting area: Button colour: *yellow metal*
Grodek Jagiellonski

Raised on 1 January 1883 from one battalion each of 9th, 30th, 55th and 80th Regiments.

The first Colonel-in-Chief, General Emmerich von Kaiffel, did not take up his appointment until 1885 and held it until 1892. There was another period of three years without a Colonel until in 1895, General von Albori assumed command.

General Adolf Horsetzky von Hornthal No 90

A German regiment Facing colour: *amaranth red*
Recruiting area: *Jaroslau* Button colour: *yellow metal*

Raised on 1 January 1883 from battalions from the 10th, 40th, 45th and 77th Regiments.

The first Colonel-in-Chief was General Prince Ludwig von Windisch-Graetz who held the appointment until 1904. He was succeeded by General Horsetzky.

(Title vacant) No 91

A German regiment Facing colour: *parrot green*
Recruiting area: *Budweis* Button colour: *yellow metal*

The regiment was formed on 1 January 1883 from an amalgamation of battalions taken from 11th and 75th Regiments as well as from detachments from 24th and 34th Feldjaeger Battalions.

From 1885 to 1902 the Colonel-in-Chief of the 91st was General Ludwig Frohlich von Elmbach who was succeeded by General Hubert von Czibulka in 1904.

General von Hortstein No 92

A German regiment Facing colour: *white*
Recruiting area: *Komotau* Button colour: *white metal*

The regiment was created out of the amalgamation of battalions taken from 12th, 26th, 42nd and 74th Regiments. The Colonel-in-Chief was General Gustav von Koenig.

(Title vacant) No 93

A German regiment Facing colour: *dark brown*
Recruiting area: Button colour: *yellow metal*
Maehrisch-Schoenberg

The regiment was formed on 1 January 1883 from an amalgamation of battalions drawn from the 13th, 20th, 56th and 57th Regiments.

Command of the regiment was first bestowed upon General Alfred von Joelson.

General Albert von Koller No 94

A German regiment Facing colour: *white*
Recruiting area: *Turnau* Button colour: *yellow metal*

The regiment was formed on 1 January 1883 from an amalgamation of battalions taken from 25th, 66th and 67th Regiments as well as detachments from 37th Feldjaeger Battalion.

The first Colonel-in-Chief of the regiment was Alfonso, King of Spain, who held the appointment from 1883 to 1885, and who was succeeded by General Prince Leopold von Croy. He held the colonelcy from 1889 to 1894. In 1897 General von Merta was appointed to command the 94th and in 1900 General von Klobus took up the post.

General von Kövess No 95

A German regiment Facing colour: *amaran red*
Recruiting area: *Czortkov* Button colour: *white metal*

The regiment was formed on 1 January 1883 from an amalgamation of battalions taken from the 15th, 24th, 41st and 58th Regiments.

From 1885 to 1886 the post of Colonel-in-Chief was held by General Ludwig von Cornaro. He was succeeded in 1887 by General Joseph von Rodakowski.

Ferdinand, Kronprinz von Rumänien No 96

A Hungarian regiment Facing colour: *carmine*
Recruiting area: *Carlstadt* Button colour: *yellow metal*

The regiment was formed on 1 January 1883 from an amalgamation of battalions taken from the 16th, 53rd, 70th and 78th Regiments.

From 1883 to 1889 General von Ramberg was Colonel-in-Chief of the 96th and from 1900 to 1907 the post was held by General von Catinelli.

General George von Waldstätten No 97

A German regiment Facing colour: *rose*
Recruiting area: *Trieste* Button colour: *white metal*

The regiment was raised on 1 January 1883 from battalions taken from 17th, 22nd and 70th Regiments as well as companies from the 33rd Feldjaeger Battalion.

The first Colonel-in-Chief was Milan I, King of Serbia, who held the appointment from 1883 to 1892, when he was succeeded by General von Waldstaetten.

General von Rummer No 98

A German regiment Facing colour: *light fawn*
Recruiting area: Button colour: *white metal*
Hohenmauth

Formed on 1 January 1883 from battalions taken from 18th, 21st and 71st Regiments as well as companies from the 39th Feldjaeger Battalion.

The post of Colonel of the Regiment was held from 1887

to 1902 by General von Dresdenberg and he was succeeded by General Charles Horsetzky von Hornthal.

(Title vacant) No 99

A German regiment   Facing colour: *sulphur yellow*
Recruiting area: *Znaim*   Button colour: *yellow metal*

Formed on 1 January 1883 from battalions taken from the 19th, 44th, 48th and 52nd Regiments.

The only Colonel-in-Chief of this regiment was George I, King of the Hellenes, who held the appointment from the time of the regiment's raising until 1909.

General Moritz von Steinsberg No 100

A German regiment   Facing colour: *light fawn*
Recruiting area: *Teschen*   Button colour: *yellow metal*

The regiment was formed on 1 January 1883 from battalions taken from the 50th, 51st and 64th Regiments as well as from 36th Feldjaeger Battalion.

The first Colonel-in-Chief was General Edmund von Krieghammer who was succeeded by von Steinsberg.

General Charles Dratschmidt von Bruckheim No 101

A Hungarian regiment   Facing colour: *sulphur yellow*
Recruiting area: *Bekescaba* Button colour: *white metal*

Formed on 1 January 1883 from battalions drawn from 37th, 39th, 46th and 68th Regiments.

The first Colonel-in-Chief was Sergius Alexandrovitch, Grand Duke of Russia, who held the appointment from 1884 to 1905. In that year he was succeeded by General von Bruckheim.

General Potiorek No 102

A German regiment   Facing colour: *sea grass green*
Recruiting area: *Beneschau* Button colour: *yellow metal*

The regiment was raised on 1 January 1883 from battalions taken from 26th, 69th, 72nd and 76th Regiments.

The first Colonel-in-Chief was General Adolf von Catty, who held the appointment until 1894. In 1897 General Ludwig Fabini assumed the colonelcy and he was succeeded in 1909 by General Potiorek.

|||||||||||||||||||||||||||||||||||||||||||||||||||||||||||||||||||||||||||||||||||||||||||||||||||||||||||||||||||||

INFANTRY · COMMON ARMY

3 · Tiroler Kaiserjaeger Regiments

|||||||||||||||||||||||||||||||||||||||||||||||||||||||||||||||||||||||||||||||||||||||||||||||||||||||||||||||||||||

The four regiments of Tiroler Kaiserjaeger which were on the Army List in 1914 descended from the Tiroler Jaeger Regiment which had been raised in 1801 and disbanded in 1808.

The next step in the regiment's development was in the raising of a Rifle Corps by General Franz Fenner von Fennerberg in 1813. The Fenner Corps was retitled Tiroler Jaeger Regiment Kaiser Franz during 1816 and bore, from 1835 to 1848, the name of the new Emperor, Ferdinand. The regiment was renamed when Franz Joseph ascended the throne in 1848. In 1895 the single Tiroler Jaeger Regiment Kaiser Franz Joseph was reorganised into four serially numbered regiments of Kaiserjaeger, all of which had the Emperor as their Colonel-in-Chief.

The Tiroler Kaiserjaeger Regiment No 1 was formed by the amalgamation of the first four battalions and the first replacement battalion of the existing Tiroler Jaeger Regiment 'Kaiser'; and the second regiment from the grouping of Battalions Nos 5 to 8 and the second replacement battalion.

The Tiroler Kaiserjaeger Regiment No 3 was created out of the amalgamation of Battalions Nos 9 to 12 and the third Replacement battalion; and the 4th Regiment through the amalgamation of Battalions Nos 13 to 16 and the fourth replacement battalion.

The Austrian Service had no Guards regiments such as the Household troops of the British Army or the Prussian Guard Corps of the German Imperial Army. There were certain regiments in the Austro-Hungarian Army, however, which were held to be elite. Chief among those were the regiments of Kaiserjaeger.

2nd Kaiserjaeger Regiment marching past the saluting base during the 1902 parade. The annual military parade on the Schmelz in Vienna was one of the features of the Austrian social year.

Men of the Kaiserjaeger march past their Colonel-in-Chief, The Emperor Franz Joseph, at Schoenbrunn Palace in Vienna. The Austro-Hungarian Army had no Guards regiments and the Kaiserjaeger were thus considered to be the élite of the old Imperial Army.

|||||||||||||||||||||||||||||||||||||||||||||||||||||||||||||||||||||||||||||||||||

INFANTRY · COMMON ARMY
4·Feldjaeger Battalions

The Archduke Eugene, The Hoch und Deutschmeister, reviewing the 4th Regiment of Kaiserjaeger, the 59th kuk Infantry Regiment and the 11th Feldjaeger Battalion at a parade in Tirol, 18 August 1905, in celebration of the Emperor's birthday.

|||||||||||||||||||||||||||||||||||||||||||||||||||||||||||||||||||||||||||

1st Bohemian

A German battalion
Recruiting area: *Josephstadt*
Raised in 1808

2nd Bohemian

A German battalion
Recruiting area: *Josephstadt*
Raised in 1808

3rd

Converted to become the 13th Battalion of the Tiroler Jaeger Regiment in 1893

4th Galician

A German battalion
Recruiting area: *Przemysl*
Raised in 1808

5th Moravia-Silesian

A German battalion
Recruiting area: *Cracow*
Raised in 1808

6th Bohemian

A German battalion
Recruiting area: *Prague*
Raised in 1808

7th Krain

A German battalion
Recruiting area: *Graz*
Raised in 1808

8th Carinthian

A German battalion
Recruiting area: *Graz*
Raised in 1808

9th Styrian

A German battalion
Recruiting area: *Graz*
Raised in 1808

10th Lower Austrian

A German battalion
Recruiting area: *Vienna*
Raised in 1813

This battalion carried a special Signal Horn to commemorate the bravery it showed when it took part in the fighting in Italy under Field Marshal Radetzky and, specifically, during the battle of Monte Berico.

The trumpet horn was carried from 1849 and was accorded the same honours as a Regimental Colour.

The 10th Battalion also carried the name Kopal as a permanent distinction.

11th Hungarian

A Hungarian battalion
Recruiting area: *Pozsony*
Raised in 1813

12th Bohemian

A German battalion
Recruiting area: *Josephstadt*
Raised in 1813

13th Galician

A German battalion
Recruiting area: *Cracow*
Raised in 1849

14th

Converted in October 1893 to become the 14th Battalion of the Tiroler Jaeger Regiment. Re-raised as 14th Feldjaeger Battalion in 1914.

15th

Converted in October 1893 to become the 11th Battalion of the Tiroler Jaeger Regiment.

16th Silesian

A German battalion
Recruiting area: *Cracow*
Raised in 1849

17th Moravian

A German battalion
Recruiting area: *Vienna*
Raised in 1849

18th

Converted in October 1893 to become 15th Battalion of the Tiroler Jaeger Regiment. Re-raised in 1914.

19th Hungarian

A Hungarian battalion
Recruiting area: *Pozsony*
Raised in 1849

20th Coastal and Krain

A German battalion
Recruiting area: *Graz*
Raised in 1849

21st Lower Austrian

A German battalion
Recruiting area: *Vienna*
Raised in 1849

22nd Bohemian

A German battalion
Recruiting area: *Prague*
Raised in 1849

23rd Hungarian

A Hungarian battalion
Recruiting area: *Nagyszeben*

Raised in 1848 as the Siebenburg Jaeger Battalion and converted to Feldjaeger status in 1849.

24th Hungarian

A Hungarian battalion
Recruiting area: *Budapest*

The unit was raised in 1880 and was given the number 40. It was re-numbered as 24th Battalion on 1 January 1883.

A former unit with the number 24 was the 1st Vienna Volunteer Battalion which was raised in 1848, was converted to Feldjaeger status in 1849 and used to form part of the newly raised 91st Infantry Regiment during 1883.

25th Moravian

A German battalion
Recruiting area: *Vienna*
Raised in 1849

26th

Converted on 1 October 1890 to become 12th Battalion of the Tiroler Jaeger Regiment.

27th

The unit was converted on 1 October 1893 to become the 16th Battalion of the Tiroler Jaeger Regiment. Re-raised in 1914.

28th Hungarian

A Hungarian battalion
Recruiting area: *Temesvar*
Raised in 1859

29th Hungarian

A Hungarian battalion
Recruiting area: *Kassa*
Raised in 1859

30th Galician

A German battalion
Recruiting area: *Lemberg*
Raised in 1859

31st Croatian

A Hungarian battalion
Recruiting area: *Agram*

Raised in 1859 as 1st Vienna Volunteer Battalion and converted to Feldjaeger status in the same year.

32nd Hungarian

A Hungarian battalion
Recruiting area: *Kassa*

Raised in 1859 from the 2nd and 3rd Vienna Volunteer Battalions.

Bosnia-Herzegovinian

Recruiting area: *Sarajevo*

This battalion was formed on 1 October 1903 from an amalgamation of Field Companies supplied by the Bosnia-Herzegovian Infantry regiments.

||||||||||||||||||||||||||||||||||||||||||||||||||||||||||||||||||||||||||

INFANTRY · COMMON ARMY
5 · Bosnia-Herzegovinian Regiments

||||||||||||||||||||||||||||||||||||||||||||||||||||||||||||||||||||||||||

No 1

Recruiting area: *Sarajevo*

The regiment was formed on 1 January 1894 through an amalgamation of the independent 1st Bosnia-Herzegovinian Infantry Battalion which had been formed in 1885, the 5th Bosnia-Herzegovinian Battalion, raised in 1889, and the 9th Bosnia-Herzegovinian Battalion, raised in 1892.

No 2

Recruiting area: *Banja-Luka*

The regiment was formed on 1 January 1894 through the amalgamation of the 2nd Bosnia-Herzegovinian Battalion which had been raised in 1885, the 6th Bosnia-Herzegovinian Battalion, raised in 1889, and the 10th Battalion, raised in 1892.

No 3

Recruiting area: *Dolnya-Tuza*

The regiment was formed on 1 January 1894 from the 3rd Bosnia-Herzegovinian Battalion which had been raised in 1885, the 7th Bosnia-Herzegovinian Battalion, raised in 1889, and the 11th Battalion, raised in 1892.

No 4

Recruiting area: *Mostar*

The regiment was formed on 1 January 1894 from an amalgamation of the independent 4th Bosnia-Herzegovinian Infantry Battalion which had been raised in 1885, the 8th Bosnia-Herzegovinian Battalion, raised in 1889, and the 12th Battalion, raised in 1892.

The battalions and regiments raised from Bosnia-Herzegovinia were among the bravest and most loyal of the Imperial Army. The fez headdress and the two buttons fastening the puttee were two dress distinctions peculiar to the Bosnian units.

INFANTRY · LANDWEHR

1 · Landwehr Infantry Regiments

Vienna No 1

Recruiting area: *Vienna*

Raised in 1889 from the Landwehr Infantry Battalions Vienna No 1, Korneuburg No 2 and Znaim No 18. The regiment was first titled Lower Austrian Landwehr Infantry Regiment No 1 and was retitled to that shown above during 1894.

In 1900 the 3rd Battalion was posted to the Landwehr Infantry Regiment Vienna No 24 and a new 3rd Battalion was then raised.

Linz No 2

Recruiting area: *Linz*

Raised in 1889 from the Landwehr Battalions Linz No 6, Wels No 7 and Salzburg No 8. First titled Upper Austrian and Salzburg Landwehr Infantry Regiment No 2. Received the title shown above during 1894.

The regiment reached a strength of four battalions during 1899 but was reduced again during October 1901 when its 4th Battalion was transferred to the Landesschuetzen Regiment Innsbruck No 1.

Graz No 3

Recruiting area: *Graz/Marburg*

Raised in 1889 from the Landwehr Battalions Cilli No 29, Marburg No 21 and Graz No 22. First titled Steyrmaerkisches Landwehr Infantry Regiment No 3, it received the above title in 1894.

In 1894 the 4th Battalion of Landwehr Infantry Regiment No 4 was taken on strength as 2nd Battalion of the Graz Regiment. During 1901 the 3rd and 4th Battalions of that regiment were posted to Landwehr Infantry Regiment Marburg No 26 and a new 3rd Battalion was then raised.

Klagenfurt No 4

Recruiting area: *Klagenfurt*

Raised in 1889 from the Landwehr Battalions Leoben No 23, Klagenfurt No 26 and Villach No 27 as the Styrian-Carinthian Landwehr Infantry Regiment No 4. It received the title shown above during 1894.

During that year the 2nd Battalion was posted to 3rd Landwehr Infantry Regiment and was replaced by Rudolswerth No 24 and Laibach No 25 Battalions of Trieste No 5. In 1901 those two battalions were posted to Infantry Regiment Laibach No 27. A new 3rd Battalion was raised.

In that year the regiment was then converted to become the 1st Mountain Rifle Regiment (Gebirgsschuetzen Regiment No 1).

Trieste No 5

Recruiting area: *Trieste*

Raised in 1889 from the Landwehr Battalions Rudolswerth No 24, Laibach No 25, Trieste No 72, Mitterburg (Pision) No 73 and Gorizia No 74. First titled Krain and Coastal area Landwehr Infantry Regiment No 5, it received the title shown above in 1894.

During that same year the 24th and 25th Battalions were posted away from the 5th Regiment and to the 4th Landwehr Regiment.

Eger No 6

Recruiting area: *Eger*

Raised during 1889 from the Landwehr Battalions Eger No 41, Bischofsstein No 51 and Plan No 51, and named as the Bohemian Landwehr Infantry Regiment No 6. Received the title shown above during 1894.

Pilsen No 7

Recruiting area: *Pilsen*

Raised in 1889 from the Landwehr Battalions Beraun No 34, Pilsen No 35, Klettau No 36 and Pisek No 47, and entitled Bohemian Landwehr Infantry Regiment No 7. It received the title given above during 1894.

In 1893 the Beraun Battalion was posted to 8th Landwehr Regiment and 28th Battalion was received as a replacement. In 1899 the 3rd and 4th Battalions were posted to 28th Landwehr Infantry Regiment and 29th Landwehr Infantry Regiment. A new 3rd Battalion was subsequently raised.

Prague No 8

Recruiting area: *Prague*

Raised in 1889 from the Landwehr Battalions Budweis No 28, Prague No 33, Neuhaus No 45 and Tabor No 46. First titled Bohemian Landwehr Infantry Regiment No 8 and retitled to that shown above in 1894.

In 1893 the 28th Battalion was posted to the Landwehr Infantry Regiment No 7, and 29th Battalion was received in exchange. In 1899 the 3rd Battalion was posted to the 28th Landwehr Regiment and 4th Battalion to the 29th Regiment. A new 3rd Battalion was then raised.

Leitmeritz No 9

Recruiting area: *Leitmeritz*

Raised in 1889 from the Landwehr Battalions Theresienstadt No 39, Brux No 40 and Komotan No 42. First titled Bohemian Landwehr Infantry Regiment No 9. Received the title given above during 1894.

Jungbunzlau No 10

Recruiting area: *Jungbunzlau*

Raised in 1889 from the Landwehr Battalions Jungbunzlau No 37, Boehmisch-Leipa No 38, Kuttenberg No 48 and Böhmisch-Brod No 49. First named as Bohemian Landwehr Infantry Regiment No 10, the regimental title changed to that given above during 1894.

During that year the 4th Battalion was posted to the 12th Landwehr Infantry Regiment.

Jicin No 11

Recruiting area: *Jicin*

Raised in 1889 from the Landwehr battalion Koeniggraetz No 29, Jicin No 43 and Trautenau No 44. First titled Bohemian Landwehr Infantry Regiment No 11 and retitled to that shown above in 1894.

Caslau No 12

Recruiting area: *Caslau*

Raised in 1889 from the Landwehr Battalions Hohenmauth No 30, Caslau No 31 and Deutsch-Brod No 32. The regiment was first titled Bohemian Landwehr Infantry Regiment No 12 and was retitled to that shown above in 1894.

In 1898 the 3rd Battalion was posted to the newly raised 30th Landwehr Infantry Regiment and a battalion of 10th Landwehr Infantry Regiment was received as a replacement.

Ölmutz No 13

Recruiting area: *Oelmutz*

Raised in 1889 from the Landwehr Battalions Oelmutz No 15, Schoenberg No 16 and Maehrisch-Trubau No 19. First titled as Moravian Landwehr Infantry Regiment No 13 and retitled to that shown above during 1894.

Brünn No 14

Recruiting area: *Bruenn*

Raised in 1889 from the Landwehr Battalions Kremsier No 12, Bruenn No 13 and Iglau No 14 as Moravian Landwehr Infantry Regiment No 14. The regiment received the title shown above during 1894.

In 1900 the 3rd Battalion was posted to the 25th Landwehr Infantry Regiment. A new 3rd Battalion was then raised.

Troppau No 15

Recruiting area: *Troppau*

Raised in 1889 from the Landwehr Battalions Troppau No 9, Teschen No 10, Jaegerndorf No 11 and Weisskirchen No 17 as Moravia-Silesian Landwehr Infantry Regiment No 15. Received the title shown above during 1894.

During October 1901 the 3rd Battalion was posted to the 31st Landwehr Infantry Regiment. The 4th Battalion was then renumbered as No 3.

Cracow No 16

Recruiting area: *Cracow*

Raised in 1889 from the Landwehr Battalions Cracow No 52, Tarnow No 53, Vadovice No 54 and Neu-Sandez No 60, and known as Galician Landwehr Infantry Regiment No 16. Received the title shown above during 1894.

In October 1901 the 2nd Battalion was posted to 31st Landwehr Infantry Regiment and the 3rd and 4th Battalions to 32nd Landwehr Infantry Regiment. Two new battalions were thereupon raised.

Rzeszow No 17

Recruiting area: *Rzeszow*

Raised in 1889 from the Landwehr Battalions Rzeszow No 55 and Kolbuszow No 56, Sanok No 57 and Jaroslau No 58. First titled Galician Landwehr Infantry Regiment No 17 and retitled in 1894 to that shown above.

In 1901 the 3rd Battalion was posted to 34th Landwehr Regiment and the 4th Battalion to 18th Landwehr Regiment. A new battalion was raised.

Przemysl No 18

Recruiting area: *Przemysl*

Raised in 1889 from the Landwehr Battalions Przemysl No 59, Sembor No 61, Stryj No 65 and Grodek No 68, as Galician Landwehr Infantry Regiment No 18. The regiment received the title shown above during 1894.

In October 1901 the 3rd and 4th Battalions were posted to the 33rd Landwehr Infantry Regiment and the 3rd Battalion of the 17th Landwehr Regiment was received as a replacement.

Lemberg No 19

Recruiting area: *Lemberg*

Raised in 1889 from the Landwehr Battalions Lemberg No 63, Zolkiew No 64, Zloczow No 67 and Tarnopol No 71, as Galician Landwehr Infantry Regiment No 19. The regiment received the title shown above during 1894.

In 1898 the 3rd and 4th Battalions were posted to the 35th Landwehr Infantry Regiment. A new 3rd Battalion was then raised.

Stanislau No 20

Recruiting area: *Stanislau*

Raised in 1889 from the Landwehr Battalions Stanislau No 62, Kolomea No 66, Czortkow No 69 and Bunczacz No 70 and first titled as Galician Landwehr Infantry Regiment No 20. The regiment received the title given above during 1894.

In 1898 the 4th Battalion was posted to 36th Landwehr Infantry Regiment.

St Pölten No 21

Recruiting area: *St Poelten*

Raised in 1889 from the Landwehr Battalions St Poelten No 3, Wiener-Neustadt No 4 and Krems No 5, as Lower Austrian Landwehr Infantry Regiment No 21. The regiment received the title shown above during 1894.

Czernowitz No 22

Recruiting area: *Czernowitz*

Raised in 1889 from the Landwehr Battalions Radautz No 75, Kotmann No 76, Czernowitz No 77 and Suczawa No 78, as Galician Landwehr Infantry Regiment No 22. Retitled to that shown above in 1894.

In 1898 the 4th Battalion was posted to 36th Landwehr Infantry Regiment.

Zara No 23

Recruiting area: *Zara*

Raised in May 1893 from the Landwehr Battalions Zara No 79, Spalato No 80, Ragusa No 81 and Cattaro No 82, as Dalmatian Landwehr Infantry Regiment No 23. Received the title shown above in 1894.

Vienna No 24

Recruiting area: *Vienna*

Formed in October 1900 around a nucleus of 3rd Battalion of 1st Landwehr Infantry Regiment and two other newly formed battalions.

Kremsier No 25

Recruiting area: *Kremsier*

Raised in 1900 from the 3rd Battalion of 14th Landwehr Infantry Regiment and two other battalions which had been newly raised.

Marburg No 26

Recruiting area: *Marburg*

Raised during October 1901 from the 3rd and 4th Battalions of 3rd Landwehr Infantry Regiment and a newly raised battalion.

Laibach No 27

Recruiting area: *Laibach*

Raised during October 1901 from the 3rd and 4th Battalions of 4th Landwehr Infantry Regiment and a newly raised battalion.

This regiment was then converted to become 2nd Mountain Rifle Regiment (Gebirgsschuetzen Regiment No 2)

Pisek No 28

Recruiting area: *Pisek*

Raised in October 1899 from 3rd Battalion of 7th Landwehr Infantry Regiment, 3rd Battalion of 8th Landwehr Infantry Regiment and another battalion.

Budweis No 29

Recruiting area: *Budweis*

Raised in 1899 from 4th Battalion of 7th Landwehr Infantry Regiment, 4th Battalion of 8th Landwehr Infantry Regiment and a newly raised battalion.

Hohenmauth No 30

Recruiting area: *Hohenmauth*

Raised in 1898 from 3rd Battalion of 12th Landwehr Infantry Regiment and two other newly raised battalions.

Teschen No 31

Recruiting area: *Teschen*

Raised during October 1901 from 3rd Battalion of 15th Landwehr Infantry Regiment and one newly raised battalion, as well as 2nd Battalion of the 16th Landwehr Infantry Regiment.

Neu-Sandez No 32

Recruiting area: *Neu-Sandez*

Raised during October 1901 from the 3rd and 4th Battalions of 16th Landwehr Infantry Regiment and a newly raised battalion.

Stryj No 33

Recruiting area: *Stryj*

Raised during October 1901 from the 3rd and 4th Battalions of 18th Landwehr Infantry Regiment and a newly raised battalion.

Jaroslau No 34

Recruiting area: *Jaroslau*

Raised during October 1901 from 3rd Battalion of 17th Landwehr Infantry Regiment and two newly raised battalions.

Zloczow No 35

Recruiting area: *Zloczow*

Raised during October 1898 from 3rd and 4th Battalions of the 19th Landwehr Infantry Regiment and a newly raised battalion.

Kolomea No 36

Recruiting area: *Kolomea*

Raised during October 1898 from 4th Battalion of 20th Landwehr Infantry Regiment, 4th battalion of 22nd Landwehr Infantry Regiment and a newly raised battalion.

Gravosa No 37

Recruiting area: *Gravosa and Castelnuovo*

Raised in 1906.

|||||||||||||||||||||||||||||||||||||||||||||||||||||||||||||||||||||||||||||||||||||||||||||||||||||

INFANTRY · LANDWEHR
2 · Landesschuetzen

|||||||||||||||||||||||||||||||||||||||||||||||||||||||||||||||||||||||||||||||||||||||||||||||||||||

The Landesschuetzen units in the Imperial Service formed part of the Austrian Landwehr organisation and had several distinctions not enjoyed by other units. The first of these was the right of the men of each company to elect their own officers. This jealously guarded privilege went back to the 16th century and to the time of the Emperor Maximilian. The second distinction was that the Landesschuetzen units of Tirol and Vorarlberg could not be employed in a military role outside the territory of those provinces. Statutes governing this concession were regularly renewed between 1870 and 1913.

The number of Landesschuetzen formations to be raised was fixed by decree, dated 18 December 1870, as ten independent Rifles battalions and two Mounted Rifles companies. The yearly recruiting contingent of 413 men was not always met and the number of companies with a battalion was often reduced because of the shortage of men. By 1873 the establishment of each battalion had been fixed and for each regular battalion there was a reserve battalion and a permanent depot station. The average strength of a battalion in that year was 16 officers and 984 men. The seven men who served on the permanent staff at battalion headquarters brought the numbers up to 1,007.

To distinguish the Landesschuetzen units from the ordinary Landwehr in matters of dress, Joseph von Philipovic, the Military Commandant of Tirol, ordered that a vulture's feather, or the curled tail feathers of the capercailie, would be worn on the headdress. Such innovations, such infringements of dress regulations, conflicted with the policy of the War Department which ordered that the practice of wearing feathers in the cap was to cease.

Training and equipping of Landesschuetzen units developed to a point where, during the 1878 autumn manoeuvres, the men demonstrated the excellence of their training and their own hardihood by sleeping out in the snow without tents.

It had been a tradition that men for the Landesschuetzen units were recruited from local sources. The regular army's regiments of Kaiserjaeger might—and did—recruit from the whole Empire, but Landesschuetzen were tied very closely to particular villages and valleys. At first the battalions refused to accept outsiders but as early as 1889, it was clear that unless such recruits were accepted it would be impossible to meet the contingent numbers. The Landesschuetzen units then accepted men from neighbouring provinces and by 1 May 1893 not only were the companies up to full strength but the possibility existed that this situation would continue. This allowed the independent battalions to be formed into three regiments. An attempt to revert to purely local recruiting resulted in an inevitable shortfall in numbers which led to the disbandment of IIIrd Regiment during 1901. The men from that regiment were then posted to the other regiments and brought them up to strength. Another scheme to maintain the Landesschuetzen numbers was to draft men from other Landwehr battalions, but this was not a success. Company strengths during the first years of the 20th century seldom rose above 62 and this continuing shortfall in men made it impossible to detach companies or even platoons to man the fortresses along the border with Italy, as had been proposed.

Austria's political position vis-à-vis that country deteriorated and the Imperial manoeuvres, carried out at the end of August 1905, were intended both to impress and to warn the Italians. More than 20,000 soldiers took part, including both Landesschuetzen regiments which demonstrated the mountaineering skills which they had gained. The excellent showing of those regiments demonstrated that the defence of Tirol might well be entrusted to Landesschuetzen regiments, so long as these were trained, equipped and prepared for mountain warfare. To increase the number of mountain warfare formations the 4th (Klagenfurt) and the 27th (Laibach) Landwehr Regiments were brought onto establishment.

By 1 May 1906 the Landesschuetzen regiments, now reorganised as alpine troops, were at last authorised to demonstrate their association with the mountains by wearing a set of capercailie feathers on the left side of the cap. A second distinction granted to them was the wearing of an edelweiss badge on the tunic collar. There were other, more practical changes. The long unwieldy rifle was replaced by the shorter carbine and machine-gun detachments were set up.

The announcement that the Landesschuetzen units would be alpine troops generated a great response among the local civilian population whose members had only recently ventured into the high mountain peaks in search of recreation. There was a rush of volunteers to the now specialist Landesschuetzen units and company strengths rose from about sixty men to nearly twice that number. The continuing support for the new mountain troops then enabled IIIrd Regiment to be reformed on 1 March 1909.

The great and general enthusiasm was not lost upon the military commanders in Vienna, nor upon Conrad von Hoetzendorff who was one of the initiators of specialist mountain troops. The strength of battalions now allowed the commanders to detach men to garrison the permanent defensive works along the frontier with Italy. Each of the regiments was allotted a stretch of mountainous area which it would defend in time of war and in which its constituent battalions and the regimental depot were located. The IInd Regiment held the area from the Stilfserjoch to Lake Garda. The Ist Regiment covered the ground between Lake Garda and the Dolomites, while IIIrd Regiment was responsible for the territory between the Dolomites and the Austrian province of Carinthia.

Although the mountains were wild lonely places and although, in those days, the villages were poor and offered little in the way of amenities, the morale of the men in alpine units was always high. For most of them it really was the case of guarding their home and hearth. Each regiment had an unofficial motto. That of Ist Regiment was 'Victory or death in an alpine dawn'. The IInd Regiment carried as its motto 'On the rocky heights where the eagle flies', and the IIIrd 'Always watchful and filled with the lust of battle'.

Daily life in the regiments revolved round a summer and a winter schedule. In the summer the battalions patrolled in the high mountains keeping watch and sleeping out in the open or in the huts of the alpine societies. When winter came the patrols went down into the valleys and were bivouacked in the villages and little towns of the area. Winter training included competitions in marksmanship and from 1908 onwards there were valuable cash prizes to be won. One of the most prestigious was the Emperor's Target, awarded for skill in musketry. Those competitors with high marks were allowed to keep their service firearms as a reward. There were also prizes for proficiency with a machine gun.

With the outbreak of war in August 1914, the Landesschuetzen regiments were not kept to guard behind the southern frontier with Italy. Despite the assurances that they would not be employed on battlefields outside their provinces of Tirol and Vorarlberg, they were sent to the Eastern Front to face the Russians, leaving their native provinces unprotected. When Italy came into the war against Austria in 1915, the defence of the alpine regions depended upon the under-age boys and the old men of local Rifle Clubs—the Standschuetzen—and they, few in number though they were, defended the mountains until reinforcements could be brought from the other battle fronts to hold the attacking Italians.

LANDESSCHUETZEN REGIMENTS

Innsbruck No I

Recruiting areas: *Innsbruck and Salzburg.*

Formed in 1893 from four Landesschuetzen battalions and titled Tiroler Landesschuetzen Regiment No I. Received the title shown above in 1894.

Bozen No II

Recruiting areas: *Brixen and Trient*

Formed in 1893 from three Landesschuetzen battalions and titled Tiroler Landesschuetzen Regiment No II. Received the title shown above in 1894.

Innichen No III

Recruiting areas: *Brixen and Trient*

This regiment was first raised during 1893 and then disbanded in 1901. The component battalions were posted to the other two regiments of Landesschuetzen. The regiment was reformed in 1909.

INFANTRY · LANDWEHR (HONVED)
Landwehr (Honved) Regiments

Four types of uniform worn by the Infantry of the Landwehr (Honved), c1890. From left to right: Officer in marching order. Other Rank in the early pattern tunic whic...

Budapest No 1

A Hungarian regiment
Recruiting area: *Budapest*

Raised in 1886 from four Landwehr battalions and formed into the 1st Half Brigade. In 1889 a fourth battalion was raised. The title shown above was given in 1890.

Gyula No 2

A Hungarian regiment
Recruiting area: *Bekes-Gyula*

Raised in 1886 from three Landwehr battalions and formed into the 2nd Half Brigade. Received the title given above during 1890.

Debreczen No 3

A Hungarian regiment
Recruiting area: *Debreczen*

Raised in 1886 from four Landwehr battalions and formed into 3rd Half Brigade. Received the title given above during 1890.

Grosswardein No 4

A Rumanian regiment
Recruiting area: *Grosswardein*

Raised in 1886 from three Landwehr battalions and formed into the 4th Half Brigade. Received the title shown above during 1890.

Szeged No 5

A Hungarian regiment
Recruiting area: *Szeged*

Raised in 1886 from three Landwehr battalions and formed into the 5th Half Brigade. Received the title shown above during 1890.

Maria-Theresiopol No 6

A Serbian regiment
Recruiting area: *Maria-Theresiopol*

Raised in 1886 from three Landwehr battalions and formed into the 6th Half Brigade. Received the title given above during 1890.

Versec No 7

A Serbian regiment
Recruiting area: *Versec*

Raised in 1886 from three Landwehr battalions and formed into the 7th Half Brigade. Received the title shown above during 1890.

Lugos No 8

A Rumanian regiment
Recruiting area: *Lugos*

Raised in 1886 from four Landwehr battalions and formed into the 8th Half Brigade. Received the title shown above during 1890.

Kaschau No 9

A Hungarian regiment
Recruiting area: *Kaschau*

Raised in 1886 from four Landwehr battalions and formed into the 9th Half Brigade. Received the title shown above during 1890.

Miskolcz No 10

A Hungarian regiment
Recruiting area: *Miskolcz*

Raised in 1886 from three Landwehr battalions and formed into the 10th Half Brigade. Received the title shown above during 1890.

...as replaced by one without breast cords; ...ivate soldier in field service marching ...der; a bandsman.

(...alman collection)

Munkacs No 11

A Hungarian regiment
Recruiting area: *Munkacs*

Raised in 1886 from three Landwehr battalions and formed into the 11th Half Brigade. Received the title shown above during 1890.

Szatmar No 12

A Rumanian regiment
Recruiting area: *Szatmar Nemeti*

Raised in 1886 from three Landwehr battalions and formed into the 12th Half Brigade. Received the title shown above in 1890.

Pozsony No 13

A Slovenian regiment
Recruiting area: *Pozsony*

Raised in 1886 from four Landwehr battalions and formed into the 13th Half Brigade. Received the title given above during 1890.

Nyitra No 14

A Slovenian regiment
Recruiting area: *Nyitra*

Raised in 1886 from three Landwehr battalions and formed into the 14th Half Brigade. Received the title shown above during 1890.

Trencsen No 15

A Slovenian regiment
Recruiting area: *Trencsen*

Raised in 1886 from three Landwehr battalions and formed into the 15th Half Brigade. Received the title shown above during 1890.

Neusohl No 16

A Rumanian regiment
Recruiting area: *Neusohl*

Raised in 1886 from three Landwehr battalions and formed into the 16th Half Brigade. Received the title shown above during 1890.

Szekesgehervar No 17

A Hungarian regiment
Recruiting area: *Szekesgehervar*

Raised in 1886 from four Landwehr battalions and formed into the 17th Half Brigade. Received the title shown above during 1890.

Ödenburg No 18

A Hungarian regiment
Recruiting area: *Oedenburg*

Raised in 1886 from three Landwehr battalions and formed into the 18th Half Brigade. Received the title shown above during 1890.

Fünfkirchen No 19

A Hungarian regiment
Recruiting area: *Fuenfkirchen*

Raised in 1886 from four Landwehr battalions and formed into the 19th Half Brigade. Received the title shown above during 1890.

Nagy-Kanisza No 20

A Hungarian regiment
Recruiting area: *Nagy-Kanisza*

Raised in 1886 from three Landwehr battalions and an independent company and formed into the 20th Half Brigade. Received the title shown above in 1890.

Koloszvar No 21

A Rumanian regiment
Recruiting area: *Koloszvar*

Raised in 1886 from four Landwehr battalions and formed into the 21st Half Brigade. Received the title shown above during 1890.

Maros-Vasarhely No 22

A Rumanian regiment
Recruiting area: *Maros-Vasarhely*

Raised in 1886 from three Landwehr battalions and formed into the 22nd Half Brigade. Received the title shown above during 1890.

Nagyszeben No 23

A Rumanian regiment
Recruiting area: *Nagyszeben*

Raised in 1886 from three Landwehr battalions and formed into the 23rd Half Brigade. Received the title shown above during 1890.

Brasso No 24

A Rumanian regiment
Recruiting area: *Brasso*

Raised in 1886 from four Landwehr battalions and formed into the 24th Half Brigade. Received the title shown above during 1890.

Agram No 25

A Serbian regiment
Recruiting area: *Agram*

Raised in 1886 from three Landwehr battalions and formed into the 25th Half Brigade. Received the title shown above during 1890.

In 1892 the 2nd and 3rd Battalions were posted to 27th Landwehr Regiment and the 2nd and 3rd Battalions of that regiment were received by the 25th in exchange.

Carlstadt No 26

A Serbian regiment
Recruiting area: *Carlstadt*

Raised in 1886 from three Landwehr battalions and formed into the 26th Half Brigade. Received the title shown above during 1890.

Sissek No 27

A Serbian regiment
Recruiting area: *Sissek*

Raised in 1886 from three Landwehr battalions and formed into the 27th Half Brigade. Received the title shown above in 1892, after being first titled Belovar Regiment.

In 1892 the 2nd and 3rd Battalions of the regiment were posted to 25th Landwehr Regiment and received the 2nd and 3rd Battalions of that regiment in exchange.

Esseg No 28

A Rumanian regiment
Recruiting area: *Esseg*

Raised in 1886 from three Landwehr battalions and formed into the 28th Half Brigade. In 1890 the regiment was known as Vinkov Landwehr Infantry Regiment No 28 and received the title shown above during 1894.

Budapest No 29

A Hungarian regiment
Recruiting area: *Budapest*

Raised in 1913.

Budapest No 30

A Hungarian regiment
Recruiting area: *Budapest*

Raised in 1913.

Veszprem No 31

A Hungarian regiment
Recruiting area: *Veszprem*

Raised in 1913.

Des No 32

A Rumanian regiment
Recruiting area: *Bistritz*

Raised in 1913.

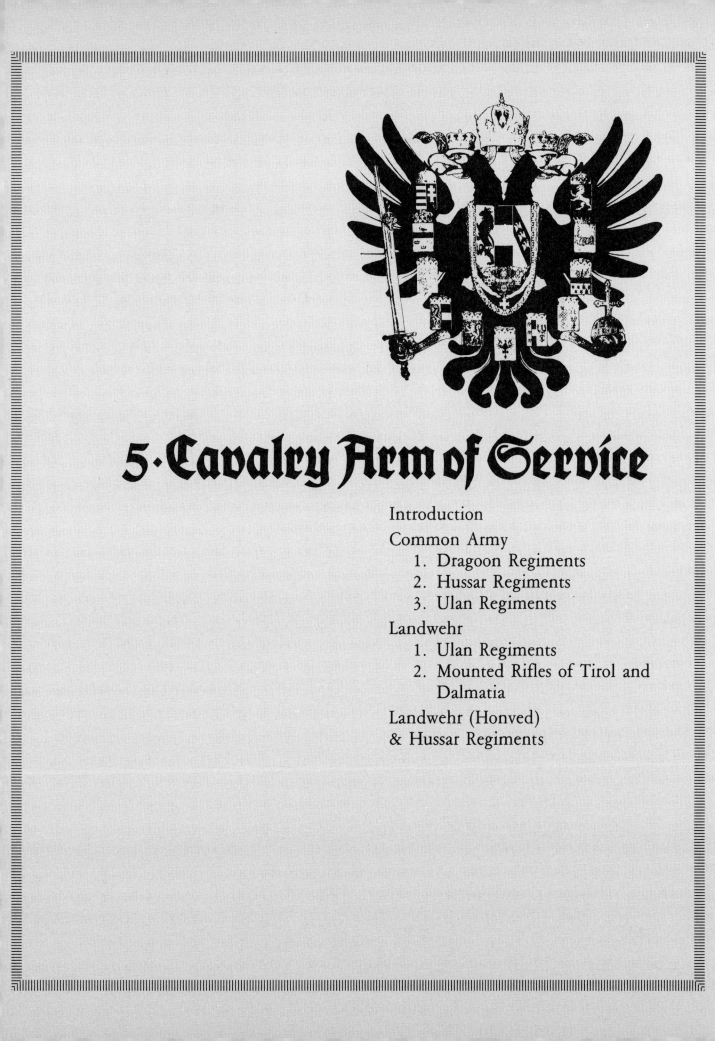

5·Cavalry Arm of Service

Introduction

Common Army
1. Dragoon Regiments
2. Hussar Regiments
3. Ulan Regiments

Landwehr
1. Ulan Regiments
2. Mounted Rifles of Tirol and Dalmatia

Landwehr (Honved)
& Hussar Regiments

Cavalry Arm of Service

The Austro-Hungarian Cavalry Arm was an intellectual body. The Imperial horsemen may not have been as numerous as those of other forces. They may not have produced the same fearsome effect as did, for example, the German cuirassiers, but the Emperor's horsemen had mental ability and were encouraged to produce original ideas. It was in the Habsburg cavalry that regimental pioneer troops were first raised to carry out light demolitions and constructions. Another innovation was the introduction of flotation bags to support individual soldiers during river crossings or to build rafts for ferrying equipment. Exercises in training horses to swim were developed in the Imperial Army. It was an Austrian cavalryman who invented a light bridge which could be thrown as a single unit across small obstacles and heavier pontoon bridging teams formed part of the Pioneer section in 6th Dragoons, 3rd and 7th Ulans as well as in the 1st, 2nd and 16th Hussars.

Another important innovation was the formation of special courier troops. A common complaint by cavalry commanders in all armies was that, on active service, the strength of their units was frittered away by having to detach men for escort, guard and orderly duties. The Austrian Service overcame that problem by forming messenger troops of one officer and fifty men who, at general mobilisation, were posted from their own regiment to a higher command.

Cavalry regiments were allocated either to infantry divisions where they were grouped under the heading of 'Divisional Cavalry', or they were grouped in brigades to form cavalry divisions. The regiments which were allotted as divisional cavalry carried out scouting, reconnaissance and outpost duties. Cavalry divisions served as a mass, to undertake long range reconnaissance, or to protect the main body of the army from enemy attack.

The nineteen cavalry brigades on the peacetime establishment of the Common Army formed Cavalry Divisions Nos 1, 2, 3, 4, 6, 7, 8 and 10. The 9th Cavalry Division was only raised during general mobilisation and both the 5th and 11th Divisions were formed from the Landwehr (Honved) establishment.

The Imperial Army had at one time contained eight types of cavalry but in the middle decades of the 19th century that number had been reduced to five and, by the end of that century, to three. Although the Cuirassier regiments had been abolished, Dragoons were retained to serve as a link with the centuries of German/Austria's mounted glory. Concessions to Magyar sensibilities maintained the Hussars and, perhaps to please the Slav peoples

Artist's sketch of a Squadron of Landwehr (Honved) Hussars on parade, 1913. (Kalman collection).

Josef, Graf Bellacic de Buzim, in the Hussar pattern winter attila which carried the same cords and braiding as the standard garment.

of the Empire, the Ulan, without his lance but still wearing the shapka, found a place on the cavalry establishment. Those three types of Horse helped to preserve the fiction that differences between the light and heavy cavalry were being maintained. It was a fiction for, although all three types kept their own dress style, the role of the Austro-Hungarian cavalry was that of mounted riflemen.

It would be pleasant to believe that Austria's military leaders organised the cavalry to carry out that role because they had foreseen the coming decline in importance on the battlefield of the mounted man. But this would be untrue. Those commanders who appreciated that the ability of a mounted rifleman to kill an enemy at long range was more to be prized than the rare opportunity for a rider to carry a steel blade to within striking distance of the enemy, were as few in number in the Habsburg armies as they were in the world's other military forces.

When all the reorganisations had been completed the Common Army

The Archduke Karl in Hussar attila, being cheered by officers of the Budapest garrison in 1914.

cavalry establishment was forty-two regiments strong, a figure no higher than it had been at the time of the Empress Maria Theresia. That total was broken down into:

Fifteen regiments of Dragoons, numbered serially.

Sixteen regiments of Hussars, numbered serially.

Eleven regiments of Ulans numbered serially, 1 to 8, and 11 to 13. Regiments 9 and 10 on the Ulan establishment did not exist.

The Austrian Landwehr organisation contained six regiments of Ulans and two half regiments of Mounted Rifles; one each from Tirol and Dalmatia. There was no provision for cavalry units on the Austrian Landsturm establishment.

Ten regiments of Hussars were on the Landwehr (Honved) establishment. The Hungarian Landsturm was not intended to be grouped regimentally although plans, produced in 1912, foresaw a build-up of that force to a strength of thirty squadrons.

The several reorganisations brought about changes and improvements. In 1884 cavalry armament was standardised as sabre, carbine and/or pistol. In 1892 saddle-bags of fodder were introduced and, in the same year, 1-200,000 maps were issued for cavalry reconnaissance. By 1899 a magazine carbine was on issue to all mounted units.

As early as 1913 machine-gun detachments had been raised by the following regiments:

Dragoon Regiments Nos 1, 2, 3, 5, 6, 11, 12 and 15.

Hussar Regiments Nos 1, 5, 9, 10, 12 and 14.

Ulan Regiments Nos 1, 3, 6 and 8.

At the turn of the century instructions were issued regarding the dyeing of horses to a dark, neutral shade in time of war. It seems strange that horses

Opposite page
Above
Eduard, Freiherr Bersina von Siegenthal, Colonel-in-Chief of kuk 6th Hussar Regiment. Of particular note is the barrelled and looped sash and the cartridge belt worn from the left shoulder to the right hip.

Below
A Dragoon regiment on parade, Bohemia 1910.

were to be painted as a camouflage measure, when no similar provision had been made to conceal the rider in his distinctive bright uniform. It had been proposed in 1909 to issue a grey standard combat dress to all the cavalry, but this had not been carried out by August 1914, except for the regimental machine-gun units.

When the cavalry entered the field in 1914 it did so coloured in blue, red and gold, for its active-service dress was also its parade dress. In the early days of the war, isolated attempts at concealment were made. Iron-grey overalls of the type which had been worn on active service in Bosnia during the 1870s were issued to several units. Other regiments covered their helmets, shapkas or shakoes with grey cloth or paint. Some units, chiefly those on detached duties at headquarters, did retain their parade headdress until quite late in the war. Some kept it even until the armistice.

In the summer of 1914 the cavalry of Austria-Hungary, riding out to fight the first major war for nearly half a century, was confident of its ability and conscious of the glorious traditions of the army to which it belonged. Its service had been a long and proud one. The earliest battle honour awarded to the cavalry had been in 1619, to the 8th Dragoons, the former Dompierre Cuirassiers. During the nigh-on three centuries which had passed from the Thirty Years War to the First World War the Emperor's horsemen had, time and time again, fought and won against such enemies as Frederick the Great and Napoleon Bonaparte. Even on such stricken fields as Koeniggraetz, from which even their elan and determination had been unable to pluck the laurels of victory, the self-sacrificing bravery of the Habsburg cavalry in pressing home attacks against all odds brought respectful praise from their opponents.

But many years before the First World War it had been apparent to unbiased military thinkers that the outcome of future battles would not and, indeed, could not be decided by cavalry masses fighting in the way traditional to that arm. The Russo-Japanese War had demonstrated that the importance of the mounted man had been reduced vis-à-vis the infantryman and that a handful of soldiers, well dug in and armed with a machine gun, could dominate a battlefield. Cavalry in the mass could still perform certain strategically important tasks such as wide-ranging reconnaissance before a battle, or could carry out vital tactical tasks such as a protecting screen for the slower-moving infantry. But it was clear that military decisions would no more be gained through a cavalry mêlée fought with swords or lances, nor could victory be achieved by gallant horsemen charging entrenched infantry who were armed with machine guns. The habits and traditions of three centuries die hard. Years of training and an instinctive reaction to certain military situations are hard to overcome under active service conditions. Thus, when the First World War came, regiments still tried to resolve problems through mounted action and still charged with the sword. Jaroslavice, in August 1914, was the last time that large numbers of men of the Habsburg cavalry regiments crossed blades with their Emperor's enemies. Thereafter, the opportunities for attack by one body of mounted men against another vanished completely as machine guns forced the armies to move below ground and barbed wire inhibited their deployment.

Soon after the battle of Jaroslavice the first dismounted rifle troops were formed; a move that was not to halt until almost the entire cavalry arm was fighting in an infantry role. For, despite the early successes which the Imperial cavalry had had on the Eastern Front, the shortage of infantry and the

introduction of positional warfare on that Front, as well as in the south, demanded a scaling down in horsed strength and the employment of the dismounted cavalrymen in an infantry role.

Three centuries of tradition, of legend, of colour passed. The era of the beau sabreur was over, so far as the Austrian Service was concerned. The reality was dead but the romantic image of the Emperor's horsemen lingered on for decades after the end of the First World War—even if only in song, film, or operetta.

Dragoon NCO reporting to a Staff Officer during the opening campaigns in Galicia, August 1914. At that stage of the war the Cavalry Arm of Service was still wearing full dress uniform in the field.

CAVALRY · COMMON ARMY
1 · Dragoon Regiments

Kaiser Franz No 1

A German regiment
Recruiting area:
  Josephstadt

Facing colour: *dark red*
Button colour: *white metal*

The regiment was raised in 1768 as 2nd Carbiniers. General Count Michael Altmann commanded it until 1774 when the Archduke Joseph of Tuscany succeeded him. In 1790 the Crown Prince Franz became the new Colonel and held the post for two years when Franz II, the Holy Roman Emperor, assumed the colonelcy. In 1798 the regiment was converted to Curassier status. In 1835 the Emperor Ferdinand took over the regiment and was succeeded in 1848 by Franz Josef I. During the latter's incumbency the regiment was converted to Dragoon status (1 October 1867) and was given the number 1.

There had been former Dragoon regiments with the number 1. The unit which had held that number from 1788 to 1802 became Ulan Regiment No 6. Dragoon Regiment No 9 carried the number 1 from 1802 until 1860 and Dragoon Regiment No 13 carried it from 1860 to 1867.

The name and number of the regiment were carried as permanent distinctions to commemorate the Emperor Franz who died in 1835.

The regiment was authorised to carry, on a specially presented trumpet, a medal to commemorate the Golden Jubilee of H.M. Franz Joseph I.

General Count Eduard Paar No 2

A German regiment
Recruiting area: *Prague*

Facing colour: *black*
Button colour: *white metal*

Raised in 1677 as a Curassier regiment by Field Marshal Count Anton Caraffa. In 1693 Colonel Count Franz Schrattenburg assumed command and he was succeeded in the same year by Field Marshal Prince Max von Braunschweig-Lueneburg und Hannover. General Georg von Offeln was appointed to lead the regiment in 1726 and seven years later Field Marshal Duke Carl von Braunschweig-Lueneburg-Beven-Wolfenbuettel took over the post. Field Marshal Prince Theodor Lubomirski took up the colonelcy in 1736 and in 1745 General Ludwig von Bretlach became the new commander. He was succeeded in 1767 by General Count Carl Caramelli and he, in 1789, by the Archduke Franz Josef von Este. The regiment was renumbered in 1798 as 2nd Curassiers.

In 1846 General Heinrich Sunstenau von Schuetzenthal was appointed as Colonel-in-Chief and he was succeeded two years later by Maximilian Joseph, King of Bavaria. The Prussian Field Marshal, Count Friedrich Wrangel, took up the post in 1864 and during the period of his command the regiment converted to Dragoon status, receiving the number 2. General Count Tassilo Festetics de Tolna assumed command of the regiment in 1877 and in 1883 General Count Nicholas Pejacsevic von Veroecze was appointed to the position, which he held until 1890.

There had been a former Dragoon regiment, with the number 2, on establishment. From 1798 to 1801 the Light Dragoon Regiment Kronprinz Ferdinand held the number and was disbanded in 1801. From 1802 to 1867 the same number had been held by two regiments. One of these became 15th Hussars (1802 to 1860) and from 1860 to 1867 the regiment which became Dragoon Regiment No 14 also held the number 2.

Friedrich August, König von Sachsen No 3

A German regiment
Recruiting area: *Vienna*

Facing colour: *dark red*
Button colour: *yellow metal*

The regiment was raised in 1768 as 1st Carbiniers by Field Marshal Duke Albert of Sachse-Teschen. Thirty years later the regiment changed its status to that of a Curassier regiment and was given the number 3.

In 1822 there began the relationship between the 3rd Dragoons and the Royal House of Saxony when Friedrich August Albert, Royal Prince and Co-Regent of Saxony, took up the appointment of Colonel-in-Chief. He was succeeded in 1836 by Friedrich August who, in turn, was followed by Johann, King of Saxony, in 1856. During his time as Colonel the regiment converted to become Dragoon Regiment No 3. In 1873 Albert, King of Saxony, took up the post; in 1902 Georg, King of Saxony; and in 1905 Friedrich August, King of Saxony.

There had been former Dragoon regiments with the number 3. From 1798 to 1802 Dragoon Regiment No 9 had held that number, and from 1802 to 1860 Dragoon Regiment No 11.

Kaiser Ferdinand No 4

A German regiment   Facing colour: *grass green*
Recruiting areas: *Linz and* Button colour: *yellow metal*
Salzburg

The regiment was raised in 1672 by General Cristoph von Harant and ten years later command was taken up by General Aeneas Piccolomini d'Aragona. In 1690 General Count Laurenz Hofkirchen took up the post and three years later command passed to General Count Johann Herberstein before passing, in 1700, to Field Marshal Count Leo von Uhlenfeld.

General Comte de Gondrecourt held the post in 1716 and commanded for five years. In 1723 Colonel Prince Johann Modena d'Este became the commander and, in 1727, Field Marshal Seherr von Thoss replaced him. General Franz von St Ignon took up post in 1743 and in 1745 Field Marshal Count Johann Baptist Serbelloni had the appointment. Field Marshal Georg Prince of Mecklenburg-Strelitz became the Colonel-in-Chief in 1778 and in 1786 he was succeeded by General Count Moritz Kavanagh.

There was a conversion to Curassier status between the years 1798 to 1802 during which period the regiment was first numbered 12 and then No 4. In 1801 Field Marshal Crown Prince Ferdinand became the Colonel-in-Chief and in 1835 General Raban von Spiegel. His period in office was brief for within a year General Carl von Mengen had taken up post and held it until 1848 when Kaiser Ferdinand assumed command. This appointment he held until 1875 and was succeeded by Field Marshal The Archduke Albrecht, who commanded the 4th Dragoons from 1875 to 1895. On 1 October 1867 the regiment received the number 4.

There had been other regiments on the Imperial establishment which had held the number 4. From 1798 to 1802 that number was held by Ulan Regiment No 7 and from 1802 to 1860 by the Dragoon Regiment Leopold II, Grand Duke of Tuscany, which was disbanded in 1860.

The name and number of the regiment were carried as a permanent distinction to commemorate the Emperor Ferdinand who died in 1875 while in command of the regiment.

Nikolaus I, Kaiser von Russland No 5

A German regiment   Facing colour: *Imperial*
                                       yellow
Recruiting area: *Graz*   Button colour: *white metal*

Raised in 1721 by General Emmanuel Mendoza Conde de Galbes, the regiment was first considered as a Curassier formation. In 1726 Field Marshal Count Kaspar Cordova

assumed command and was succeeded in 1756 by General Count Carl O'Donell. General Jakob von Brockhausen assumed command in 1773 and in 1779 General Nicholas von Haag assumed the colonelcy. Two years later Field Marshal Prince Friedrich von Nassau-Usingen held the post and during his period as commander the regimental number changed to No 9 (1798) and then to No 5 (1802).

In 1806 General The Marquis Sommariva became the Colonel-in-Chief and in 1829 General Count Maximilian Auersperg. During 1849 Nicholas I, Tsar of Russia, became the new commander and was followed by General Count Franz Schaffgotsche in 1855. During the period that General Alexander von Koller commanded it the regiment became a Dragoon regiment with the number 5 (1 October 1867).

There had been other Dragoon regiments on establishment which had held the number 5. From 1798 to 1801 the Light Dragoon Regiment, Duke of Modena, which was disbanded in 1801; and from 1802 to 1860 the 13th Dragoon Regiment.

The name and number of the regiment were carried as permanent distinctions to commemorate the Colonel-in-Chief, Nicholas I, who died in 1855.

Friedrich Franz IV, Grossherzog von Mecklenburg-Schwerin No 6

A German regiment   Facing colour: *black*
Recruiting area: *Vienna*   Button colour: *yellow metal*

Raised in 1701 as a Curassier regiment by Field Marshal Prince Phillip von Hessen-Darmstadt from whom command passed in 1737 to General Count Franz Miglio. Eight years later General Hannibal von Schmerzing took up the appointment and was succeeded in 1762 by General Count Joseph D'Ayasasa. During 1779 General Heinrich von Schackhin assumed the colonelcy and in 1793 this passed to General Carl von Leirerich.

The regiment was renumbered as 10th Curassiers in 1798 and renumbered once again in 1802 to become the 6th Regiment. In 1808 General Freidrich von Gottesheim assumed command and held the post for only one year before it passed to General Prince Moritz von Liechtenstein. Ten years later General Count Ludwig Wallmoden-Gimborn held the appointment which passed in 1862 to General Alexander Prince von Hessen.

On 1 October 1867 the unit was converted to become 6th Dragoons. In 1889 Albrecht, Prince von Preussen and Regent of the Brauschweig Duchy, took over command of the regiment.

There had been other Dragoon regiments which had carried the number 6. From 1798 to 1801 that number had been held by the disbanded Light Dragoon Regiment, Prince of Sache-Coburg-Saalfeld. From 1802 until 1860 that number had been carried by the regiment which converted to become 12th Dragoons.

Carl V, Herzog von Lothringen und Bar No 7

A German regiment   Facing colour: *sulphur yellow*

Recruiting area: *Prague*   Button colour: *white metal*

Raised in 1663 as a Curassier regiment by General Hans Heinrich von Garnier who was succeeded in 1664 by Colonel Count Johann Nostitz. Six years later Field Marshal Count Johann Dunewald became the Colonel-in-Chief and in 1691 General Heinrich Truchsess von Wetzhausen took over command. General Prince Christian von Braunschweig-Lüneburg und Hannover took over the post in 1697 and after a period in office of only six years handed over command to General Count Lamoral von Thurn und Taxis. General Peter de Viard held the appointment from 1711 until 1718 and General Count Andreas Hamiltion was commander of the regiment from 1718 until 1738. There was a rapid succession of commanders and in 1798 the regiment was numbered Curassier Regiment No 7, during the incumbency of General Prince Carl von Lothringen. In 1826 General Count Heinrich Hardegg held the colonelcy and in 1854 he was succeeded by Wilhelm, Duke of Braunschweig. During his period of office the regiment became a Dragoon unit and was given the number 7.

There had been other units on the Dragoon establishment which had held the number 7. These were the regiment which eventually became Hussar Regiment No 15, from 1798 to 1802, and from 1851 to 1860 the unit which eventually became 14th Dragoons.

The regimental title and number were carried as a permanent distinction to commemorate Carl V of Lorraine and Bar who had died in 1690.

General Raimund Montecuccoli, Fürst und Reichsgraf No 8

A German regiment   Facing colour: *scarlet*

Recruiting area: *Josephstadt*   Button colour: *yellow metal*

Raised from a force known as the Floretine Company which had been recruited for the Grand Duke Cosmo II of Medici during 1618, there was an expansion in 1619 to a force of 200 Curassiers and 300 Arquebussiers. The first commander was Colonel Count Jakob Duval. The regiment was reformed during 1623 and was commanded in 1624 by General Count Giacomo Strozzi. In 1626 there was a

conversion to Curassier status. In 1635 the commander was Colonel Johann Puechaimb and he was succeeded in 1661 by Colonel Christian Zeiss. In 1673 command passed to General Count Adam von Heberstein and within a year it had gone to Field Marshal Duke Alexander Bournonville. There was a reformation of the regiment during 1679 and in 1698 General Prince Joseph von Lothringen was appointed to command it.

After a succession of a great many commanders the next important stage in the regiment's history occurred a century later when, during 1798, it was given the number 8 in the Curassier establishment. In 1813, Constantin, the Tsarevitch and Grand Prince of Russia, assumed command and in 1831 he was succeeded by General Count Ignaz Hardegg. There were two Colonels-in-Chief during 1848 when General Count Carl Auersperg succeeded General Hardegg and Carl, Prince von Preussen, succeeded Auersperg.

On 1 October 1867 there was a conversion when the regiment became the 8th Dragoons. From 1883 to 1899 the post of Colonel-in-Chief was held by General Count Leopold Sternberg.

There had been other Dragoon regiments on establishment which had carried the number 8. From 1798 to 1802 the regiment which became 11th Dragoons, and from 1854 to 1860 the Dragoon Regiment, Ferdinand IV Grand Duke of Tuscany, which was disbanded.

The 8th Dragoons was a unit in the Austrian service which had a number of traditions not shared by any other regiment. The 8th had the privilege of marching through Vienna and the Hofburg in that city with Colours flying and trumpets playing. It was also allowed to set up a recruiting point in the Hofburgplatz for three consecutive days. The regimental Colour could be lodged in the Hofburg and the Regimental Colonel could receive an audience of the Sovereign without making an appointment. Neither could the regiment be reduced in number nor disbanded.

The regiment also carried the name and number as a permanent distinction to commemorate the service of the great Austrian military commander. He died in 1680.

Feldmarschall Erzherzog Albrecht No 9

A German regiment   Facing colour: *grass green*

Recruiting area: *Lemberg*   Button colour: *yellow metal*

The regiment which became 9th Dragoons was raised as Curassiers in 1682 and was commanded by Duke Julius von Sachse-Lauenburg. During 1689 The Marchese John Baptist Doria assumed the colonelcy which passed, three years later, to Field Marshal Count Franz Gransfeld. Don Emanuel, The Infant of Portugal, took up the post in 1719 and he was succeeded by General Eberhard von Berlichingen during 1766.

During his term of office the regiment was converted to become Dragoons (1779) and six years later Colonel The Archduke Joseph of Tuscany became the Colonel-in-Chief and he was succeeded in 1795 by Field Marshal Archduke Johann Baptist. In the years from 1798 to 1802 the regiment converted to Light Dragoon status but then reverted and was given the number 1.

During the period in office of General Count Stadion zu Thanhaussen there was a reversion to Curassier status and once again a reversion, on 1 October 1867, as a result of which the regiment was renumbered as No 9. In 1868 General Prince Carl Salms-Braunfels became the Colonel-in-Chief and was succeeded in 1895 by the Archduke Albrecht.

There had been another regiment which had carried the number and status. This had been formed from the headquarters troops of other Dragoon units in 1799 and had been commanded by Johann Prince von Liechtenstein. That unit was disbanded in 1801.

The regimental title and number were carried as permanent distinctions to commemorate the great reformer of the Austrian Army, who died in 1895.

General Fürst Johannes von Liechtenstein No 10

A German regiment   Facing colour: *sulphur yellow*
Recruiting area: *Prague*   Button colour: *yellow metal*

The regiment was formed in 1631 around a nucleus of troops of Dragoons, by Christian Reichsherr von Illo. By 1634 the unit had reached a strength of ten companies and was commanded by Colonel Michael d'Espaigne. In 1640 General Johann de la Corona took over command and he held it for thirteen years. Colonel Peter von Buschiere, who succeeded him, held the post until 1661 when he was succeeded by General Baron Jaques Gerart. In 1676 General Count Johann Schultz assumed the command and held it for ten years. Between 1686 and 1775 there were three other Colonels and during that latter year the status of the regiment changed to that of Chevaux Leger. In 1788 there was another change of status to that of Light Dragoons and the regiment was numbered 12th of that series. A reversion to Chevaux Legers status occurred during 1802.

In 1804 General Count Klenau became the Colonel-in-Chief and was succeeded in 1840 by General Prince Karl von Liechtenstein, during whose period of office the unit became 9th Ulan Regiment. During the colonelcy of General Prince Montnuovo there was a reversion to become 10th Dragoons and when he laid down the post in 1895,

it was bestowed upon General Prince Rudolf of Liechtenstein (1904).

There had been two former 10th Dragoon Regiments. The first was formed during 1798 and was disbanded in 1802. It later became the 8th Ulans. The second unit which had carried the name and title of 10th Dragoons was raised during 1867 and disbanded in 1873 when it was converted to become 15th Hussars.

The regimental title and number were carried as permanent distinctions to commemorate Prince John Joseph of Liechtenstein who died in 1836.

Kaiser Franz Joseph No 11

A German regiment   Facing colour: *scarlet*
Recruiting area: *Vienna*   Button colour: *white metal*

Raised as a Dragoon regiment during 1688 by Count Donatus Heissler von Heitersheimb, who was succeeded in 1692 by Colonel Pillip von der Porten. During the following year General Count Franz Serenyi assumed command of the regiment and eight years later he was succeeded by General Count Carl Colonna zu Fels. In 1718 there began the long association of the regiment with the ruling House of Wurttemberg when Duke Eberhard Ludwig took up the post of Colonel-in-Chief.

In 1798, during the period of office of Friedrich Wilhelm—later to become King of Wurttemberg—the regiment was converted to Light Dragoon status and given the number 8. In 1802 it became full Dragoon and was renumbered 3. Friedrich Wilhelm was the last of the House of Wurttemberg to hold the colonelcy of the 11th, for in 1843 the Archduke Franz Josef assumed command and retained it when he became Emperor in 1848.

A former 11th Dragoon Regiment had been on the army list from 1798 to 1802, and eventually became 14th Dragoons.

The 11th Dragoons had the distinction of carrying, on the trumpet banner of a specially presented instrument, a gold medal to commemorate the Golden Jubilee of Franz Josef in 1898.

Nikolaus Nikolayewitsch Grossfürst von Russland No 12

A German regiment   Facing colour: *Imperial yellow*
Recruiting area: *Cracow*   Button colour: *yellow metal*

Raised in 1798 from a French regiment and known as the Royal German Dragoons, the unit was taken into Imperial Service during 1798 with the status of a Curassier regiment and numbered 12 on that establishment. It was renumbered 6 during the same year.

In 1799 General Michael von Milas was Colonel-in-Chief and during his period in office (1802) there was a change of status to that of Dragoons and a renumbering to No 6. General Count Johann Riesch then succeeded to the post and was followed by a series of other officers. Under the command of General Count Horvathy-Tholdy (1850 to 1865) the regiment reverted to become 12th Curassiers.

In 1865 General Count Erwin von Neipperg took over the post of Colonel and on 1 October 1867 the regiment underwent the final conversion and became Dragoon Regiment No 12.

There had been a former Dragoon Regiment No 12 on establishment. This unit, which held the number from 1798 to 1802, became Dragoon Regiment No 10.

Feldmarschall Prinz Eugen von Savoyen und Graf von Soissons No 13

A German regiment   Facing colour: *madder red*
Recruiting area: Button colour: *white metal*
    Josephstadt

The regiment was raised in 1682 by Colonel Johann von Kueffstein who was succeeded in the post by Prince Eugen during 1683. From 1737 to 1772 Field Marshal Count Ferdinand Asorenibt-Linden commanded the regiment and from 1773 to 1781 it was led by General Count Carl von Richecourt und Ney. There followed in succession General Count Ferdinand Tighe (1781 to 1811), General Johann von Mohr (1815 to 1842), General Count Franz Schlik zu Bassano (1843 to 1847), General Friedrich, Landgraf von Furst-enberg (1849 to 1866) and General Prokop Dobrzensky von Dobrzenitz from 1873.

The regiment had been numbered 15 when on the Light Dragoon establishment (1798 to 1802) and then between 1802 and 1860 it had served as 5th Dragoons. There was a renumbering in 1860 when the number 1 was bestowed upon it but in September 1867 the new number 13 was given.

There had been a former 13th Dragoon Regiment (1798 to 1802) and the unit which had held that title and number became 16th Hussar Regiment.

The regimental title and number were carried as permanent distinctions to commemorate the great contemporary of Marlborough who died on 21 April 1736.

Alfred, Fürst zu Windisch-Graetz No 14

A German regiment   Facing colour: *madder red*
Recruiting area: *Prague*   Button colour: *yellow metal*

Raised in 1726 as a Dragoon regiment by Field Marshal The Marquise Johann Westerloo, command then passed to Prince Ferdinand de Ligne in 1732. In 1757 General Count Benedict Daun became the Colonel-in-Chief and he was followed by General Prince Phillip Loewenstein-Werkheim. During the colonelcy of General Count St Ignon (1759 to 1779) the regiment became Chevaux Leger but then reverted to Dragoon status in 1765. In 1790 General Count Maximilian Baillet de Latour held the appointment of Colonel-in-Chief and during the period of his command there was a reconversion to Chevaux-Leger status. During the time the number 4 was given to the regiment. Seven years later (1798) the regiment had undergone another change of status and was 11th Regiment of Light Dragoons. In 1802 there was a reversion to Chevaux Leger status and the regiment was numbered 4.

From 1826 the Colonel-in-Chief was overseas and could not command the regiment in person. A deputy Colonel exercised command during the years of absence. In 1851 the regiment became 7th Dragoons and three years later part of the regiment was detached to become the cadre of the newly raised 8th Dragoons. From 1860 to the end of 1867 the regiment held the number 2 and was renumbered to that shown above in 1867. From 1862 to 1868 General Count Carl Coudenhove commanded the regiment.

From 1798 to 1802 there had been a 14th Dragoon Regiment. This was the Dragoon Regiment, Grand Duke of Tuscany, which was disbanded in 1802.

The 14th Dragoons had a number of privileges, the most significant of which was that it alone had the right to carry a Standard for the bravery shown by its soldiers at the battle of Kolin. Another privilege connected with that battle was the right of the men of the 14th Dragoons not to wear moustaches. This right was reaffirmed by Franz Josef on 5 October 1850.

A golden medal of honour awarded by the Emperor Leopold II was carried on the Standard.

The regimental title and number were carried as permanent distinctions to commemorate the Prince of Windisch-Graetz who died in 1862.

Erzherzog Joseph No 15

A German regiment   Facing colour: *white*
Recruiting area: *Vienna*   Button colour: *yellow metal*

The regiment was raised in 1891 and was commanded from the time of its establishment until 1904 by General Anton von Bechtolsheim. He was succeeded in 1905 by the Archduke Joseph.

CAVALRY · COMMON ARMY

2 · Hussar Regiments

Kaiser Franz Joseph No 1

A Hungarian regiment	Shako colour: *dark blue*
Recruiting area: *Temesvar*	Attila colour: *dark blue*
	Olivets: *of yellow metal*

The regiment was raised in 1756. Its first Colonel, Franz I, the Holy Roman Emperor, established the precedent that the regiment should be commanded by the Sovereign. The appointment thus passed from Franz I to Joseph II and from him to Leopold II. In 1792 Franz II took up the appointment which was then inherited by Ferdinand. The Emperor Franz Joseph I assumed the colonelcy in 1848.

The Hussar Regiment No. 1 carried on the banner of a specially presented silver trumpet a medal bestowed upon it commemorating Franz Joseph's Golden Jubilee.

Friedrich Leopold, Prinz von Preussen No 2

A Hungarian regiment	Shako colour: *white*
Recruiting area: *Nagyszeben*	Attila colour: *light blue*
	Olivets: *of yellow metal*

The regiment was raised in 1743 and was commanded from 1749 by General Count Anton Kalnoky. In 1784 Colonel the Archduke Leopold Alexander, Palatin of Hungary, assumed the colonelcy and he was succeeded in 1795 by Field Marshal The Archduke Joseph Anton, Palatin of Hungary. In 1847 Ernst August, King of Hannover, assumed command and held the appointment until 1852 when Nicholas Nicholaievitch took up the post. He was Colonel-in-Chief until 1893 when he was succeeded by Friedrich Leopold, Prince of Prussia.

Graf Andreas Hadik von Futak No 3

A Hungarian regiment	Shako colour: *white*
Recruiting area: *Temesvar*	Attila colour: *dark blue*
	Olivets: *of yellow metal*

The regiment was raised in 1702 by General Count Forgach de Ghymes. Two years later General Martin von Lehoczky took over the appointment and held it until 1712, when General Paul von Babocsay assumed command. He was succeeded in 1727 by General Stephan von Dessewffy and in 1748 General Joseph Festetics de Tolna assumed command of the regiment. General Count Anton Szechenyi became the Colonel-in-Chief in 1757, and in 1767 General Ferdinand von Ujhaxy took up the appointment. General Count Emmerich Esterhazy who had been appointed Colonel-in-Chief in 1768 was succeeded in 1794 by Archduke Ferdinand Carl d'Este who held the colonelcy until 1850 when Carl, Prince of Bavaria, assumed the command. General Count Ludwig Folliot de Crenneville was awarded the appointment in 1866 and held it until 1876, when General Prince Emmerich von Turn und Taxis became the new Colonel-in-Chief.

The regimental name and number were retained as permanent distinctions to commemorate Field Marshal Graf Hadik von Futak who died in 1790.

Artur, Herzog von Connaught und Strathearn No 4

A Hungarian regiment	Shako colour: *madder red*
Recruiting area: *Temesvar*	Attila colour: *light blue*
	Olivets: *of white metal*

The regiment was raised in 1734 by General Count Johann Havor who commanded it until 1744, when General Joseph von Dessewffy succeeded him. Twenty-four years later General Count Ferdinand Ujhazy took up the post and held it until 1773, when General Martin von Grewen was appointed. General Sigbert Vecsey von Hajnacskeo took over command of the regiment in 1791 and held the post until 1803 when General Prince Friedrich von Hesse-Homburg became the new Colonel-in-Chief. Twenty-six years later General Leopold von Geramb was appointed and in 1839 Alexander, Tsarevitch of Russia, succeeded him. After an incumbency of ten years General Count Franz Schlik zu Bassano took over command and in 1862, General Viktor Cseh von Szent Katolna was the new commander. General Leopold von Edelsheim-Gyulai took over command in 1867 and held it until 1893 when Arthur, Duke of Connaught, was appointed.

Feldmarschall Count Joseph Radetzky von Radetz No 5

A Hungarian regiment	Shako colour: *madder red*
Recruiting area: *Pozsony*	Attila colour: *dark blue*
	Olivets: *of white metal*

The regiment was raised in 1798 and the first Colonel-in-

Common Army Hussars on active service in Poland, August 1914.
(Kalman collection)

Chief was General Carl von Ott. In 1809 one of Austria's most celebrated military commanders, Radeztky von Radetz, took over the appointment. He was followed in 1814 by George, The Prince Regent, who continued to serve the regiment when he became King. The appointment of General Radetzky in 1830 was short-lived and in 1831 Charles, King of Sardinia, took over. Radetzky resumed the colonelcy of his old regiment in 1848 and upon his death it passed to William, Prince Montenuovo.

The name and number of the 5th Hussars were retained for all time to commemorate Field Marshal Radetzky who died in 1858.

Wilhelm II, König von Württemberg No 6

A Hungarian regiment   Shako colour: *ash grey*
Recruiting area: *Kassa*   Attila colour: *light blue*
                                   Olivets: *of yellow metal*

The regiment was raised in 1734 by General Count Alexander Karolyi de Nagy-Karoly. He held the colonelcy for four years and was succeeded in 1738 by General Count Franz Karolyi de Nagy-Karoly. In 1750 General Count Rudolf Palffy took up post and held it until 1868 when Hadik von Futak became the Colonel-in-Chief. He led the regiment until 1791 when General Count Ernst

Blankenstein was appointed. In 1814 Crown Prince Wilhelm von Wurttemberg became the first member of that House to take command of the 6th Hussar Regiment and he was followed in 1864 by Carl I of Wurttemberg, and in 1891 by Wilhelm II of that family.

Wilhelm II, Deutscher Kaiser und König von Preussen No 7

A Hungarian regiment
Recruiting area: *Budapest*
Shako colour: *light blue*
Attila colour: *light blue*
Olivets: *of white metal*

The first commander of the 7th Hussars, which had been raised in 1798, was Field Marshal Prince Johann von Liechtenstein. He held the appointment from 1801 to 1836 when it passed to General Prince Henry von Reuss-Koestritz. He, in turn, was succeeded by General Carl von Simbschen in 1857. In 1864 a member of the Prussian royal family assumed the colonelcy, thus setting a precedent which was followed for the remainder of the regiment's life. The first of the Prussian royal family, Friedrich Karl, Prince von Prussia, held the post from 1864 to 1885 and was succeeded by Wilhelm, Prince von Prussia who became Wilhelm, Crown Prince of the German Empire and Crown Prince of Prussia in 1888.

General Tersztyanszky No 8

A Hungarian regiment
Recruiting area: *Budapest*
Shako colour: *madder red*
Attila colour: *dark blue*
Olivets: *of yellow metal*

The regiment was raised in 1696 by General Paul Deak de Mihaly who commanded it until 1706 when Colonel Andreas von Viszlay took up the appointment. He was succeeded in the same year by General Johann von Splenyi de Mihaldy who held the post until 1730 when General Franz von Zungsberg became the Colonel-in-Chief. In 1735 General Emmerich von Deweffy held the post and then, four years later, General Johann Baranyay von Bodorfalva was appointed to lead the regiment. In 1766 General Carl von Hauendorf took up the colonelcy and he held it for nine years, to be succeeded by Field Marshal Count Dagbert Wurmser. Nearly a quarter of a century later, in 1799, General Count Friedrich Nauendorf took over command and was succeeded in 1802 by General Michael von Kienmayer. General Duke Ferdinand of Sachse-Coburg-Gotha assumed command in 1828 and during 1851 Kurfurst Friedrich Wilhelm von Hessen-Cassel was appointed to command the regiment. His period as Colonel ended in 1875 when General Alexander von Koller was appointed. He was succeeded in 1890 by General Count

Moritz, Graf Palffy ab Erdod, Colonel-in-Chief of 14th Hussar Regiment, in the undress uniform of his appointment. Note the fur kutsma with its feather, which was worn for a short period before the felt shako was introduced.

Andreas Palffy ab Erdoed, and in 1903 General Prince Alois Esterhazy von Galantha assumed command.

Feldmarschall Graf Leopold Nadasdy auf Fogoras No 9

A Hungarian regiment
Recruiting area: *Poszony*
Shako colour: *white*
Attila colour: *dark blue*
Olivets: *of white metal*

The regiment was raised in 1688 by General Count Adam Czobor who was succeeded in 1688 by General Count Johann Palffy. Twelve years later Field Marshal Laidslaus von Ebergenyi took up the post and in 1724 this passed to Field Marshal Count Georg Csaky de Keresztszegh.

During 1741 Field Marshal Count Franz Nadasdy auf Fogoras became the new Colonel-in-Chief and in 1783 General Count Johann Erdody de Monyorokerek succeeded him. The post then passed in 1806, to General Prince of Antrodocco, and then to General Georg von Wieland in 1832. One year later and the post was occupied by Nicholas I, Tsar of Russia, who held it for sixteen years, being succeeded in 1849 by General Prince Franz von Liechtenstein. In 1887 General Lamoral, Prince of Thurn and Taxis, assumed command.

The name and number of the regiment were retained as permanent distinctions to commemorate the Field Marshal who had commanded the regiment in 1741 and who died in 1783.

Friedrich Wilhelm III, König von Preussen No 10

A Hungarian regiment Shako colour: *light blue*
Recruiting area: *Budapest* Attila colour: *light blue*
Olivets: *of yellow metal*

The regiment was raised in 1741 and was commanded by General Johann von Beleznay. He was succeeded in the post by General Emmerich von Morocz in 1754 and he, in turn, by General Count Joseph Bethlen. During 1773 General Vincent von Barco took over. In 1797 General Johann von Meszaros was appointed to lead the regiment. General Joseph Stipsicz von Ternova then assumed the colonelcy and held it until 1814 when Friedrich Wilhelm III of Prussia was appointed. From 1861 until 1868 General Carl von Loderer was Colonel-in-Chief and in 1873 Wilhelm, King of Prussia and newly created Emperor of Germany, re-established the links of the 10th Hussars with the royal family of Prussia. Upon his death in 1888, Friedrich, Emperor of Germany and King of Prussia, assumed the colonelcy.

The regimental name and number were retained as permanent distinctions to commemorate Friedrich Wilhelm III of Prussia who had been Colonel-in-Chief from 1814 to 1840.

Ferdinand I, König von Bulgarien No 11

A Hungarian regiment Shako colour: *ash grey*
Recruiting area: *Poszony* Attila colour: *dark blue*
Olivets: *of white metal*

The 11th Hussar Regiment developed from the Szekeler Frontier Hussar Regiment which had been raised during 1762. In 1850 the Szekeler Regiment was taken onto the Imperial establishment, and command of the 11th Hussars was given to Alexander, Duke of Wurttemberg, who held

it until 1885. In 1887 he was succeeded by General The Prince Joseph von Windisch-Graetz.

(Title vacant after 1910) No 12

A Hungarian regiment Shako colour: *white*
Recruiting area: *Kassa* Attila colour: *light blue*
Olivets: *of white metal*

Raised during 1800 as the Palatinal Hussar Regiment by Field Marshal Joseph Anton, the Palatin of Hungary, and numbered 12 during 1802. In 1847 the Archduke Stephan, Palatin of Hungary, took up the post.

Not until 1850 did the regiment carry the name of the Colonel-in-Chief. In that year it was General Count Franz Haller von Hallerkeo. During 1875 he was succeeded by General Ignaz von Fratricsevics and in 1888 Edward, Prince of Wales, became the Colonel-in-Chief. When he became King in 1901 the regimental title changed to Edward VII, King of Great Britain and Ireland, Emperor of India. He died in 1910 and no other Colonel-in-Chief was appointed.

There had been a Frontier Hussar Regiment which carried the number 12. This had existed between 1798 and 1801. That unit had been raised during 1793 from the Osterreichisch-Steyer-Wurmser'schen Freikorps and was reorganised and numbered as the Slavonic-Croatian Frontier Hussar Regiment No 12.

Wilhelm, Kronprinz des deutschen Reiches and Kronprinz von Preussen No 13 (Jazygier und Kumanier Husaren Regiment)

A Hungarian regiment Shako colour: *dark blue*
Recruiting area: *Budapest* Attila colour: *dark blue*
Olivets: *of white metal*

Raised during 1859 from the Jazygier und Kumanier Volunteer Hussar Regiment as well as from the Kecskemeter and Arad Volunteer Hussar Half Regiment. From the date of its raising on 10 September 1859 until 16 January 1860, the unit carried the title Jazygier und Kumanier Volunteer Hussar Regiment and carried the number 13. On 17 January 1860 the unit was renumbered as No 1. In October 1861 the name of the Colonel-in-Chief was added to the title. At that time it was General Prince Friedrich of Liechtenstein who held the appointment until 1885, when he was succeeded by General Theodor Galgoczy de Galantha. He held the post for a year and during 1900 the German Crown Prince took over the colonelcy.

The word 'Volunteer' was dropped from the regimental title during 1862 and it was further decreed that the sub-title would form part of the regimental name and description.

There had been a former Hussar regiment with the number 13—the Banderial Hussar Regiment—which had been formed during 1848 and which was converted in 1851 to become Ulan Regiment No 5.

General von Kolossvary No 14

A Hungarian regiment
Recruiting area: *Kassa*
Shako colour: *madder red*
Attila colour: *light blue*
Olivets: *of yellow metal*

The 14th Regiment of Hussars descended from the 1st and 2nd Debreczen and Hajduken Hussars and from the 1st and 2nd Zala-Egerszeger Volunteer Hussar Half Regiments. The title Volunteer Hussar Regiment and the number 14 were bestowed upon the unit on 10 September 1859. On 17 January 1860 this title was changed to Volunteer Hussar Regiment No 2 and on 7 July 1862 that was changed again and this time to the title given above, when it was considered that the regiment had come onto the Common Army establishment.

The first Colonel-in-Chief was General Count Moritz Palffy ab Erdoed and he was succeeded during 1872 by Vladimir, Grand Prince of Russia, from whom the appointment passed to General von Kolossvary.

Erzherzog Franz Salvator No 15

A Hungarian regiment
Recruiting area: *Kassa*
Shako colour: *ash grey*
Attila colour: *dark blue*
Olivets: *of yellow metal*

The 15th Hussars began life as a Dragoon regiment in Bayreuth during the year 1701 when it was commanded by Field Marshal Christian Markgraf von Bayreuth. In 1712 Field Marshal Georg Wilhelm Margraf von Bayreuth took command and in 1727 Field Marshal Viktor Phillipi became the Colonel-in-Chief. He was succeeded by General Count Ludwig von Balayra during 1740 and thirteen years later General Count August Porporatti took up the post. The Field Marshal Carl Pfalzgraf von Zweibrucken became Colonel in 1757 and during the period of his appointment the regimental status was changed to that of Chevaux Leger

(1760). In 1767 Colonel Christian Pfalzgraf von Zweibrucken became the regiment's Colonel and he was succeeded in 1781 by General Christian Prince zu Waldeck. During 1798 there was a conversion to Light Dragoon status and in 1802, the regimental number changed to number 2. During 1801 General Prince Friedrich von Hohenlohe-Ingelfingen took up the appointment and the regiment was passed to Maximilian Joseph I, King of Bavaria, in 1814. He was succeeded during 1825 by Ludwig I, King of Bavaria. In 1860 the regiment was converted to Curassier status and given the number 10. On 1 October 1873 there was the final conversion to Hussar status and the number 15 was bestowed upon the regiment. During 1873 command of the 15th Hussars passed to General Count Moritz von Palffy ab Erdoed.

General Graf Alexander Üxküll-Gyllenband No 16

A Hungarian regiment
Recruiting area: *Temesvar*
Shako colour: *ash grey*
Attila colour: *light blue*
Olivets: *of yellow metal*

The regiment was raised in 1798 as 13th Dragoons and was commanded by General Prince Franz Rosenberg-Orsini. There was a conversion to Chevaux Leger status in 1802 when the new unit received the number 6. In 1832 the Colonel-in-Chief was General Simon Chevalier Fitzgerald. Thirteen years later and command passed to General Count Laidslaus Wrbna und Freudenthal. In 1851, during the incumbency of General Count Edward Clams-Gallas, the regiment converted to become Ulan and received the number 10. There was a reconversion in October 1873 when the regiment came onto the Hussar establishment and was given the number 16. In 1891 General Count Uexkuell-Gyllenband assumed command.

On 29 January 1917 the Emperor Karl named his wife, the Empress Zita, as Colonel-in-Chief of the 16th Hussars, thereby breaking the tradition that the command of a regiment should be that of a male. Only the Empress Zita and the former Empress Maria Theresia were thus privileged.

Hussars of a Common Army regiment in Vienna, c1908. They are wearing the scarlet peakless field service cap which was on issue to all mounted units.

CAVALRY · COMMON ARMY
3 · Ulan Regiments

Ulan or Lancer regiments had been on the Imperial cavalry establishment since 1784. There were eleven regiments numbered serially from 1 to 8 and from 11 to 13. The 9th and 10th Regiments had been converted into 10th Dragoons and 16th Hussars respectively. Eight of the Ulan regiments were raised from Galicia, two were from Croatia and one from Bohemia.

The Albrechtian reforms simplified the lancer tunic by removing the plastron covering the chest and in 1884 the lance was withdrawn as the principal shock weapon. It was replaced by the cavalry sabre. There was, however, a reversion to traditional Ulan uniform in the reintroduction of the shapka or lancer cap whose colour, together with that of the button, identified the regiment.

Ritter von Brudermann No 1

A German regiment
Recruiting area: *Cracow*
Shapka colour: *Imperial yellow*
Button colour: *yellow metal*

Raised in 1791 from the Ulan half regiments of the Chevaux Leger regiments and commanded by General Johann von Meszaros. In 1797 General Count Maximilian Merveldt succeeded him and remained in post for eighteen years. In 1815, General Duke Ernst of Sachse-Coburg-Saalfeld took up the appointment which he relinquished in 1844. He was succeeded by General Count Carl Civalart and in 1851, as the result of an Imperial Order, General Count Carl Gruenne exercised the rights of a Colonel-in-Chief. He was then formally appointed to the post in 1865 and held it until 1884. In the following year the Crown Prince Rudolf of Austria became the Colonel. Upon his death in 1889, General Archduke Otto assumed command.

Fürst zu Schwarzenberg No 2

A German regiment
Recruiting area: *Cracow*
Shapka colour: *dark green*
Button colour: *yellow metal*

Raised from the Ulan Free Corps in 1790. The first commander was Major Bernhard von Degelmann. He was succeeded in 1793 by Lieutenant Colonel Prince Scharzenberg who held the appointment for only one year, whereupon Lieutenant Colonel Count John Keglevich assumed command. Lieutenant Colonel Anton Vogl took up post in 1796 and one year later Lieutenant Colonel Joseph von Motschlitz became Colonel-in-Chief. The regiment converted to become a standard Ulan regiment in 1798.

The Colonels-in-Chief were then General Duke Ferdinand of Sachse-Coburg-Saalfeld who held the post from 1822, succeeded in 1828 by General Franz von Vlasits. He commanded the regiment until 1840 and then, for a period of twenty-one years, General Wilhelm von Hammerstein-Ecquord held the appointment. In 1861 General Franz von Wallyemare was Colonel and he laid down the post in 1866. General Carl Zaitsek von Egbell then took command and held it until 1887.

To commemorate the bravery of the regiment in many battles, the officers were authorised to wear the shapka metal chain and three lions' heads in silver. For the rank and file the chain was in white metal.

The regimental name and number were retained as permanent distinctions to commemorate the victorious military commander, who died in 1820.

Erzherzog Carl No 3

A German regiment
Recruiting area: *Przemysl*
Shapka colour: *madder red*
Button colour: *yellow metal*

Raised in 1801, the regiment had as its first commander the Archduke Carl, Generalissimo and Field Marshal. From 1847, when the Archduke died, the post was carried by General Count Phillip Gruenne who held it until 1854. General Prince Friedrich of Liechtenstein then commanded the regiment until 1861, and from that year until 1877 the Colonel-in-Chief was General Vinzenz von Minutillo.

The regimental name and number were retained as permanent distinctions to commemorate the Archduke Carl, who died in 1847.

Kaiser Franz Josef No 4

A German regiment
Recruiting area: *Lemberg*
Shapka colour: *white*
Button colour: *yellow metal*

The regiment was raised in 1813, with the Kaiser Franz as its first Colonel-in-Chief. He was succeeded by Kaiser

Ferdinand in 1835. From 1848 the Kaiser Franz Joseph served the regiment as its Colonel-in-Chief.

The regiment carried, on the trumpet banner of a specially presented instrument, a gold medal commemorating the Emperor's Golden Jubilee.

Nikolaus II, Kaiser von Russland No 5

A German regiment   Shapka colour: *light blue*
Recruiting area: *Agram*   Button colour: *yellow metal*

Raised in 1848 as the Banderial Hussars, the regiment was converted to Ulan status on 8 January 1851. From that year until 1883 General Count Carl Wallmoden-Gimborn was the Colonel-in-Chief and two years later, in 1885, Nikolaus Alexandrovitch, Grand Prince of Russia, took up the appointment. When he became Tsar in 1894, the regimental name was altered to read 'Emperor of Russia'.

The 5th Ulan Regiment was unusual in that it was one of two regiments of Lancers raised in the Croatian area of Hungary.

Kaiser Joseph II No 6

A German regiment   Shapka colour: *Imperial yellow*
Recruiting area: *Przemysl*   Button colour: *white metal*

Raised in 1688 as a Dragoon regiment it was converted to the role of Chevaux Leger in 1765. In 1798 there was a new conversion, this time to the status of a Light Dragoon regiment with the regimental number 1. During 1802 there was a further conversion back to Chevaux Leger status but the number was retained, and it was not until June 1851 that the final conversion to a Ulan regiment was carried out. The number given to the new Ulan regiment was No 6.

The first Colonel of the Dragoon regiment was Colonel Count Hanibal Lowenschild who was succeeded in 1690 by General Count Leopold Schlik. In 1705 Field Marshal Count Gundaker Altmann took up the post and in 1748 Colonel The Archduke Joseph assumed command. In 1765, when the regiment converted to Chevaux Leger, Kaiser Joseph II became Colonel-in-Chief and in 1790 Kaiser Leopold II succeeded him. In 1792 Kaiser Franz II, who became Kaiser Franz after relinquishing the title of Holy Roman Emperor, served the regiment until 1835 when Kaiser Ferdinand became the Colonel-in-Chief. In 1848 Franz Joseph assumed command.

The regimental title and number were retained as permanent distinctions to commemorate Kaiser Joseph II, who died in 1790. As a further distinction, a gold medal to honour the Golden Jubilee of Franz Joseph was carried on the trumpet cloth of a specially presented instrument.

Erzherzog Franz Ferdinand von Österreich-Este No 7

A German regiment   Shapka colour: *dark green*
Recruiting area: *Lemberg*   Button colour: *white metal*

The regiment was raised in 1758 from specially selected detachments of the Loewenstein Dragoons, which became 14th Dragoon Regiment. During the following year the 7th Ulan became an independent Chevaux Legers Light Dragoon regiment. It received the number 4 on the Light Dragoon establishment during 1798 and in 1802 was converted back to Chevaux Leger status with the regimental number 2. It became a Ulan regiment and received the number 7 on 1 June 1851.

The first Colonel, when the regiment was converted to Chevaux Leger in 1759, was General Prince Christian Loewenstein. General Count Carl von Richecourt took over command in 1781 and eight years later it passed to General Andreas von Karaiczky. In 1801, after conversion to Light Dragoon status, command was taken by Field Marshal Prince Friedrich Hohenzollern-Hechingen and he carried the regiment through its reconversion to Chevaux Leger in 1802. In 1844 Friedrich Anton von Hohenzollern-Hechingen assumed command and he was succeeded in 1848 by General Archduke Carl Ludwig, who remained in post until 1896 when Franz Ferdinand became the Colonel-in-Chief.

Graf Auersperg No 8

A German regiment   Shapka colour: *madder red*
Recruiting area: *Lemberg*   Button colour: *white metal*

Raised in 1718 as a Dragoon regiment, its status changed to that of a Chevaux Leger regiment in 1779. During 1798 there was a reversion to Dragoon status and the regiment was numbered 10 on the Dragoon establishment. In 1802, there was a reconversion to Chevaux Leger and the regiment was renumbered as 3rd. On 1 June 1851 there was a new conversion, this time to Ulan status with the regiment number 8.

The first Colonel of the Dragoon regiment was Wilhelm Friedrich Markgraf von Brandenburg Onolzbach. In 1723 he was succeeded by Carl Wilhelm Markgraf von Brandenburg-Onolzbach, and three years later Field Marshal Johann Duke of Sachse-Gotha. General Johann Graf Bettoni took over command during 1767 and in 1773 Field Marshal Joseph Prince Lobkowitz became the Colonel-in-Chief. He was succeeded by General Andreas O'Reilly during 1803 and in 1832 General Count Bartholeus Alberti-de-Poya took up post. In 1836 General Paul von Wennardt became Colonel and in 1846 Vice Admiral The Archduke

Ferdinand Max assumed the colonelcy. Maximilian, formerly Archduke of Austria and then Emperor of Mexico, became the Colonel-in-Chief in 1864, and shortly after his execution General Count Carl Bigot de St Quentin assumed command of the regiment and held the appointment until 1884, when it passed to General Viktor von Ramberg.

There was no Ulan Regiment No 9

The unit which had held that number was converted in 1873 to Dragoon status and was numbered 10 on the Dragoon establishment.

There was no Ulan Regiment No 10

The unit which had held that number was converted in 1873 and became Hussar Regiment No 16.

Alexander II, Kaiser von Russland No 11

A German regiment Shapka colour: *cherry red*
Recruiting area: *Leitmeritz* Button colour: *white metal*

The regiment was first raised in 1814 to be the 7th Chevaux Leger regiment and was converted to become an Ulan regiment on 1 June 1851. It was numbered as 11 in the Ulan establishment.

The first commander of the Chevaux Leger regiment was General Count Johann Nostitz-Rieneck who commanded until 1840, when he was succeeded by General Carl Kress von Kressenstein. During 1849 Alexander, the Tsarevitch, took the regiment into Ulan status. From 1881 to 1894 the Colonel of the Regiment was Alexander III, Tsar of Russia.

The regimental name and number were retained as permanent distinctions to commemorate the Tsar, Alexander II, who died in 1881.

Graf Huyn No 12

A Hungarian regiment Shapka colour: *dark blue*
Recruiting area: *Agram* Button colour: *yellow metal*

This, the second Croatian Ulan regiment on establishment, was raised during 1854 and was first commanded by Ferdinand II, King of the Two Sicilies. Francisco II, King of the Two Sicilies, took up the appointment which he held until 1895. He was succeeded by General Otto von Gagern who held the post until 1902. In that year General Wilhelm von Bothmer became Colonel-in-Chief.

General von Böhm-Ermolli No 13

A German regiment Shapka colour: *dark blue*
Recruiting area: *Lemberg* Button colour: *white metal*

The regiment was raised in 1860 as the Volunteer Ulan Regiment and was taken on strength as an Imperial unit in 1862.

The first Colonel-in-Chief was Ludwig, Count of Trani, Prince of the Two Sicilies. He was succeeded in 1886 by General Count Hermann Nostitz-Rieneck who held the post until 1896. In 1898 General Count Paar took over command.

||||||||||||||||||||||||||||||||||||||||||||||||||||||||||||||||||||||||||||||||||

CAVALRY · LANDWEHR

1·Ulan Regiments of the Landwehr

||||||||||||||||||||||||||||||||||||||||||||||||||||||||||||||||||||||||||||||||||

Under a military law passed in 1870, twenty-five squadrons of Landwehr cavalry were to be recruited from a number of provinces of the German area of the Empire, but excluding both Tirol and Vorarlberg.

Twelve of the original squadrons were organised, uniformed and named as Dragoon units, with the remaining thirteen formed as Ulans. A reorganisation of the Landwehr Cavalry organisation during 1894 amalgamated the twenty-five squadrons into six serially numbered Ulan regiments. In the historical notes set out below, it will be seen that the dates on which the regiments are considered to have been raised are either 1883 or 1885. The amalgamation into regiments was ordered to be carried out in 1883, but was completed by only three regiments in that year. A period of two more years elapsed before the other three Landwehr Ulan regiments came onto establishment.

No 1

Raised during October 1885 in Cracow. The regiment's original recruiting area, to the east of Cracow, was extended during 1894, and again in 1901 to include other parts of eastern Galicia.

No 2

Was raised during October 1885 in Hohenmauth. The original recruiting area around Przemysl was extended in 1894 to include some parts of Bohemia and was further extended, during 1901, to include other districts of that country.

No 3

The regiment was raised in Sambor during 1883.

It was intended that the regiment should recruit in the border areas of eastern Galicia but, since insufficient numbers of men were obtained, it was decided in 1889 to include the districts around Przemysl, Jaroslav and Sambor, together with three other districts.

No 4

Raised in Cracow during 1883 as the 2nd Landwehr Dragoon Regiment. The unit was converted to Ulan status in 1894, and was numbered 4 in the Landwehr Ulan establishment.

The original recruiting areas were in Moravia in Silesia, but in 1889 these areas were extended temporarily to include Cracow and Troppau. In 1894 those districts were confirmed as being part of the regimental recruiting area and in 1901 this was further extended to include Teschen and Neu Sandec.

No 5

Raised in Stockerau in 1883 as 1st Landwehr Dragoon Regiment and converted to Ulan status in 1894, receiving the number 5.

The original recruiting districts of Upper and Lower Austria, Styria, Carinthia, Krain and the coastal areas were extended in 1889 and again, in 1900, to include Vienna, Kremsier, Marburg and Laibach.

No 6

Raised in Wels during 1885 as 3rd Landwehr Dragoon Regiment and converted to Ulan status in 1894, receiving the number 6.

The original recruiting area in Bohemia was later extended to include parts of northern Austria and southern Czechoslovakia, especially the Sudetenland. A subsequent extension of the recruiting area included the Innsbruck region.

||||||||||||||||||||||||||||||||||||||||||||||||||||||||||||||||||||||||||||||||||||||||||||||

CAVALRY · LANDWEHR

2 · Mounted Rifles of Tirol and Dalmatia

||||||||||||||||||||||||||||||||||||||||||||||||||||||||||||||||||||||||||||||||||||||||||||||

In addition to Ulan regiments, the Austrian Landwehr organisation also had on its establishment two other cavalry units: the Tirolean Mounted Rifles and the Dalmatian Mounted Rifles.

The Tirolean Mounted Rifles were raised under a law passed in 1871 which ordered the recruiting of two companies. A cadre common to both was formed in Innsbruck.

The unit horses were a special breed. Smaller than the standard cavalry mount they had great staying power for they were required to carry their riders and equipment for long periods in difficult terrain.

The companies were named initially as Horsed Riflemen of Tirol and Vorarlberg but by 1910 this title had changed to Tirolean Mounted Rifles.

The Dalmatian Mounted Rifles were raised in 1874 as The Cadre of the Mounted Rifles in Dalmatia to carry out reconnaissance in time of war. An expansion to field squadron strength and a replacement troop was planned to take place upon general mobilisation.

During 1894 the unit was renamed The Mounted Dalmatian Rifle Squadron and with the raising of a second squadron there came a new title: The Mounted Dalmatian Rifles Half Regiment.

Recruits for the unit were obtained from Dalmatia and the horses they rode were of a special breed, famous for their hardiness and smaller even than the beasts issued to the Tirolean Mounted Rifles.

CAVALRY · LANDWEHR (HONVED)

Hussar Regiments of the Landwehr (Honved)

The battle plans of the Imperial authorities did not foresee the employment of Hussar units of the Landwehr (Honved) in any role other than Divisional cavalry. It was not the intention to create large formations such as regiments, for the tasks of Divisional cavalry were to act as messengers or escorts or to carry out local patrols of a defensive nature; duties for which major units would have been unsuitable.

In time there came the realisation that the Landwehr units of both Austria and Hungary were as proficient and as able as the Imperial and Royal regiments. There was a re-evaluation of Landwehr roles and it was decided to amalgamate the squadrons into regiments. In 1874 the orders were issued and very soon ten regiments had been formed. Nine of these were Hussar; one was Ulan. That unit, which bore the description Ulan until 1882, had been created out of four Lancer squadrons which had been raised in Croatia-Slovenia.

In 1890 the regiments of Landwehr Hussars were authorised to carry, as part of their official title, the name of the garrison town.

In 1912 it was proposed to double the Landwehr cavalry establishment and the first stage of that expansion was begun during the following year.

The Hussar regiments of the Landwehr (Honved) could only be identified by the colour of the shako, for the colour of the attila and the olivets which fastened it were standard for all: dark blue and yellow metal respectively.

Budapest No 1

Recruiting area: Shako: *grey*
  Budapest
  (1st Half Regt)
  Bekes-Gyula
  (2nd Half Regt)

Formed from Nos 1, 19, 2 and 34 Independent Squadrons in the year 1874 and first entitled Landwehr Cavalry Regiment No 1. In 1877 the 2nd Half Regiment was sent to the 4th Regiment and the 1st Half Regiment of the 2nd Regiment was taken on strength as a replacement.

In 1880 the regiment received the title Landwehr Hussar Regiment No 1. This was changed to Budapest Landwehr Hussar Regiment No 1 in the year 1894.

Debreczin No 2

Recruiting area: Shako: *light blue*
  Grosswardein
  (1st Half Regt)
  Debreczin
  (2nd Half Regt)

Formed in 1874 from the 20th, 33rd, 7th and 16th Squadrons and first entitled Landwehr Cavalry Regiment No 2. In 1877 the 1st Half Regiment was sent to the 1st Regiment and the 1st Half Regiment of No 3 Regiment was received in replacement.

In 1880 the title of Landwehr Hussar Regiment No 2 was given and the title changed to Debreczin Landwehr Hussar Regiment No 2 in the year 1894.

Szegedin No 3

Recruiting area: Shako: *white*
  Lugos
  (1st Half Regt)
  Versec
  (2nd Half Regt)

Formed from the 3rd, 5th, 6th and 8th Squadrons and given the title of Landwehr Cavalry Regiment No 3 in 1874. In 1877 the 1st Half Regiment was posted to No 2 Regiment, and the 2nd Half Regiment of No 4 Regiment was received as replacement.

In 1880 the regiment received the name Landwehr Hussar Regiment No 3 and this was changed to Szegedin Landwehr Hussar Regiment No 3 in 1894.

Kecskemet No 4

Recruiting area: Shako: *madder red*
  Maria Theresiopel
  (1st Half Regt)
  Szegedin
  (2nd Half Regt)

In 1874 the regiment was formed from the 4th, 9th, 10th and 35th Squadrons and entitled Landwehr Cavalry Regiment No 4. It handed over its 2nd Half Regiment to No 3 Regiment, and received the 2nd Half Regiment of 1st Regiment in exchange.

In 1880 it was entitled Landwehr Hussar Regiment No 4 and this was changed to the title given above in 1894.

Kassa No 5

Recruiting area: Shako: *madder red*
  Kassa and Munkacs
  (1st Half Regt)
  Miskolcz and
  Szatmar
  (2nd Half Regt)

Formed in 1874 from the 17th, 18th, 14th, and 15th Squadrons and first entitled Landwehr Cavalry Regiment No 5.

  That title was changed to Landwehr Hussar Regiment No 5 in 1880, and to the title given above in the year 1894.

Waitzen No 6

Recruiting area: *Waitzen*   Shako: *dark blue*

Formed in 1874 as Landwehr Cavalry Regiment No 6, from the 22nd, 38th, 21st and 37th Squadron.

  Renamed Landwehr Hussar Regiment No 6 in 1880, and given the title shown above in 1894.

There were formerly two Ulan regiments on the establishment of the Landwehr (Honved) but these were then converted to Hussar status. This detachment of Landwehr (Honved) Ulans is wearing ulan pattern tunics and headdress (tatarka) of Common Army pattern. The lance as a weapon was abolished in the Imperial Service during 1888.
(Kalman collection)

Papa No 7

Recruiting area: Shako: *grass green*
   Stuhlweissenburg
   (1st Half Regt)
   Oedenburg
   (2nd Half Regt)

Formed in 1874 from the 23rd, 24th, 27th, and 39th Squadrons and named Landwehr Cavalry Regiment No 7.

In 1880 renamed Landwehr Hussar Regiment No 7, and given the title shown above in 1894.

Fünfkirchen No 8

Recruiting area: Shako: *madder red*
   Fuenfkirchen
   (1st Half Regt)
   Nagykanizsa
   (2nd Half Regt)

Formed from the 25th, 26th, 28th, and 40th Squadrons and named Landwehr Cavalry Regiment No 8 in 1874.

Renamed Landwehr Hussar Regiment No 8 in 1880, and given the title shown above in 1894.

Honved Hussar patrol. (Kalman collection)

Maros-Vasarhely No 9

Recruiting area: Shako: *madder red*
Maros-Vasarhely
(1st Half Regt)
Klausenburg
(1st Half Regt)
Hermannstadt
2nd Half Regt)
Kronstadt
(2nd Half Regt)

Formed from the 12th, 13th, 11th and 36th Squadrons in 1874 and received the title Landwehr Hussar Regiment No 9.

Retitled Landwehr Hussar Regiment No 9 in 1880, and the title shown above in 1894.

Varasdin No 10

Recruiting area: Shako: *madder red*
Agram and
Carlstadt
(1st Half Regt)
Sissek and
Essegg
(2nd Half Regt)

Formed from the 29th, 30th, 31st and 32nd Squadrons in 1874 and entitled Landwehr Cavalry Regiment No 10.

Entitled Landwehr Lancer Regiment No 10 in 1880, and two years later the regimental description was changed to Landwehr Hussar Regiment No 10. In 1894 the regiment was given the title shown above.

6·Artillery Arm of Service

||||||||||||||||||||||||||||||||||||||||||||||||||||||||||||||||||||||||||||||||||||||||||

Artillery Arm of Service

||||||||||||||||||||||||||||||||||||||||||||||||||||||||||||||||||||||||||||||||||||||||||||||||||||||

For the purposes of this work the term Field Artillery is restricted to those weapons and units used in the forward combat zone, *ie* Field Guns, Field Howitzers, Mountain Artillery and Heavy Howitzers, although some mention is made of the Fortress Artillery.

The Artillery Arm was old in the Austrian Service. The first uniform for gunners dated from 1734 and two regiments bore the battle honour 'Aspern 1809'. Nevertheless, it was not considered as an Arm of Service but as an auxiliary. Its potency was, thus, long underestimated. This led to stagnation and, indeed, the modern formal organisation of the Arm can be said to date only from 1854 when a reformation of existing units produced twelve Field Artillery and one Coastal Artillery regiment.

The war of 1866 exposed the deficiencies caused by the stagnation referred to and by the misunderstanding of the role of artillery on a modern battlefield. One positive result of that disastrous war was that there came about, at last, a general appreciation of the power of the guns to prepare the way for an attack, to support an infantry assault and to sustain a defence by breaking up enemy movements or by neutralising his artillery. One basic decision taken after the Prussian War drew a clear distinction between the roles of the various branches of artillery. Thus the Field was no longer expected to perform both its own as well as fortress duties. Instead, a separate branch was formed to serve the heavy pieces in the Imperial fortresses leaving the Field to concentrate upon its task of close support. The Fortress Artillery was organised into twelve battalions; nine of which were raised in 1867 and the remainder by conversions from Coastal Artillery regiments in 1868.

To conform to the new tactical ideas that the most flexible and efficient self-contained military formation was the Division, plans were drawn up for Divisional artillery groupings and these were carried through on 1 May 1885 when the field was grouped into fourteen Brigades, each containing a Corps Artillery regiment and two independent Heavy half regiments. The Brigade and Corps Artillery Regiment both carried the Corps number but the battalions of the Heavy half regiment were numbered in series, those with 1st Artillery Brigade being numbered 1st and 2nd, etc.

The widely-held belief in Austrian military circles that war with Italy was inevitable, and the knowledge of how strongly the Italians had fortified their side of the frontier, convinced General Auffenburg-Komarov that the Imperial Army could not reduce those fortifications using the artillery pieces on issue at that time. In his book *Oesterreich-Ungarns Teilnahme am Weltkrieg* he described how he, together with Conrad von Hoetzendorff, secretly arranged the design, development and construction of the 30.5cm mortar. The contract was placed with Skoda during December 1912 and by the outbreak of the war, sufficient pieces had been produced to form twelve batteries, each of two guns. Some of those weapons were supplied to the German army and played a great part in assisting its advance through France and Belgium.

Conrad carried out an intensive reorganisation of the Artillery Arm. A reformation and restructuring of the artillery units produced the result that at the outbreak of war each Infantry Division of the Common Army had under command a Field Artillery Brigade consisting of a Field Gun regiment and a Field Howitzer half regiment. Each Landwehr Infantry Division had a Field Artillery Brigade with a Common Army Field Gun regiment, a Landwehr Field Gun half regiment and a Landwehr Field Howitzer half

A Field Artillery battery in the open during the manoeuvres held shortly before the outbreak of war in July 1914.

regiment. The Landwehr (Honved) Infantry Divisions each contained a Field Artillery Brigade with one or two Common Army half regiments of Field Guns and a Landwehr (Honved) Field Gun regiment. There were no Field Howitzer units on the Landwehr (Honved) establishment in 1914.

Each Cavalry Division controlled a Horse Artillery half regiment and each Corps had a Heavy Howitzer half regiment. Some Corps were also equipped with mountain artillery weapons.

The units of the Austro-Hungarian artillery in 1914, are listed in the following pages but to summarise the establishment, there were in the Field Artillery: forty-two regiments of Common Army, eight half regiments of Landwehr and eight full regiments of Landwehr (Honved). Fourteen Howitzer regiments were on the Common Army establishment and eight half regiments on that of the Landwehr. Fourteen half regiments of Heavy Howitzer artillery on the Common Army establishment. Nine half regiments of Horse Artillery with the Common Army and one half regiment with the Landwehr (Honved). In Mountain Artillery the Common Army had ten regiments and one independent half regiment, while in Fortress Artillery the Common Army had six regiments and ten battalions on establishment. When it marched out on active service the strength of the Artillery Arm was 397 Field and 74 Mountain batteries, controlling 2,562 pieces of ordnance. That is approximately one gun section per battalion of infantry.

Despite the improvements which Conrad brought about there had not been time enough to raise the artillery to that level of organisation or of armament that would enable it to meet the demands of a major war. The Imperial Army was also inferior in number, both relatively and absolutely, to that of the other major powers and its infantry divisions had lower artillery ordnance establishments than those of its principal enemies: Russia and Italy.

The development of weapons had been neglected and this time lack of money was not the principal cause. The financial restrictions, serious though they were, were accompanied by differences of opinion between certain artillery experts on the one side, and the General Staff on the other, as to the type of weapons that were required. As a consequence two thirds of the Field Artillery guns were still flat trajectory; an error in appreciation which placed the Imperial Artillery Arm in a subservient position, vis à vis its enemies. In addition the guns were generally outranged by the weapons of other nations. For example the 4½ miles maximum range of the M5 was

Korpskommandant
F.Z.M. Stephan Ljubicic.

PHOT. JAHUDKA
WIEN, 1914.

Artillery General Ljubicic, a Corps Commander at the outbreak of war, wearing the undress shako.

exceeded by at least 1,000yds by the equivalent Russian piece. Although new models: a 7cm mountain gun, a 10cm light and a 15cm heavy field howitzer, a 10cm gun and a motor drawn 15cm gun and howitzer had all been introduced before the outbreak of war, these had not reached the stage of mass production, nor were the arsenals and factories of the Empire geared to produce the number of shells that were required. Serious shortages were encountered after only a few weeks of active service expenditure.

Although both the Landwehr and the Landwehr (Honved) were held to be on a par with the Common Army there were no regiments of Heavy Field Artillery on either establishment before the war and it was not until 1916 that the first of these was raised.

The weapons of the Fortress Artillery left that branch of the service in a situation even more unhappy than that of the Field Artillery. The guns in the Przemysl fortress still used black powder and those in the forts at Peterwardein were of the 1861 pattern. Only at Pola were there modern 24cm coastal pieces and these were removed soon after the outbreak of war, for use on the Russian front. Only the Alpine forts facing Italy were armed with modern 10cm howitzers fitted into retracting turrets.

The Rennweg Barracks in Vienna, for nearly a century the Depot of the Artillery Arm of Service.

General Franz Wilsdorf in the uniform of a Colonel of Artillery. He was Colonel-in-Chief of 8th Artillery Regiment.

||||||||||||||||||||||||||||||||||||||||||||||||||||||||||||||||||||||||||||||||||

ARTILLERY · COMMON ARMY
1 · Field Gun Regiments

||||||||||||||||||||||||||||||||||||||||||||||||||||||||||||||||||||||||||||||||||

No 1

A German regiment
Recruiting area: *Cracow*

The regiment was formed on 1 May 1885 as the Independent Half Regiment No 1 out of the former 7th Field Artillery Regiment. It became Divisional Artillery Regiment No 1 on 1 January 1894, and was retitled Field Gun Regiment No 1 on 6 April 1908.

No 2

A German regiment
Recruiting area: *Cracow*

Formed on 1 May 1885 as the Independent Half Regiment No 20 out of the former 2nd Field Artillery. It became Divisional Artillery Regiment No 2 on 1 January 1894, and was retitled Field Gun Regiment No 2 on 6 April 1908.

No 3

A German regiment
Recruiting area: *Cracow*

The regiment was formed on 1 January 1892 as the Independent Half Regiment No 41 out of the former 10th Corps Artillery Regiment. It became Divisional Artillery Regiment No 3 on 1 January 1894, and was retitled Field Gun Regiment No 3 on 6 April 1908.

No 4

A German regiment
Recruiting area: *Vienna*

The regiment was formed on 1 May 1885 as the Independent Half Regiment No 4 from the former 11th Field Artillery Regiment. It became Divisional Artillery Regiment No 4 on 1 January 1894, and was retitled Field Gun Regiment No 4 on 6 April 1908.

No 5

A German regiment
Recruiting area: *Vienna*

The regiment was formed on 1 May 1885 as the Independent Half Regiment No 19 out of the former 2nd Field Artillery Regiment. It became Divisional Artillery Regiment No 5 on 1 January 1894, and was retitled Field Gun Regiment No 5 on 6 April 1908.

No 6

A German regiment
Recruiting area: *Vienna*

The regiment was formed on 1 January 1892 as the Independent Half Regiment No 39 out of the former 2nd Corps Artillery Regiment. It became Divisional Artillery Regiment No 6 on 1 January 1894, and was retitled Field Gun Regiment No 6 on 6 April 1908.

No 7

A German regiment
Recruiting area: *Graz*

The regiment was formed on 1 May 1885 as the Independent Half Regiment No 5 out of the former 6th Field Artillery Regiment. It became Divisional Artillery Regiment No 7 on 1 January 1894, and was retitled Field Gun Regiment No 7 on 6 April 1908.

No 8

A German regiment
Recruiting area: *Graz*

The regiment was formed on 1 May 1885, as the Independent Half Regiment No 6 out of the former 6th Field Artillery Regiment. It became Divisional Artillery Regiment No 8 on 1 January 1894, and was retitled Field Gun Regiment No 8 on 6 April 1908.

No 9

A German regiment
Recruiting area: *Graz*

The regiment was formed on 1 January 1892 as the Independent Half Regiment No 29 out of the former 3rd Corps Artillery Regiment. It became Divisional Artillery Regiment No 9 on 1 January 1894, and was retitled Field Gun Regiment No 9 on 6 April 1908.

No 10

A Hungarian regiment
Recruiting area: *Budapest*

The regiment was formed on 1 May 1885 as Independent Half Regiment No 7 out of the former 5th Field Artillery Regiment. It became Divisional Artillery Regiment No 10 on 1 January 1894, and was retitled Field Gun Regiment No 10 on 6 April 1908.

No 11

A Hungarian regiment
Recruiting area: *Budapest*

The regiment was formed on 1 May 1885 as the Independent Half Regiment No 8 out of the former 5th Field Artillery Regiment. It became Divisional Artillery Regiment No 11 on 1 January 1894, and was retitled Field Gun Regiment No 11 on 6 April 1908.

No 13

A Hungarian regiment
Recruiting area: *Pozsony*

The regiment was formed on 1 May 1885 as the Independent Half Regiment No 10 out of the former 3rd Field Artillery Regiment. It became Divisional Artillery Regiment on 1 January 1894, and was retitled Field Gun Regiment No 13 on 6 April 1908.

No 14

A Hungarian regiment
Recruiting area: *Pozsony*

The regiment was formed on 1 May 1885 as the Independent Half Regiment No 9 out of the former 3rd Field Artillery Regiment. It became Divisional Artillery Regiment No 14 on 1 January 1894, and was retitled Field Gun Regiment No 14 on 6 April 1908.

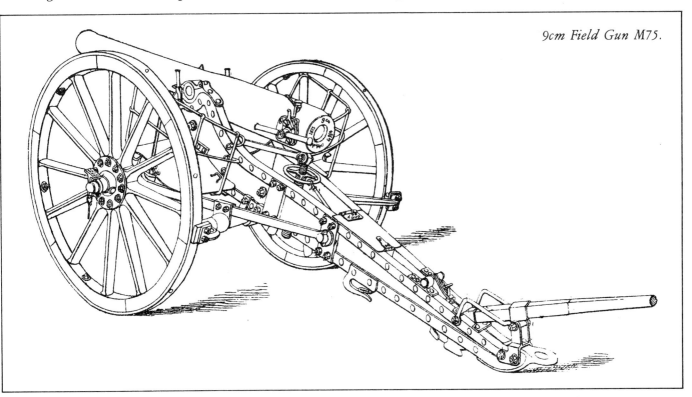

9cm Field Gun M75.

No 12

A Hungarian regiment
Recruiting area: *Budapest*

The regiment was formed on 1 January 1892 as the Independent Half Regiment No 30 out of the former 4th Corps Artillery Regiment. It became Divisional Artillery Regiment No 12 on 1 January 1894, and was retitled Field Gun Regiment No 12 on 6 April 1908.

No 15

A Hungarian regiment
Recruiting area: *Pozsony*

The regiment was formed on 1 January 1892 as the Independent Half Regiment No 31 out of the former 5th Corps Artillery Regiment. It became Divisional Artillery Regiment No 15 on 1 January 1894, and was retitled Field Gun Regiment No 15 on 6 April 1908.

No 16

A Hungarian regiment
Recruiting area: *Kassa*

The regiment was formed on 1 May 1885 as the Independent Half Regiment No 11 out of the former 10th Field Artillery Regiment. It became Divisional Artillery Regiment No 16 on 1 January 1894, and was retitled Field Gun Regiment No 16 on 6 April 1908.

No 17

A Hungarian regiment
Recruiting area: *Kassa*

The regiment was formed on 1 May 1885 as the Independent Half Regiment No 12 out of the former 10th Field Artillery Regiment. It became Divisional Artillery Regiment No 17 on 1 January 1894, and was retitled Field Gun Regiment No 17 on 6 April 1908.

No 19

A Hungarian regiment
Recruiting area: *Temesvar*

The regiment was formed on 1 May 1885 as the Independent Half Regiment No 13 out of the former 13th Field Artillery Regiment. It became Divisional Artillery Regiment No 19 on 1 January 1892, and was retitled Field Gun Regiment No 19 on 6 April 1908.

No 20

A Hungarian regiment
Recruiting area: *Temesvar*

The regiment was formed on 1 May 1885 as the Independent Half Regiment No 14 out of the former 13th Field Artillery Regiment. It became Divisional Artillery Regiment No 20 on 1 January 1894, and was retitled Field Gun Regiment No 20 on 6 April 1908.

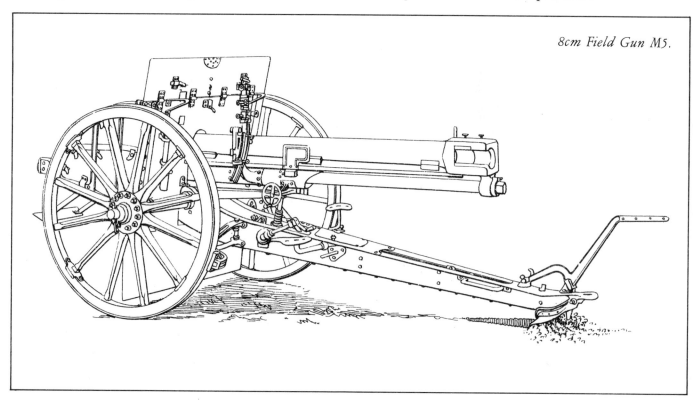

8cm Field Gun M5.

No 18

A Hungarian regiment
Recruiting area: *Kassa*

The regiment was formed on 1 January 1892 as the Independent Half Regiment No 40 out of the former 6th Corps Artillery Regiment. It became Divisional Artillery Regiment No 18 on 1 January 1894, and was retitled Field Gun Regiment No 18 on 6 April 1908.

No 21

A Hungarian regiment
Recruiting area: *Temesvar*

The regiment was formed on 1 January 1892 as the Independent Half Regiment No 32 out of the former 7th Corps Artillery Regiment. It became Divisional Artillery Regiment No 21 on January 1894, and was retitled Field Gun Regiment No 21 on 6 April 1908.

24 A gun of the Horse Artillery and its crew. The losses in the Horse Artillery during the Battle of Chulm were so severe that the Officer in the foreground of this painting was the only commissioned rank to have survived the battle.

Above:
25 A battery of the Horse Artillery taking up a new firing position. The Horse Artillery was the only branch of the Artillery to wear the horse-hair plume on active service. Note that the trumpeter carried a red, and not a black, plume.

Above right:
26 A Field Officer of the Horse Artillery in parade dress, *c*1892.

The watercolours on the right are from the Kalman collection.

Above left:
27 Soldier in a Landwehr (Honved) Infantry regiment wearing parade dress.

Above right:
28 Soldier of the Landwehr (Honved) wearing the 1869 pattern Infantry uniform.

Below:
29 Landwehr (Honved) soldier dressed in the 1873 pattern Cavalry uniform.

Left:
30 Soldier of the 7th Regiment of Landwehr (Honved) Hussars in the 1895 pattern uniform.

Centre:
31 Infantryman of the Landwehr (Honved) in field service order, 1914.

Right:
32 Soldier of the Landwehr (Honved) Artillery in field service dress, 1913.

(*Kalman collection*)

Right:
33 Watercolour showing a General Officer of the Landwehr (Honved) wearing a white tunic, escorted by an Officer of the Honved General Staff *(foreground)* and a Honved Hussar Officer *(background)*.
(*Kalman collection*)

The following seven paintings are by the artist Moritz Ruhl.

34 GENERAL OFFICERS.
1 Inspector General of Artillery in gala dress.
2 Auditor General in gala dress.
3 Adjutant General in gala dress.
4 Field Marshal in gala dress.
5 Inspector General of Engineers in gala dress.
6 General Officer standard uniform.
7 General Officer in field service dress.
8 General Officer in Hungarian uniform gala dress.
9 General Officer in Hungarian parade dress.
10 General Officer in standard Hungarian uniform.
11 General Medical Officer in gala dress.

Above: 35 GENERAL STAFF, AIDES-DE-CAMP, ADJUTANTS. Parade uniform, or active service dress

1 General Staff Captain; field service dress.
2 Chief of the General Staff; field service dress.
3 Major of the General Staff; parade dress.
4 Senior Adjutant or a member of the Military Chancery; parade dress.
5 General Staff Officer Hungarian Infantry; parade dress.
6 General Administrator; parade dress.
7 Personal Adjutant or Aide-de-Camp; parade dress.
8 Captain of the Hungarian General Staff; parade dress.
9 War Office official; parade dress.

Below: 36 INFANTRY OF THE COMMON ARMY
Parade dress.

1 Kaiserjaeger, Jaeger or Austrian Landwehr.
2 Long service Sergeant of a Hungarian regiment.
3 A Bosnia-Herzogovinian battalion.
4 to 6 German Infantry regiments (Sergeant Standard bearer, a Corporal and a Lieutenant).
7 Soldier from a Bosnia-Herzogovinian Infantry regiment.
8 A Field Officer in a Jaeger or Landwehr unit.
9 Officer of the Landesschuetzen, or of 4th Landwehr Infantry regiment.
10 and 11 Officer and man of the Landwehr (Honved).

Above: 37 INFANTRY. Field service dress:

1 German Infantry marching order.
2 Junior NCO; Kaiserjaeger, Feldjaeger, Austrian Landwehr or of a machine-gun detachment.
3 Mule handler; machine-gun detachment.
4 Soldier of the Landesschuetzen or 4th Landwehr Regiment.
5 Bosnia-Herzegovinian infantryman with 6 Bosnia-Herzegovinian Jaeger.
7 Infantry Officer; Austrian Landwehr or Landwehr (Honved).
8 Ensign; Jaeger or Austrian Landwehr.
9 Infantryman; Landwehr (Honved) unit.
10 Infantryman; Hungarian regiment of the Common Army.

Below: 38 1 Bandmaster of an Hungarian Infantry regiment of the Common Army.
2 Gun number of a Cavalry machine-gun detachment.
3 Proposed uniform for the Cavalry Arm of Service.
4 Other Rank; Honved Hussars.
5 and 6 Officers of a Honved Hussar regiment.
7 and 9 Officers of an Ulan regiment. 7 Field Officer.
8 Field Officer; Common Army Hussar regiment.
10 and 11 Dragoon Officers. 10 Parade uniform.
11 Field service dress. Worn round the helmet, a manoeuvre band.
12 Ensign; Common Army Hussars.

Above: 39 CAVALRY UNIFORMS

1 and 2 Mounted Tirolean or Dalmatian Rifles.
3 to 5 Ulans. 4 Corporal. 3 and 5 Either Landwehr Ulan or Common Army. 6 to 10 Dragoons.
6 Time serving Sergeant in a Cavalry pattern greatcoat.
10 Farrier identifiable by the lace around the cuff.
11 to 13 Hussars of the Common Army.

Below: 40 ARTILLERY UNIFORMS

1 Gunner of the Fortress Artillery in marching order.
2 Sergeant of a gun or howitzer battery in parade dress.

3 Dismounted Gunner of the Mountain Artillery.
4 Gunner of a Horse Artillery battery.
5 Artillery Master Gunner. 6 Gunner in a gun or howitzer battery, mounted or carried on the limber, in marching order. 7 Technical Artilleryman.
8 Artillery Engineer or an Officer in parade dress.
9 Artillery Officer in field service dress.
10 Gunner in a Horse Artillery battery, wearing a stable cap. 11 Artillery Officer in parade dress.
12 Trumpeter. 13 Sergeant in the Fortress Artillery in the old pattern uniform.

No 22

A German regiment
Recruiting area: *Prague*

The regiment was formed on 1 May 1885 as the Independent Half Regiment No 15 out of the former 1st Field Artillery Regiment. It became Divisional Artillery Regiment No 22 on 1 January 1894, and was retitled Field Gun Regiment No 22 on 6 April 1908.

No 23

A German regiment
Recruiting area: *Prague*

The regiment was formed on 1 May 1885 as the Independent Half Regiment No 16 out of the former 1st Field Artillery Regiment. It became Divisional Artillery Regiment No 23 on 1 January 1894, and was retitled Field Gun Regiment No 23 on 6 April 1908.

No 25

A German Regiment
Recruiting area: *Josephstadt*

The regiment was formed on 1 May 1885 as the Independent Half Regiment No 17 out of the former 4th Field Artillery Regiment. It became Divisional Artillery Regiment No 25 on 1 January 1894, and was retitled Field Gun Regiment No 25 on 6 April 1908.

No 26

A German regiment
Recruiting area: *Josephstadt*

The regiment was formed on 1 May 1885 as the Independent Half Regiment No 24 out of the former 4th Field Artillery Regiment. It became Divisional Artillery Regiment No 26 on 1 January 1894, and was retitled Field Gun Regiment No 26 on 6 April 1908.

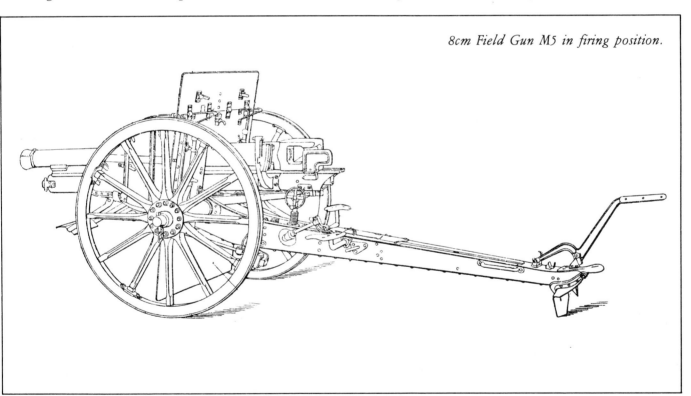

8cm Field Gun M5 in firing position.

No 24

A German regiment
Recruiting area: *Prague*

The regiment was formed on 1 January 1892 as the Independent Half Regiment No 33 out of the former 8th Corps Artillery Regiment. It became Divisional Artillery Regiment No 24 on 1 January 1894, and was retitled Field Gun Regiment No 24 on 6 April 1908.

No 27

A German regiment
Recruiting area: *Josephstadt*

The regiment was formed on 1 January 1892 as the Independent Half Regiment No 24 out of the former 9th Corps Artillery Regiment. It became Divisional Artillery Regiment No 27 on 1 January 1894, and was retitled Field Gun Regiment No 27 on 6 April 1908.

No 28

A German regiment
Recruiting area: *Przemysl*

The regiment was formed on 1 May 1885 as the Independent Half Regiment No 2 out of the former 7th Field Artillery Regiment. It became Divisional Artillery Regiment No 28 on 1 January 1894, and was retitled Field Gun Regiment No 28 on 6 April 1908.

No 29

A German regiment
Recruiting area: *Przemysl*

The regiment was formed on 1 May 1885 as the Independent Half Regiment No 3 out of the former 11th Field Artillery Regiment. It became Divisional Artillery Regiment No 29 on 1 January 1894, and was retitled Field Gun Regiment No 29 on 6 April 1908.

No 30

A German regiment
Recruiting area: *Przemysl*

The regiment was formed on 1 January 1892 as the Independent Half Regiment No 38 out of the former 1st Corps Artillery Regiment. It became Divisional Artillery Regiment No 30 on 1 January 1894, and was retitled Field Gun Regiment No 30 on 6 April 1908.

No 31

A German regiment
Recruiting area: *Lemberg*

The regiment was formed on 1 May 1885 as the Independent Half Regiment No 21 out of the former 9th Field Artillery Regiment. It became Divisional Artillery Regiment No 31 on 1 January 1894, and was retitled Field Gun Regiment No 31 on 6 April 1908.

No 32

A German regiment
Recruiting area: *Lemberg*

The regiment was formed on 1 May 1892 as the Independent Half Regiment No 22 out of the former 9th Field Artillery Regiment. It became Divisional Artillery Regiment No 32 on 1 January 1894, and was retitled Field Gun Regiment No 32 on 6 April 1908.

No 33

A German regiment
Recruiting area: *Lemberg*

The regiment was formed on 1 January 1892 as the Independent Half Regiment No 42 out of the former 11th Corps Artillery Regiment. It became Divisional Artillery Regiment No 33 on 1 January 1894, and was retitled Field Gun Regiment No 33 on 6 April 1908.

No 34

A Hungarian regiment
Recruiting area: *Nagyszeben*

The regiment was formed on 1 May 1885 as the Independent Half Regiment No 23 out of the former 8th Field Artillery Regiment. It became Divisional Artillery Regiment No 34 on 1 January 1894, and was retitled Field Gun Regiment No 34 on 6 April 1908.

No 35

A Hungarian regiment
Recruiting area: *Nagyszeben*

The regiment was formed on 1 May 1885 as the Independent Half Regiment No 24 out of the former 8th Field Artillery Regiment. It became Divisional Artillery Regiment No 35 on 1 January 1894, and was retitled Field Gun Regiment No 35 on 6 April 1908.

No 36

A Hungarian regiment
Recruiting area: *Nagyszeben*

The regiment was formed on 1 January 1892 as the Independent Half Regiment No 35 out of the former 12th Corps Artillery Regiment. It became Divisional Artillery Regiment No 36 on 1 January 1894, and was retitled Field Gun Regiment No 36 on 6 April 1908.

No 37

A Hungarian regiment
Recruiting area: *Agram*

The regiment was formed on 1 May 1885 as the independent Half Regiment No 25 out of the former 12th Field Artillery Regiment. It became Divisional Artillery Regiment No 37 on 1 January 1894, and was retitled Field Gun Regiment No 37 on 6 April 1908.

No 38

A Hungarian regiment
Recruiting area: *Agram*

The regiment was formed on 1 May 1885 as the Independent Half Regiment No 26 out of the former 12th Field Artillery Regiment. It became Divisional Artillery Regiment No 38 on 1 January 1894, and was retitled Field Gun Regiment No 38 on 6 April 1908.

No 39

A Hungarian regiment
Recruiting area: *Agram*

The regiment was formed on 1 January 1892 as the Independent Half Regiment No 36 out of the former 13th Corps Artillery Regiment. It became Divisional Artillery Regiment No 39 on 1 January 1894, and was retitled Field Gun Regiment No 39 on 6 April 1908.

No 40

A German regiment
Recruiting area: *Innsbruck*

The regiment was formed on 1 May 1885 as the Independent Half Regiment No 27 out of the former 1st Field Artillery Regiment. It became Divisional Artillery Regiment on 1 January 1894, and was retitled Field Gun Regiment No 40 on 6 April 1908.

No 41

A German regiment
Recruiting area: *Innsbruck*

The regiment was formed on 1 May 1885 as the Independent Half Regiment No 28 out of the former 4th and 6th Field Artillery Regiments. It became Divisional Artillery Regiment No 41 on 1 January 1894, and was retitled Field Gun Regiment No 41 on 6 April 1908.

No 42

A German regiment
Recruiting area: *Vienna*

The regiment was formed on 1 January 1892 as the Independent Half Regiment No 37 out of the former 14th Corps Artillery Regiment. It became Divisional Artillery Regiment No 42 on 1 January 1894 and was retitled Field Gun Regiment No 42 on 6 April 1908.

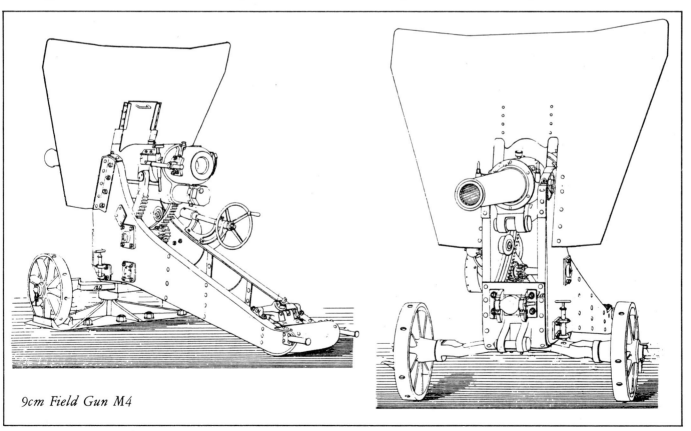

9cm Field Gun M4

||||||||||||||||||||||||||||||||||||||||||||||||||||||||||||||||||||||||||||

ARTILLERY · COMMON ARMY

2 · Field Howitzer Regiments

||||||||||||||||||||||||||||||||||||||||||||||||||||||||||||||||||||||||||||

The fourteen Field Howitzer regiments on the peacetime establishment of the Common Army were numbered serially. Each regiment had four batteries and the war establishment was for six howitzers per battery. The standard armament at the outbreak of war was the obsolescent steel bronze 10cm, M99 recoilless howitzer.

Upon mobilisation each regiment formed two independent half regiments, each of two batteries—except for the 14th Regiment—which formed only one half regiment with its two batteries numbered serially. The third and fourth batteries of that regiment were formed into two mountain howitzer batteries.

During 1914 new Field Howitzer batteries were raised. Some were equipped with the modern military pieces which had been ordered by the Chinese and Turkish governments but which had not been delivered. They were confiscated by the Austrian government and such batteries were known as Turkish or Chinese howitzer batteries. During this time reserve batteries were formed for each regiment and the obsolescent M99 was replaced by the modern steel M14.

Sergius Michailovitch Grossfürst von Russland No 1

A German regiment
Recruiting area: *Cracow*

The regiment was raised in 1854 as 2nd Field Artillery Regiment out of the existing 1st Field Artillery Regiment. The first Colonel-in-Chief was General Duke Ludwig who was succeeded by The Archduke Rudolf. From 1889 to 1904 General Carl Fischer assumed command.

On 1 May 1885 the unit was renamed and renumbered to become Corps Artillery Regiment No 10, and on 1 January 1894 became Corps Artillery Regiment No 1.

Retitled as Field Howitzer Regiment No 1 on 6 April 1908.

A former artillery regiment with the number 1 was raised in 1772 and disbanded in 1854. Elements of that formation were used to form the 1st, 2nd and 3rd Field Artillery Regiments.

General Count Gustav von Geldern-Egmond zu Arcen No 2

A German regiment
Recruiting area: *Vienna*

The unit was raised in 1854 as 11th Field Artillery Regiment and was commanded by General Vinzenz von Fitz. He was succeeded in 1865 by General Anton Juptner von Jonstorff. At the end of his twelve-year period of office, General The Archduke Johann assumed command of the regiment and in 1889 it was bestowed upon General August von Weigl.

During the period of the Archduke's incumbency the unit became Corps Artillery Regiment No 2 (1 May 1885) and received the title shown above on 6 April 1908.

Erzherzog Wilhelm No 3

A German regiment
Recruiting area: *Graz*

Raised in 1854 as 6th Field Artillery Regiment, the colonelcy was bestowed upon The Archduke Wilhelm. On 1 May 1885 the unit became Corps Artillery Regiment No 3, and was retitled as Field Howitzer Regiment No 3 on 6 April 1908.

The regiment carried the title and number as permanent distinctions to commemorate the Archduke Wilhelm who died in 1894.

(Title vacant) No 4

A Hungarian regiment
Recruiting area: *Budapest*

The unit was raised in 1854 as 5th Field Artillery Regiment out of the existing 4th Artillery Regiment. The first Colonel-in-Chief was General August von Stwrtnik. Between 1871 and 1894 the regiment was commanded by General Wilhelm Lenk von Wolfsberg. He was succeeded in 1895 by General Alfred von Kropatschek.

During the period of von Wolfsberg's incumbency the unit became Corps Artillery Regiment No 4 (1 May 1885) and was given the title shown above on 6 April 1908.

The former 4th Artillery Regiment was raised in 1802 and disbanded in 1854. Detachments from the regiment helped to form the Field Artillery Regiments Nos 5, 6 and 7.

Erzherzog Albrecht No 5

A Hungarian regiment
Recruiting area: *Pozsony*

The unit was raised in 1854 as 3rd Field Artillery Regiment out of the existing 1st Artillery Regiment, and was commanded by General Vinzenz von Augustin. He was succeeded in 1860 by General Alois Pichler and he, in turn, by the Archduke Albrecht in 1887.

On 1 May 1885 the unit became Corps Artillery Regiment No 5 and was then retitled to that shown above on 6 April 1908.

The former 5th Artillery Regiment was raised in 1816 and when it was disbanded in 1854, elements from it were used to form Field Artillery Regiments Nos 10 and 12.

The regiment carried the title and number as permanent distinctions to commemorate the Archduke Albrecht who died in 1895.

Erzherzog Franz Ferdinand von Österreich-Este No 6

A Hungarian regiment
Recruiting area: *Kassa*

Raised in 1854 as 10th Field Artillery Regiment and commanded by General Natalis Bervaldo-Bianchini. Eleven years later command passed to the Archduke Maximilian Joseph d'Este who was succeeded in 1864 by General Joseph Hutschenreiter von Glinzendorf. From 1880 to 1896 command of the regiment was invested in General Carl Tiller von Turnfort. In 1898 The Archduke Franz Ferdinand assumed command.

On 1 May 1885, during the period in office of General Tiller von Turnfort, the unit became Corps Artillery Regiment No 6, and was retitled to that shown above on 6 April 1908.

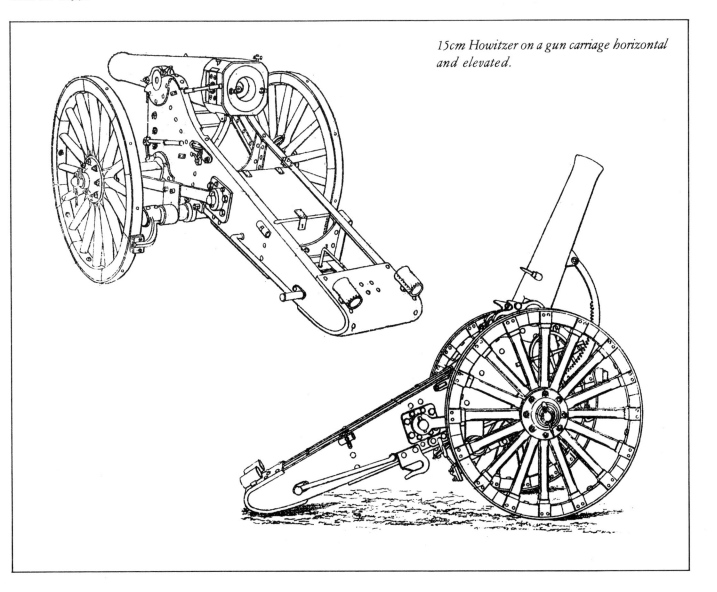

15cm Howitzer on a gun carriage horizontal and elevated.

Prinz Leopold von Bayern No 7

A Hungarian regiment
Recruiting area: *Temesvar*

Raised in 1872 as 13th Field Artillery Regiment and commanded by Leopold of Bavaria. On 1 May 1885 the unit became Corps Artillery Regiment No 7 and on 6 April 1908 received the title shown above.

Kaiser Franz Joseph No 8

A German regiment
Recruiting area: *Prague*

Raised in 1854 as 1st Field Artillery Regiment out of the existing 1st and 2nd Artillery Regiments. On 1 May 1885 the unit became Corps Artillery Regiment No 8 and was reclassified to that shown above on 6 April 1908.

The regiment carried the special distinction of a golden medal worn on the ribbon of the Franz Joseph's Order and the Royal Cypher was carried on the guns. Both distinctions were awarded in 1904, to commemorate the Golden Jubilee of the Emperor as Colonel-in-Chief of the regiment.

Fürst Joseph Wenzel von Liechtenstein No 9

A German regiment
Recruiting area: *Josephstadt*

Raised in 1854 as 4th Field Artillery Regiment out of the existing 3rd Artillery Regiment. The first Colonel-in-Chief was General Franz von Hauslab who was succeeded in 1883 by General Carl von Schmarda. On 1 May 1885 the unit became Corps Artillery Regiment No 9 and became Field Howitzer Regiment No 9 on 6 April 1908.

The regiment carried the title and number as permanent distinctions to commemorate the Prince of Liechtenstein who died in 1772.

(Title vacant) No 10

A German regiment
Recruiting area: *Przemysl*

Raised in 1854 as 7th Field Artillery Regiment, and commanded by Luitpold, Prince of Bavaria who laid down the office in 1905. The unit became Corps Artillery Regiment No 1 on 1 May 1885 and was reclassified and renumbered to that shown above on 6 April 1908.

General Joseph Smola No 11

A German regiment
Recruiting area: *Lemberg*

Raised in 1854 as 9th Field Artillery Regiment and first commanded by General Johann von Pittinger. He was succeeded in 1864 by General August von Schmidt. Four years later General Johann von Herle was appointed and in 1870 General Count Artur Bylandt-Rheidt had assumed the position. During his period of office the regiment was renamed as Corps Artillery Regiment No 11 (1 May 1885) and was then reclassified as No 11 Field Howitzer Regiment on 6 April 1908.

The regiment carried the title and number as permanent distinctions to commemorate the General, who died in 1820.

Georg V, König von England No 12

A Hungarian regiment
Recruiting area: *Nagyszeben*

Raised in 1854 as 8th Field Artillery Regiment. Command of the regiment was assumed in 1857 by General Joseph von Branttem from whom it passed in 1861 to General Franz von Wilsdorf. Fourteen years later General Carl Hofmann von Donnersberg had taken over command, which was held by General Friedrich Kreutz between 1885 and 1898. On 1 May 1885 the unit became Corps Artillery Regiment No 12 and received the title and number shown above on 6 April 1908.

Erzherzog Leopold Salvator No 13

A Hungarian regiment
Recruiting area: *Agram*

Raised in 1854 as 12th Field Artillery regiment and commanded by General Johann Vernier de Rougemont et Orchamp. In 1875 General Leopold Hofmann von Donnersberg was appointed to command the 13th. Between 1880 and 1888 the regiment was led by General Otto von Hartlieb and he was succeeded by General Prince Rudolf Lobkowitz.

During the incumbency of von Hartlieb the regiment became Corps Artillery Regiment No 13 (1 May 1885) and was renamed to that shown above on 6 April 1908.

General von Krobatin No 14

A German regiment
Recruiting area: *Vienna*

Raised in 1885 out of the existing 4th, 8th and 12th Field Artillery Regiments. The unit became 14th Field Howitzer Regiment on 6 April 1908.

The first commander of the 14th was General Rudolf Gerlich von Gerlicheburg and he was succeeded in 1891 by General Carl von Ludwig.

ARTILLERY · COMMON ARMY
3· Horse Artillery Half Regiments

The Horse Artillery Half Regiments of the Common Army were numbered 1, 2, 4, 5, 6, 7, 9, 10 and 11. Each half regiment numbered three batteries and each battery comprised of four guns. These were of the type which were on issue to Field Gun regiments.

At the outbreak of war in 1914 there was an increase in the number of half regiments and a raising of battery establishments to four per half regiment. These increases continued throughout the First World War until there were nine regiments on establishment.

There were no Horse Artillery formations on the establishment of the Austrian Landwehr and only a single one on the strength of the Landwehr (Honved).

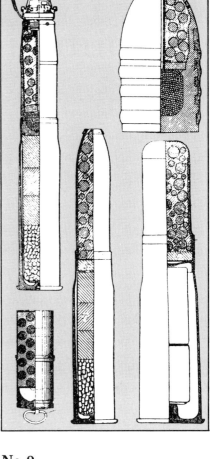

High explosive, shrapnel and standard shells in the Austrian Service.

No 1
A German unit
Recruiting area: *Cracow*

The unit was formed on 6 April 1908 from an amalgamation of the Horse Artillery batteries of 1st Corps Artillery Regiment.

No 2
A German unit
Recruiting area: *Vienna*

The unit was formed on 6 April 1908 from an amalgamation of the Horse Artillery batteries of 2nd Corps Artillery Regiment.

No 4
A Hungarian unit
Recruiting area *Budapest*

The unit was formed on 6 April 1908 from an amalgamation of the Horse Artillery batteries of 4th Corps Artillery Regiment.

No 5
A Hungarian unit
Recruiting area: *Poszony*

The unit was formed on 6 April 1908 from an amalgamation of the Horse Artillery batteries of 5th Corps Artillery Regiment.

No 6
A Hungarian unit
Recruiting area: *Kassa*

The unit was formed on 6 April 1908 from an amalgamation of the Horse Artillery batteries of 6th Corps Artillery Regiment.

No 7
A Hungarian unit
Recruiting area: *Temesvar*

The unit was formed on 6 April 1908 from an amalgamation of the Horse Artillery batteries of 7th Corps Artillery Regiment.

No 9
A German unit
Recruiting area: *Leitmeritz*

Formed in April 1908 from the batteries of 9th Corps Artillery Regiment

No 10
A German unit
Recruiting area: *Przemysl*

Formed on 6 April 1908 from an amalgamation of the Horse Artillery batteries of 7th Corps Artillery Regiment.

No 11
A German unit
Recruiting area: *Lemberg*

The unit was formed on 6 April 1908 from an amalgamation of the Horse Artillery batteries of 11th Corps Artillery Regiment.

ARTILLERY · COMMON ARMY
4·Mountain Artillery

10cm Mountain Howitzer M10 show
how it was made ready for a road ma

The establishment immediately preceding the First World War was ten full regiments and one independent half regiment which was raised from Dalmatia. The full regiments were numbered 3, 4, 6, 7, 8, 10, 11, 12, 13 and 14.

Each regiment was made up of six batteries, four of which were equipped with the obsolete 7cm, M99 Mountain gun and the remainder with the M8 or M10 Mountain howitzer. Both batteries of the Dalmatian Half Regiment were armed only with Mountain guns.

When the Mountain Artillery went onto a war footing new batteries were raised. A fifth battery for each of Nos 11, 12 and 13 Regiments, and two new batteries each for Regiments Nos 3, 8 and 14.

There were no Mountain Artillery units on either the Landwehr or the Landwehr (Honved) establishments.

No 3

A German regiment
Recruiting area: *Graz*

Formed on 6 April 1908 out of the former 1st and 2nd Instruction Cadres of Divisional Artillery Regiment No 7 and the 1st Instruction Cadre of Divisional Artillery Regiment No 9.

No 4

A German regiment
Recruiting area: *Lemberg*

Formed on 6 April 1908 out of the former 1st Artillery Inspectorate and No 1 Mountain Battery from each of the following Corps Artillery Regiments: Nos 1, 8, 10 and 11.

No 6

A Hungarian regiment
Recruiting area: *Nagyszeben*

The regiment was formed out of the former 3rd Artillery Inspectorate and No 1 Mountain Battery from each of the following Corps Artillery Regiments: Nos 2, 7, 12 and 13.

No 7

A Hungarian regiment
Recruiting area: *Temesvar*

Raised in 1908.

No 8

A German regiment
Recruiting area: *Prague*

Raised in 1908.

No 10

A German regiment
Recruiting area: *Przemysl*

Raised in 1913.

No 11

A German regiment
Recruiting area: *Lemberg*

Raised in 1908.

No 12

A Hungarian regiment
Recruiting area: *Nagyszeben*

Raised in 1908.

No 13

A Hungarian regiment
Recruiting area: *Agram*

Raised in 1911.

The Tirol und Vorarlberg Regiment 'Kaiser' No 14

A German regiment
Recruiting area: *Innsbruck*

Raised out of the former Fortress Artillery Battalion No 9 on January 1891.

Independent Mountain Gun Half Regiment

A Hungarian regiment
Recruiting area: *Agram*

Raised in 1913 in Dalmatia.

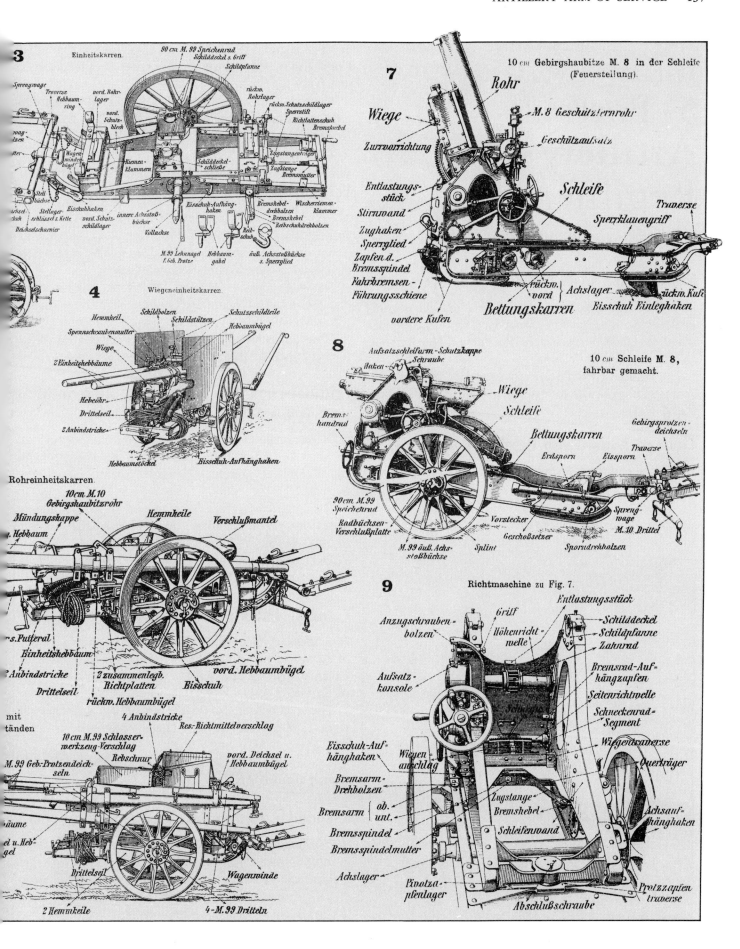

3

Einheitskarren.

90 cm M. 99 Speichenrad
Schilddeckel s. Griff
Schildpfanne
Sprengwage
Traverse
vord. Rohr-
Hebbaum-
lager
ring
vord.
Schutz-
blech
rückw.
Rohrlager
rückw. Schutzschildlager
Sperrstift
Richtlattenschuh
Bremskurbel
Zugstangenträger
Zugstange
Bremsmutter
Schilddeckel-
schließe
Stell-
büchse
Stellager
Eisschuhhaken
schlüssel s. Kette
vord. Schutz-
schildlager
Wagen-
minder-
bügel
Riemen-
klammern
Deichselscharnier
Vollachse
innere Achsstoß-
büchse
M. 99 Lehnnagel
f. Geb. Protze
Eisschuh-Aufhäng-
haken
Hebbaum-
gabel
äuß. Achsstoßbüchse
s. Sperrglied
Bremshebel-
drehbolzen
Bremshebel
Reibschuhdrehbolzen
Wischerriemen-
klammer
Reib-
schuh

4

Wiegeneinheitskarren.

Hemmkeil
Schildbolzen
Schildstützen
Schutzschildteile
Spannschraubenmutter
Hebbaumbügel
Wiege
2 Einheitshebbäume
Hebeöhr
Drittelseil
2 Anbindstricke
Hebbaumstöckel
Eisschuh-Aufhänghaken

Rohreinheitskarren.

10 cm M. 10
Gebirgshaubitzrohr
Hemmkeile
Verschlußmantel
Mündungskappe
g. Hebbaum
r. s. Putteral
Einheitshebbaum
2 Anbindstricke
Drittelseil
2 zusammenlegb.
Richtplatten
Eisschuh
vord. Hebbaumbügel
rückw. Hebbaumbügel
mit
ständen
4 Anbindstricke
Res.-Richtmittelverschlag
10 cm M. 99 Schlosser-
werkzeug-Verschlag
M. 99 Geb.-Protzendeich-
seln.
Rebschnur
vord. Deichsel u.
Hebbaumbügel
äume
l u. Heb-
gel
Drittelseil
Wagenwinde
2 Hemmkeile
4 M. 99 Dritteln

7

10 cm Gebirgshaubitze M. 8 in der Schleife
(Feuerstellung).
Rohr
Wiege
M. 8 Geschützkernrohr
Zurrvorrichtung
Geschützaufsatz
Entlastungs-
stück
Schleife
Stirnwand
Traverse
Zughaken
Sperrklauengriff
Sperrglied
Zapfen d.
Bremsspindel
Fahrbremsen-
Führungsschiene
rückw.
vord.
Achslager
rückw. Kufe
Eisschuh Einleghaken
Bettungskarren
vordere Kufen

8

10 cm Schleife M. 8,
fahrbar gemacht.
Aufsatzschleifarm-Schutzkappe
Schraube
Haken
Wiege
Schleife
Brems-
handrad
Bettungskarren
Gebirgsprotzen-
deichseln
90 cm M. 99
Speichenrad
Erdsporn
Eissporn
Traverse
Radbüchsen-
Verschlußplatte
Vorstecker
Sprengwage
M. 99 äuß. Achs-
stoßbüchse
Geschoßsetzer
Splint
Sporndrehbolzen
M. 10 Drittel

9

Richtmaschine zu Fig. 7.
Griff
Entlastungsstück
Anzugschrauben-
bolzen
Höheurichtwelle
Schilddeckel
Schildpfanne
Zahnrad
Aufsatz-
konsole
Bremsrad-Auf-
hängzapfen
Seitenrichtwelle
Schneckenrad-
Segment
Eisschuh-Auf-
hänghaken
Wiegen-
anschlag
Wiegentraverse
Querträger
Bremsarm-
Drehbolzen
Bremsarm ob.
unt.
Zugstange
Bremshebel
Achsauf-
hänghaken
Bremsspindel
Schleifenwand
Bremsspindelmutter
Achslager
Pivotza-
pfenlager
Abschlußschraube
Protzzapfen
traverse

ARTILLERY · COMMON ARMY

5 · Fortress Artillery Regiments

Kaiser Franz Josef No 1

A German regiment which drew its men from the province of Lower Austria and from Moravia. The recruiting area was that of 2nd Corps and the Regimental Headquarters and Depot were in Vienna.

The regiment was formed on 1 January 1891 from an amalgamation of the former Fortress Artillery Battalions Nos 3 and 4.

General Eduard von Beschi No 2

A German regiment which drew its men from the provinces

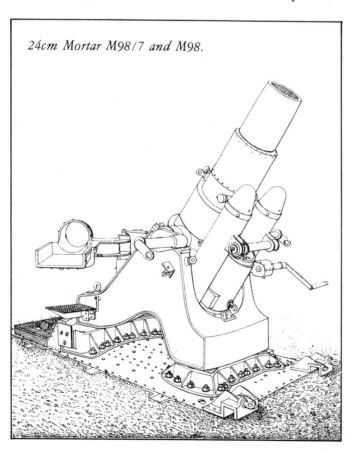

24cm Mortar M98/7 and M98.

of Moravia and Galicia. The recruiting area was that of 1st Corps and the Regimental Headquarters and Depot were in Cracow.

The regiment was formed on 1 January 1891 from an amalgamation of the former Fortress Artillery Battalions Nos 6 and 7.

Feldmarschall Franz Ulrich Kinsky, Fürst zu Vchinitz und Tettau No 3

A German regiment which drew its men from Bohemia and Galicia. There were two recruiting areas: Josephstadt (9th Corps) and Lemberg (11th Corps). The regimental Headquarters and Depot were at Przemysl.

The regimental title was carried as a permanent distinction to commemorate Field Marshal Prince Kinsky who died in 1792.

The regiment was formed from an amalgamation of the former Fortress Artillery Battalions Nos 2 and 8.

Feldmarschall Joseph, Graf Colloredo-Mels und Wallsee No 4

A German regiment which drew its men from the provinces of Styria and Krain. The recruiting area was that of 3rd Corps and the Regimental Headquarters and Depot were in Pola.

The regimental title was carried as a permanent distinction to commemorate the Field Marshall, who died in 1818.

The regiment was formed from an amalgamation of the former Fortress Artillery Battalions Nos 9 and 11.

General Theodor von Rouvroy No 5

A German regiment which drew its men from the provinces of Styria and Carinthia. The recruiting area was that of 3rd Corps and the Regimental Headquarters and Depot were in Cattaro.

The regimental title was carried as a permanent distinction to commemorate General von Rouvroy who died in 1789.

The regiment was formed from an amalgamation of the former Fortress Artillery Battalions Nos 2 and 10.

General Adolf Kollarz No 6

A Hungarian regiment which drew its men from its principal recruiting area of Poszony, that is 5th Corps. The Regimental Headquarters and Depot were at Komaron.

The regiment was formed from an amalgamation of the former Fortress Artillery Battalions Nos 1 and 5.

ARTILLERY ·COMMON ARMY

6· Fortress Artillery Battalions

No 1

A German battalion which was formed on 1 January 1891 from the former 9th Fortress Artillery Battalion.

Although the battalion was described as being from Upper Austria and Salzburg the recruiting area was Innsbruck (14th Corps) and the Battalion Headquarters was in Trient.

No 2

A Hungarian battalion which was formed on 1 January 1891 from the former 1st and 12th Artillery Battalions.

The battalion recruited in 7th Corps area (Temesvar) and had its Headquarters in Gyulafehervar.

No 3

A Hungarian battalion formed on 1 January 1894 from an amalgamation of the former 1st and 12th Fortress Artillery Battalions.

The battalion recruited in 5th Corps area (Poszony) and had its Headquarters in Peterwardein.

No 4

A German battalion formed in 1909. Although described as a Bohemian battalion, it recruited in Innsbruck (14 Corps) area.

No 5

A German battalion formed in 1909. Although described as a Bohemian-Galician battalion, it recruited in Innsbruck (14 Corps) area.

No 6

A German battalion from Poland formed in 1911. Although described as a Galician battalion, it recruited in Innsbruck (14 Corps) area.

No 7

A Hungarian battalion formed in 1911. Although described as a Hungarian unit, it recruited in Innsbruck (14 Corps) area.

No 8

A German battalion formed in 1913. Although described as being a Slovenian unit, it recruited in Graz (3 Corps) area.

No 9

A German battalion formed in 1914. Although described as a German unit from Bohemia, it recruited in Cracow (1 Corps) area.

No 10

A German battalion formed in 1914. It recruited in Graz (3 Corps) area.

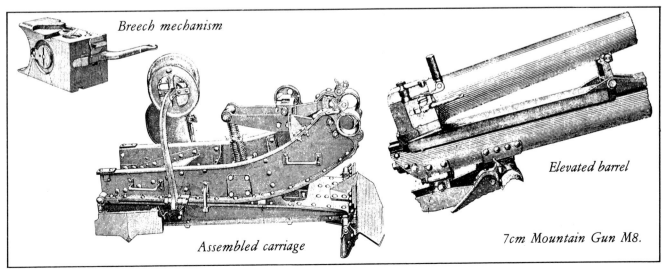

Breech mechanism

Assembled carriage

Elevated barrel

7cm Mountain Gun M8.

||||||||||||||||||||||||||||||||||||||||||||||||||||||||||||||||||||||||||||||

ARTILLERY · LANDWEHR AND HONVED

Artillery Units of the Landwehr and Landwehr (Honved)

||||||||||||||||||||||||||||||||||||||||||||||||||||||||||||||||||||||||||||||

The Field Gun and Field Howitzer half regiments of the Landwehr shared the same recruiting areas. Their formation years were 1909 for the Field Howitzer units and 1913 for those of the Field Artillery. The numbers shown indicate the Landwehr Infantry Divisions to which the half regiments were attached.

Division	Recruiting area
No 13	Vienna
No 21	Prague
No 22	Graz
No 26	Leitmeritz
No 43	Lemberg
No 44	Prague
No 45	Przemysl
No 46	Cracow

Field Gun Regiments of the Landwehr (Honved)

Division	Raised	Recruiting District
No 1	1913	Honved I
No 2	1914	Honved V
No 3	1914	Honved III
No 4	1914	Honved IV
No 5	1914	Honved V
No 6	1914	Honved VI
No 7	1914	Honved IV
No 8	1913	Honved II

Horse Artillery Half Regiments of the Landwehr (Honved)

Division	Raised	Recruiting District
No 1	1914	Honved II

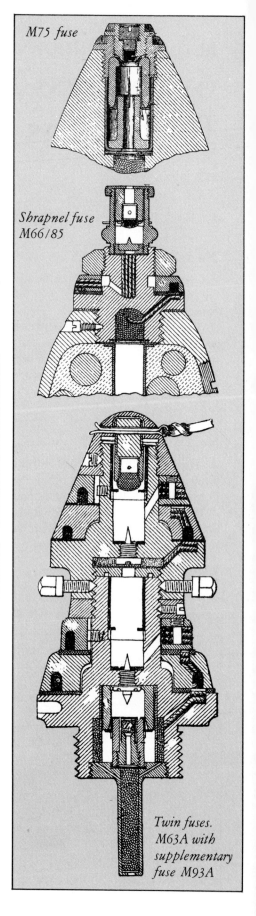

M75 fuse

Shrapnel fuse M66/85

Twin fuses. M63A with supplementary fuse M93A

7·Establishments

Introduction

Diagrams and
tables of Establishments

||||||||||||||||||||||||||||||||||||||||||||||||||||||||||||||||||||||||||||||||||||||||||||||||||||

Establishments

||||||||||||||||||||||||||||||||||||||||||||||||||||||||||||||||||||||||||||||||||||||||||||||||||||||||||||||||

Due to fluctuations in the numbers of men recruited to serve in the army and because peacetime establishments were increased by authority of the Minister for War when a regiment went out on active service to a frontier area, or for any one of a number of other factors, it is not possible to state with absolute accuracy the establishments of units in the armies of Austria-Hungary. In common with most other military bodies the Imperial force had a peacetime and a wartime establishment, but the figures quoted in the official tables were often only a norm to be attained. Depending upon circumstances, a unit's strength could fall below or even exceed the figures which had been laid down by the War Ministry.

Differences in unit role also influenced not only its strength in numbers but also its establishment of equipment. Thus, for example, a regiment equipped to fight in the high mountains did not require horse-drawn carts as did a standard infantry unit, but was outfitted with pack animals.

Let us accept then that circumstances can affect not only the numerical strength of a unit but also its composition and let us also take the year 1914 as the one on which our establishment figures are based.

Common Army Infantry

Organisation was based on the number four. There were four battalions to a regiment (I to IV), each of which had four companies (1 to 16). A company had four platoons made up of four sections. The machine gun company was also made up of four detachments although only three were fielded in peacetime. The fourth machine-gun group was activated for manoeuvres or upon mobilisation being declared.

There was also on a unit's establishment a Depot, known as the Ersatz battalion cadre, which was activated upon mobilisation and which was responsible for the training and outfitting of replacements to the battle line, as well as for the setting up of ration and ammunition columns.

The establishment of officers in a Regimental Headquarters in peacetime was a colonel in command, four battalion commanders of field rank, and another officer of equivalent rank together with three captains. These four officers could deputise for any one of the battalion commanders who was ill or on a course, or could be employed at the colonel's discretion on some other supernumary duty. Also in the headquarters' group was the regimental adjutant as well as the adjutants of each battalion, a regimental pioneer officer, the supply officer, five medical officers and the regimental paymaster, all of subaltern officer rank.

The establishment of Other Ranks at Regimental Headquarters included a warrant officer responsible for discipline, the musicians of the regimental band, batmen and various types of clerk. The peacetime establishment of a Regimental Headquarters was 21 officers and 73 men. The strength of a regiment was 85 officers and 1,562 rank and file. A company was made up of a commander, usually a captain and three subalterns. In addition to the commissioned ranks there were 93 men. In sensitive frontier areas this figure was increased to 129 rank and file.

The Depot cadre was commanded by a field officer and had, in addition, two officers from the Recruiting Board, a paymaster and a medical officer. Thirteen Other Ranks were attached to the Depot.

The increases in numbers when establishments changed to a war footing raised the strength of a company of 4 officers and 236 men. This war establishment did not remain constant throughout the war. As well as a higher number of machine guns, the employment of trench mortars and specially raised storm troop detachments had their effect upon the strength of regiments and of their constituent battalions and companies.

Corps machine-gun training school shortly after the outbreak of war. In peacetime an army school of machine-gun training had been set up at Bruck an der Leitha, but with the expansion of the machine-gun arm it was found necessary for each Corps to set up its own school. The specialist badge worn by machine gunners can be seen clearly on the collar of the man seated in the right foreground.

Cavalry

The standardisation of the Imperial Cavalry Arm meant that the same establishments applied to the Dragoon, Hussar and Ulan regiments.

The basic organisation was a regimental staff commanding two half regiments known as Divisions. Each Division was made up of three field squadrons. There was also on the regimental strength a telegraph and a pioneer section and the usual Ersatz cadre. Command of a cavalry regiment was invested in a colonel with a lieutenant colonel or a major commanding each Division. Field squadrons were commanded by a captain and lieutenants were in charge of both the telegraph and the pioneer detachments.

Cavalry regulations were explicit. Field squadrons were to be employed, exclusively, in a combat role. The other tasks for which cavalry were required, escort duties and message carrying, were carried out by troops drawn from each regiment under the command of a subaltern. The peacetime establishment of a field squadron was 5 officers and 166 rank and file. Only 156 members of a squadron were mounted. The remainder were carried on regimental transport.

There was little difference between the peacetime and wartime establishments of cavalry regiments and strengths stayed level until the time came when the regiments had to be disbanded and the men put into the trenches as infantry. Establishments then rose to the infantry level.

Signals Section on active service using the standard hand set. The rifle is a Mauser, known as 'Mexican' because the whole consignment was manufactured for the Mexican government but confiscated on the outbreak of war.

The Artillery

The organisation of a regiment of Field Artillery was a Regimental Headquarters, four battalions of guns and two cadres, one of which was the standard Depot for the training of replacements. The other was the cadre for the regimental ammunition park.

The strength of the headquarters of an Artillery regiment was two field officers, the regimental adjutant, supply officer, paymaster and medical officer. There were also Other Ranks acting as clerks to the paymaster and batmen to the officers. The Ersatz cadre was commanded by a captain in charge of ten permanent staff men. The ammunition park cadre had a strength of two officers and nine men. Battery strengths, in peacetime, were 5 officers and 100 Other Ranks. Those numbers rose, on a war footing, to 6 officers and 190 rank and file. The number of guns also rose, from 4 to 8.

The establishment of a battery of Horse Artillery was higher than that in the Field Artillery. 6 officers and 122 men with 123 horses, and those numbers increased when the unit went onto war establishment. The strength then was 180 men and 220 horses.

The peacetime strength of a battery of Mountain Artillery was 4 officers and 86 men, with 20 horses. That establishment increased to 101 men and 54 beasts upon mobilisation.

In peacetime a regiment of Fortress Artillery was usually three battalions strong. In such a case the number of officers was 67 and the number of Other Ranks 1,270. In a two-battalion regiment the numbers were 47 and 850 respectively. In time of war the establishment of a battalion increased from 20 officers and 420 men to 26 officers and 1,000 men. In addition to the standard cadres, Fortress battalions also had cadres for howitzer detachments.

Soldier of the Train, attached to an Infantry Division. The trousers were in calvary scarlet, the blouse in blue and the pelisse in brown. Facing colour was sky blue, button colour was white metal.

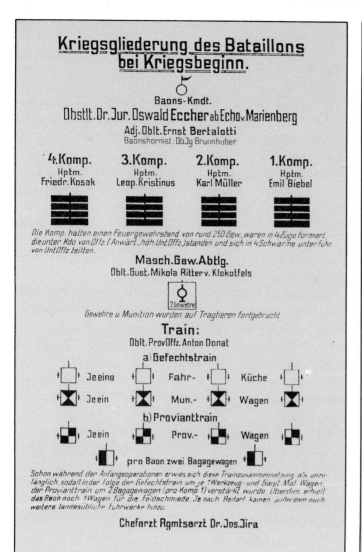

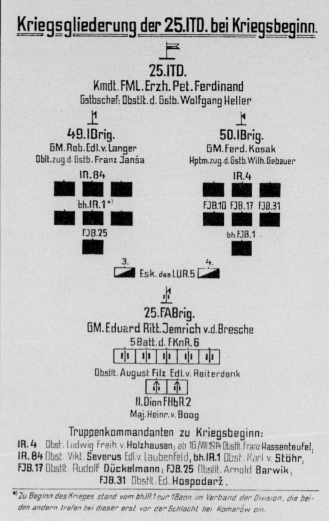

THE WAR ESTABLISHMENT OF 11TH FELDJAEGER BATTALION AT THE OUTBREAK OF WAR IN 1914.
The Commanding Officer. Adjutant and Battalion bugler. Four Companies numbered serially. Each Company with four platoons had a strength of some 250 rifles. Platoon commanders were either Aspirant Officers or senior NCOs. Each of the four Sections in a platoon was led by an NCO.

The machine-gun detachment was commanded by a Subaltern Officer. The two machine guns and ammunition were brought forward on horse or mule back.

The Train was in two parts: Battle and Provision.
The Battle Train: Each Company had two carts, one to carry stores, the other to carry the ammunition supply. A field kitchen was on issue to each Company.
The Supply Train: One cart per Company carried the rations and each battalion had, in addition, two baggage carts.

The establishment shown above was the standard one not only for Feldjaeger battalions specifically, but also for battalions within an Infantry regiment.

THE WAR ESTABLISHMENT OF 25TH INFANTRY DIVISION AT THE OUTBREAK OF WAR IN 1914.
General Officer Commanding (The Archduke Peter Ferdinand)
Chief of Staff (Lieutenant Colonel Heller)

49th Infantry Brigade:
84th Infantry Regt (3 battalions)
1st Bosnia-Herzegovinian Infantry Regt (3 battalions) 25th Feldjaeger Bn

50th Infantry Brigade:
4th Infantry Regt (3 battalions)
10th, 17th and 31st Feldjaeger Bns (in lieu of a second Infantry regiment) 1st Bosnia-Herzegovinian Feldjaeger Bn
The 3rd and 4th Squadrons of 5th Landwehr Ulan Regt

25th Field Artillery Brigade:
5 battalions of No 6 Field Gun Regt
2nd Half Regt of 2nd Field Howitzer Regt

The establishment shown above was standard for Infantry Divisions of the Austro-Hungarian Army at the outbreak of war.

Situation der Artillerie im August 1914

K.u.k. Feldkanonenregiment. Nr.

K.u.k. FHbR. Nr.

K.u.k. Rt.A.D.Nr.

K.u.k.s.H.D.Nr.

K.u.k. GbArtRgt.Nr.

K.k. Landwehr-Feldkan.Div.Nr. Feldhb.Div.

K.u.k.Dalmat.GbKan.Div.

K.ung.Landwehr-FeldkanRgt.Nr. Rt.ADiv.Nr.

K.u.k. Festungsartillerieregiment Nr.

K.u.k. Festungsartilleriebaon Nr.

Zeichenerklärung:

FeldKan. oder GbgsKanBatterie

FeldHb. oder GbgsHbBatterie

FstgsArtKomp. eingeteilt als SicherheitsBes.i.Fs.Pl.

" " " " bei einer 30'5 cm aut.MsBt.

" " " " 24 cm MsBt.

" " " " 12 cm M.80 KnBt.

15 cm M 99 sHbBt. der sHbDiv. oder FstgsArtKomp. eingeteilt bei einer solchen Batterie

Diagram showing the organisation of the Artillery Arm of Service, August 1914.

TABLES OF ESTABLISHMENTS

Peacetime establishments of Infantry or Jaeger units based on regiments with a four-battalion establishment

	Officers	Men
Common Army Infantry Regiment	85	1562
Jaeger Regiment	85	1562
Bosnia-Herzegovinian Regiment	86	1569
Feldjaeger Battalion	23	383

(The figures do not include the Ersatz cadre units)

Wartime establishments of Infantry or Jaeger units

	Officers	Men	Horses	Carts/Vehicles
Company	4	236	1	—
Battalion of				
Infantry	19	960	30	10
Jaeger	20	960	31	10
Feldjaeger				
Battalion	22	970	34	11

Peacetime establishments of an Infantry or Jaeger Company

	Standard Estab.	Increased Estab.	Ersatz cadre
Captains	1	1	1
Lieutenants	3	3	1 (2) Jaeger
Cadet Probationer	1	1	
Colour Sergeant	1	1	
Pay Sergeant	1	1	2
Sergeants	2	3	
Corporals	6	8	1 (2) Jaeger
Lance Corporals	6	9	
Private soldiers	70	100	6 (12) Jaeger
Company bugler	1	1	
Company drummer	1	1	
Batmen	4	4	2 (3) Jaeger
TOTALS Officers	4	4	2 (3) Jaeger
Men	93	129	11 (19) Jaeger

Battery limber iron construction wheel.

Field limber M75.

Peacetime establishments of a Landwehr Infantry or Jaeger Company

	Officers	NCOs and Men
Company Commander	1	
Subalterns	3	
Colour Sergeant		1
Pay Sergeant		1
Sergeants		2
Corporals		4
Lance Corporals		4
Cadet Probationer		1
Private soldiers		40
Company bugler		1
Batmen		4
TOTALS	4	58

Peacetime establishments of the Cavalry

	FIELD SQUADRON			ERSATZ CADRE		
	Officers	Men	Horses	Officers	Men	Horses
Captains and subalterns	5		11	1		3
Sergeant Majors		2	2		1	1
Sergeants		4	4		1	1
Corporals		12	12			
Trumpeters		1	1			
Lance Corporals		4	4			
Troopers		122	122			
Pay Sergeant		1			1	
Farrier		1				
Batmen		5			4	
Squadron HQ Staff		13			11	
Saddler		1				
TOTALS	5	166	156	1	18	5

Peacetime establishment of a Landwehr (Honved) Infantry Company

Company Commander	1	
Subalterns	3	
Colour Sergeants		1
Pay Sergeants		1
Sergeants		2
Corporals		3
Lance Corporals		3
Cadet Probationer		1
Private soldiers		35
Company bugler		1
Batmen		4
TOTALS	4	51

Wartime establishments of the Cavalry

	Officers	Men	Horses
Regiments complete with all HQ Staffs and with 6 Sqdns	41	1093	1105

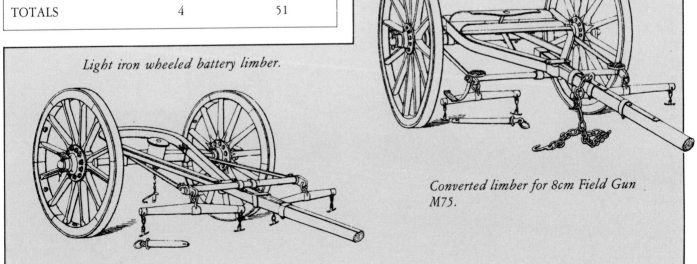

Light iron wheeled battery limber.

Converted limber for 8cm Field Gun M75.

Peacetime establishments of a Landwehr and Landwehr (Honved) Cavalry Squadron

(There were no Dragoon units on the Landwehr establishment. The cavalry units represented were Hussars, Ulan, Mounted Tirolean Rifles and the Mounted Dalmatian Rifles)

	Ulan	Mount. Tirol.R.	Mount. Dalm.R.	Hussars
Officers	5	5	5	4
Sergeant Majors	1	1	1	1
Pay Sergeants	1	1	1	1
Sergeants	2	2	2	1
Corporals	3	3	5	2
Lance Corporals	2	2	2	2
Cadet Probationers	1	1	1	1
Squadron trumpeter	1	1	1	1
Troopers	55	55	57	50
Farriers	1	1	—	1
Armourer	—	—	1	—
Saddler	1	1	1	1
Batmen	5	5	5	4
TOTALS	78	78	82	69

Field and Horse Artillery units Peacetime establishment

	Field Battery	Horse Battery	Ammunition Park	Ersatz Cadre
Officers	5	6	2	1
Sergeant Majors	2	1		
Paymaster Sergeant	1	1	1	1
Sergeants	3	3	1	1
Corporals	9	11	1	1
Battery trumpeter	1	1		
Gunners	50	60	2	4
Drivers	28	37	2	2
Batmen	4	5	2	1
Artificers				
saddlers	1	1		
smiths	1			
farriers				
TOTALS Men	105	127	11	11
Horses	53	123	5	4

War establishment of Field and Horse Artillery units

Officers	6	5
Rank and file	190	180
Horses	140	220
Artillery pieces	8	6
Ammunition carts	8	6
Other vehicles	5	6

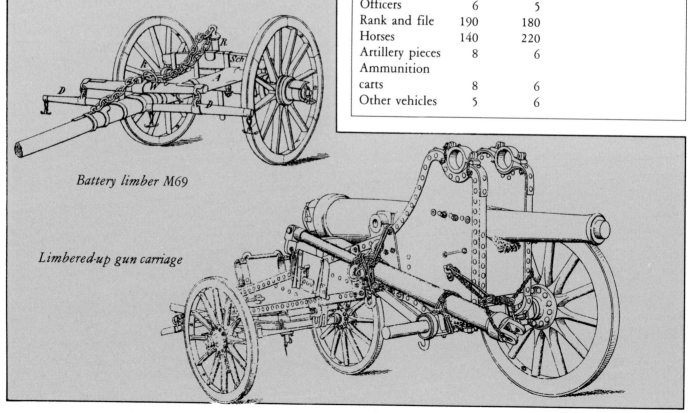

Battery limber M69

Limbered-up gun carriage

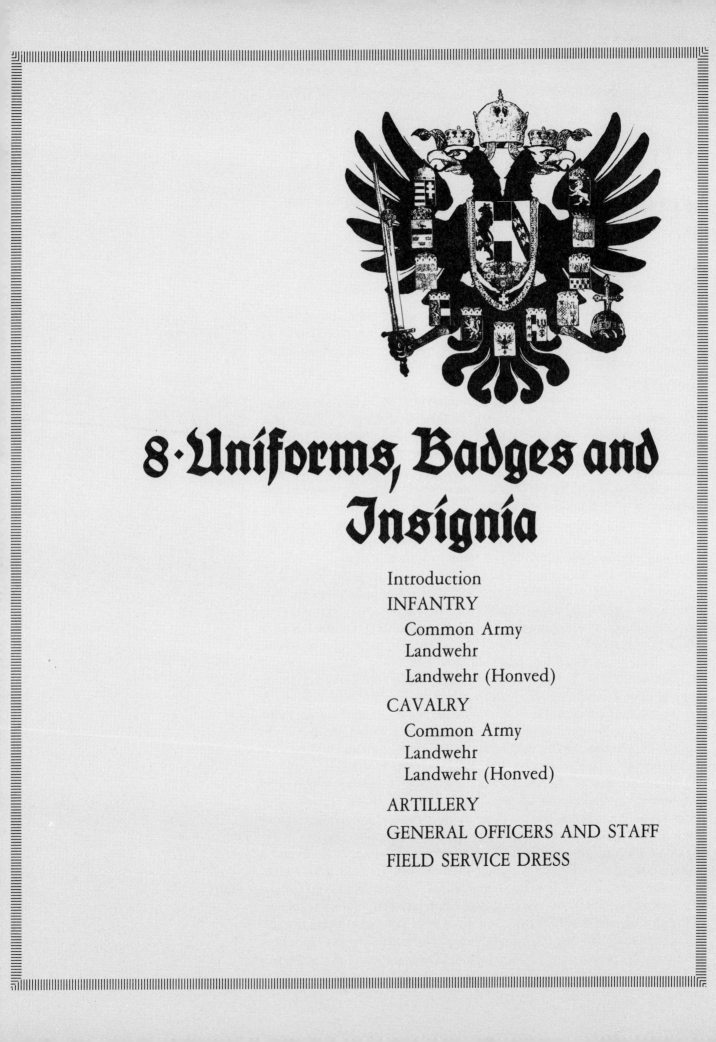

8·Uniforms, Badges and Insignia

Uniforms, badges and insignia

Compared to the uniforms worn by some of the world's military forces, the dress of the armies of Austria-Hungary in the late 19th and early 20th centuries, was not especially elaborate, even though native civilian critics referred to it as the 'paint box' army, because of the many shades of facing colour by which regiments were identified.

Even before Archduke Albrecht's great reforms there had been moves towards change and to standardisation in matters of dress, but it was not until 1868 that the traditional white tunic worn by the Habsburg infantry and curassiers, was discarded. With it went the green tunic of the ulan regiments. Henceforth the standard colour was blue. For the line infantry this was a dark shade. For the Bosnia-Herzegovinian units, the dragoons and ulans, a light tone, and for the hussars either light or dark, depending upon the regiment. The artillery and jaeger were the exceptions to that uniformity. Jaeger units retained the pike grey colour they had worn for decades and the artillery their traditional brown tunic with its red facings.

The uniforms which are described in detail below are those which were issued as a result of Albrecht's reform. A study of military dress discloses that although over the course of decades minor amendments are introduced, the basic design of a uniform remains usually unaltered. Thus, the full dress uniforms worn by the regiments of the Austro-Hungarian Army in 1914 were, essentially, those which had been introduced in 1868.

Identification of the regiments in the Imperial and royal forces depended, firstly, upon establishing the wearer's arm of service. This was very easy. A more specific identification to determine the regiment, and any specialist abilities he might have, required a certain degree of knowledge, but it was in the appreciation of the smaller distinctive marks: cuff bands, brassards and the like, that the greatest difficulties were encountered.

In the first stage of identification mounted troops, for example, were easily recognised by the red trousers with which they were issued. The shape of the headdress as well as the cut of the tunic identified whether the wearer was a dragoon, a ulan or a hussar.

A brown tunic with red facings, blue trousers of dragoon pattern and a shako bearing a black horse-hair plume, determined the field artilleryman. A simple, dark blue tunic with coloured facings, light blue slacks and a shako showed the wearer to be in a Common Army, German infantry regiment. The same type of dark blue tunic and shako worn with tight-fitting trousers decorated with elaborate thigh knots, showed the wearer to be in a Hungarian line infantry regiment. A fez worn with light blue tunic and trousers which

48

were cut full to the knee and tight round the calf was the dress of the men of Bosnian regiments. A grey tunic faced with green slacks piped in green and a black cap decorated with cock feathers established that the wearer was from a Jaeger or from an Austrian Landwehr or Landesschuetzen unit. A double-breasted blue tunic piped in red was worn by Landwehr (Honved) infantry regiments.

The second stage of identification depended upon a knowledge of facing and button colours. To distinguish the 102 Common Army infantry regiments, only nine basic colours were used: red, brown, yellow, green, blue, grey, black, hazel and white. Those nine were expanded by shading so that there were ten shades of red, two of brown, three in yellow, six in green, two blues, two greys and two hazels. The cavalry, as well as the infantry, wore distinctive colours to identify the regiments. Dragoons had one blue, one green, three reds and two yellows. For hussars, two blues, one red, one white and one grey. Ulan regiments were identified by the following colours: one yellow, one green, two red, two blue and one white.

In Common Army line infantry regiments no more than four regiments, two each from the German and Hungarian establishments, shared the same shade of colour. One German regiment and one Hungarian regiment wore white metal buttons; the other two regiments wore buttons of yellow metal. Thus, in each case, two regiments, one German and one Hungarian, wore the same facing colour and the same button colour. To distinguish between the two, the soldiers in Hungarian regiments wore tight-fitting trousers which were fastened into lace-up boots. Further marks of distinction were the thigh knots and piping in black and yellow cord which decorated those trousers. The tunic also carried a device peculiar to Hungarian regiments: this was a cuff decoration, in cloth (lace for officers) and known as a 'bear's paw'.

On the cavalry establishment dragoon regiments wore a facing colour on the tunic cuffs and collar. The pairs of regiments having the same colour were identified by whether their tunic buttons were white or yellow metal. Hussars and ulans did not carry their identifying colour on the tunic but on their headdress. In the case of hussars, the shako colour, together with that of the attila and of the olivets which fastened it, enabled a precise identification to be made.

The increase in the range and killing power of the weapons produced in the latter half of the 19th century forced armies to replace their distinctive and colourful uniforms with ones of neutral shade: grey, brown or horizon blue. Austria was among the first to adopt the new ideas and selected a grey similar in shade to that which the jaeger had been wearing for nearly a century. It was proposed that uniforms of that colour would go into general issue and in 1909 the infantry were the first arm of service to begin the change-over. The opposition of the cavalry establishment to the grey service dress was so effective that the sabre squadrons went out to war in 1914 still wearing what was, in effect, parade dress. Only cavalry machine-gun teams were outfitted with the pike grey uniform.

In order to explain certain of the dress peculiarities of the Austro-Hungarian armies, and to avoid repetition in the text, the following general definitions are given.

Headdress

This was divided into that worn as part of the parade or full dress uniform

Common Army Hussars march past The Emperor Franz Joseph during one of the celebrations to mark his Diamond Jubilee in 1908.

and that worn as non-ceremonial or active service dress. The ceremonial or full dress headgear included the cocked hat, jaeger cap, dragoon helmet, hussar shako, ulan shapka and the parade shako worn by the infantry and artillery. In cavalry regiments the parade or full dress headgear was also that worn on active service—certainly for the first months of the First World War.

Non-ceremonial headdress included the officer's undress shako and the various types of field service cap. That of the infantry was a peaked, light blue (from 1909 a pike grey) headcovering. Cavalry stable caps were of similar pattern but had no peaks and were in madder red.

Body coverings

These could also be either full dress or field service garments.

Infantry tunics, the two types of attila and the ulanka were parade items. The blouse, either in blue, in brown or in grey, was undress. That article in grey formed part of the field service dress.

Carl, Count Coudennhouve. There was a short period when the waist sash was worn from left shoulder to right hip and the Count is wearing his sash in that fashion.

Leg coverings

These were of several patterns. Trousers, breeches, white linen slacks for summer wear, officers' salonhosen, tight-fitting Hungarian trousers, Bosnian and artillery pattern breeches.

Trousers were worn by foot troops in parade dress as well as by General Officers. Salonhosen were off-duty garments worn by officers and certain very senior NCOs.

Mounted officers, including those of field rank in the infantry, wore breeches, high boots and spurs.

Footwear

Infantry wore lace-up boots, and heavier versions of that pattern boot complete with special studding were issued to mountain troops. The artillery also wore lace-up boots and leather gaiters extending to just below the knee. Mounted troops wore high boots of various patterns: the shisman for hussars, butcher boots for dragoons and jackboots for ulans.

Parolis

These were two, lozenge-shaped gorget patches in regimental facing colour worn on the upper lapels of the greatcoat. Officer pattern parolis carried a regimental button at the top of both patches.

Sashes and Belts

In the Austrian Service the waist sash or the cartridge belt were symbols of officer status and were worn whenever possible.

The waist sash was a 6cm wide strip of silk, patterned with two black lines. Both ends of the sash terminated in a gold bullion acorn and a fringe 24cm long. On the obverse of each acorn was the Imperial cypher and on the reverse the Imperial eagle, both embroidered in gold thread. General Officers in 'German' uniform had a sash of gold thread worked with black silk.

When the sash was worn around the waist it was folded along its length to a width of 3cm and was fastened with a clip in such a way that both tassels hung from the left hip. From 1859 to 1868 the sash was worn over the shoulder and fastened on the hip, but after 1868 it was worn, once again, round the body except by certain officers. These were adjutants, aides-de-camp or officers who had been seconded to the General Staff. These wore the sash opened to its full width across the shoulder and fastened at the hip as a mark of their office. For aides-de-camp or adjutants it was worn from the left shoulder to the right hip. Officers who were seconded to the Staff wore the sash from the right shoulder to the left hip.

The other mark of officer status was the cartridge belt and box, which was worn from shoulder to hip by officers of the cavalry and of the artillery.

When the regiments marched out to war, officers still wore their distinctive waist sashes and cartridge belts. The high casualty rate among commissioned ranks led to the High Command Order of September 1914, forbidding those items of dress to be worn on active service. All ranks wore a leather waist belt. For infantry units this fastened by a square buckle; cavalry and artillery belts fastened by the tongue and prong method. On the buckles of infantry belts officers carried the Imperial cypher and Other Ranks an embossed Imperial eagle.

Sword Knots

All sword knots were made up of a strap and tassel. This latter consisted of a neck, an acorn and a fringe. For commissioned ranks in the Common Army and the Landwehr the strap was of gold lace flecked with black. Landwehr (Honved) officers had straps of gold flecked with red.

The neck, acorn and fringe were of gold bullion. The tassel neck was embroidered with gold thread showing on the obverse the Imperial cypher and on the reverse the Imperial eagle. Sword knots for non-commissioned officers were of silk or wool and the neck was of zig-zag patterned lace. Ensigns had a sword knot with a neck and acorn of yellow silk with a fringe made of gold bullion. Regimental bandmasters carried sword knots of officer pattern embroidered in silver bullion and with the silver bullion fringe worked with red silk thread. Musicians and bandsmen wore NCO pattern knots in white worked with the regimental facing colour.

Sabre straps for Other Ranks in cavalry units were of red leather, shaped and fastened like standard patten sword knots.

Emblems on Headdress

There was a wide variety of badges and emblems but the one device basic to most types of headdress was the rose. For officers this was of gold bullion thread made into five circles of diminishing size. The diameter of the largest, that is the outer circle, was 5cm. The central field of the rose was of black velvet charged with the Imperial cypher in gilt letters and number. The Other Ranks pattern was also of 5cm diameter but was of brass, having a central field of black paint. Roses of this pattern were worn with parade or full dress headdress but not on the dragoon helmet, the jaeger cap or the Bosnian fez. But when worn, as for example on the infantry full dress shako, they were placed centrally on the crown of the cap and fitted in such a way that they projected above the crown and with the outer ring resting on it.

The undress shako carried a small rosette. This was of the same pattern and diameter but was set lower on the crown so that its outer ring was level with the top of the shako. On the officer pattern undress shako, a loop of lace ran vertically from the bottom of the rosette to the central buckle of the chin strap. This loop of gold lace, flecked with black, was fastened by a small gilt button. Jaeger officers wore a small horn on that loop.

On the grey field service cap rosettes for all ranks were 3cm in diameter. The officer pattern was, once again, in gold thread but that of the Other Ranks was of brass and was pierced to show the Imperial cypher emphasised against a black painted background. NCOs and others who were permitted to wear officer pattern headdress—cadets and one-year volunteers—wore rosettes of yellow silk.

The emblem carried traditionally on the headdress of Habsburg soldiers on parade or in the field was a bunch of greenery. In summer this was a spray of oak leaves and in winter a sprig of fir twigs. These emblems fitted into a receiver generally placed behind the rose or rosette. Dragoons, ulans, and jaeger, in parade dress, wore their greenery on the left side of the headdress. A bunch of the appropriate greenery decorated the head of the staff on which the regimental Colour was carried.

The hunting horn devices worn by the several types of jaeger were of white or yellow metal—silvered or gilded, as appropriate, for officers. Kaiserjaeger,

Men of a 'German' kuk Infantry regiment marching past The Emperor Franz Joseph during the celebrations to commemorate the centennial of the battle of Leipzig— Vienna 1913. In the Imperial Service the regimental Colour was carried by an NCO and escorted by a Subaltern Officer. Note

Landesschuetzen and the Tirolean Mounted Rifles carried a white Tirolean eagle within the wind of the horn in their caps. The Dalmatian Mounted Rifles showed the Imperial eagle inside theirs. Feldjaeger battalions and Landwehr infantry regiments wore a yellow metal hunting horn cap badge and set within the wind of that instrument was a white metal numeral which identified the unit.

Care must be taken not to confuse these official cap badges with the semi-official or completely unofficial badges which were produced in vast numbers and in a variety of patterns. Among emblems of those types are the battalion, regimental, divisional and even army badges in soft metal worn on the left side of the cap, or by officers of cavalry regiments on the front of their grey field service caps. When, soon after the outbreak of war in 1914, the blue tunics and their coloured facings were withdrawn from the cavalry regiments, the need for the officers of those regiments to distinguish themselves from the rest of the army was solved by the production and purchase of regimental devices in enamelled silver. Some of those beautifully produced badges are illustrated in this book.

Proficiency and specialist Badges for Other Ranks

These were usually circular or oval in shape, made of metal, and were worn on the right breast. Among the many types there were ones for estimating distance (infantry), riding (cavalry), driving carts (artillery), gun laying (artillery), telegraphy and first aid (all arms) as well as badges for machine gunners and pioneers.

One type of non-metal proficiency distinction was that which was awarded to marksmen. This consisted of an aigulette which fitted to a button inside the tunic, passed across the chest and fastened to the left shoulder strap. From the free end of this aigulette five short cords descended and to each of these was fitted a small woollen ball. For marksmen of line infantry units the aigulette and balls were in scarlet. For Jaeger and Landwehr units they were in green. There was also a first class, or sniper's award and in this the aigulette was in gold.

The cavalry equivalent of this award was an oval badge. The senior gun numbers in the artillery arm of service wore scarlet balls of the same pattern as the infantry but in a larger size. Gun commanders wore a golden cord with a pair of acorns and a signal whistle.

Cuff insignia identified the grade or status of the wearer. The most important of those sleeve insignia was the stripe of yellow silk with a central thin black thread which was worn on each cuff by the one-year volunteers. Such men in Landwehr (Honved) regiments and battalions carried a cuff band with a red thread. Pupils of the senior Honved school also carried a similarly patterned stripe. Members of the senior classes of the Maria Theresia and of the Ludovika military academies wore plain gold cuff bands. One-year volunteers in the pharmacist and in the veterinary surgeon branches also carried, in addition to the cuff band, bands of corporal pattern lace. Cuff bands of the same pattern lace were worn on each arm by armourers, blacksmiths and saddlers.

NCOs who voluntarily increased their length of service wore on the left cuff an inverted chevron of gold lace, 1.3cm wide. Thinner chevrons in gold, 6cm wide, were awarded for 3, 6 and 9 years' service respectively and were carried above the long-service chevron awarded initially.

that at the top of the flag staff, and in the caps of the marching soldiers, sprigs of fir are carried. These were one of the two distinctive devices carried by the Habsburg armies. In winter the decoration was fir twigs. In summer it was a cluster of oak leaves.

Officers' servants and grooms wore on the right cuff an inverted red cloth chevron which was 1cm wide.

In addition to the general issue of collar badges to machine gunners, to telegraphists and musicians, there was also the edelweiss device issued to certain mountain troop units. Other mountain units, known as Standschuetzen, carried on the collar the eagle of Tirol or the arms of Vorarlberg.

Brassards

Brassards, or armbands, were worn widely in the Austrian service usually on the upper left arm, except in the case of military police and headquarters troops, where they were worn on the right arm. Among the many which were worn by every branch of the army the ones relevant to this work are:

Landsturm units which had not been equipped with uniform: road-building or pioneer detachments all carried a yellow armband with a central black stripe. Tirolean troops of the Standschuetzen groups wore a green and white armband, while Hungarian Landsturm wore a brassard in the national colours of red, white and green. Landsturm armbands usually carried a regimental number preceded by the battalion number. For independent battalions the preceding number was that of the company to which the wearer belonged.

A red cross armband identified stretcher bearers, doctors and delegates from the Red Cross organisation. Certain voluntary medical organisations served with the Austro-Hungarian Army and the two most important of those—the Orders of the Teutonic Knights and of the Knights of Malta wore armbands with their own device as well as the standard red cross armband. For the Teutonic Knights this brassard was of white with a black cross superimposed, while the Maltese Order band was red with a white Maltese cross.

Civilians attached to or who supplied the army—for example market stall-holders, canteen owners, cart drivers and the like, were issued with the same type of armband as HQ personnel or military policemen. This was yellow in colour with a central black stripe taking up one-third of the width of the band. Civil commissariat members wore a white armband with a golden Imperial cypher. War reporters had a plain white armband, while veterinary officers wore a plain white armband decorated with a brown star.

A dark blue brassard was worn by mountain guides and on that brassard were carried the initials B F (Bergfuehrer: mountain guide) with an ice pick between the letters.

Coloured bands were worn on the cap during manoeuvres: white for umpires and a red band for the enemy forces.

Rank distinctions

In the Austrian service, rank was indicated by stars and/or bands of lace carried on the tunic, the attila, the ulanka and the blouse as well as on the parade headdress but not on the undress cap.

Field marshals wore on the collar stylised acanthus leaf designs in gold bullion set upon a band of lace 5cm wide. The same leaf design was worn on the cuffs. Tunic buttons were of General Officer pattern.

General Officers carried on the tunic a band of gold bullion lace and the

Carl, Prince Liechtenstein, wearing the full dress Hungarian uniform of a General.

stars of their rank embroidered in silver bullion. On each cuff there was a 5cm wide band of gold lace. A band 8cm wide decorated the cocked hat and one, 6.6cm wide, was carried on the shako.

Rank insignia on the collar indicated:

> Three stars . . General
> Two stars . . . . Lieutenant General
> One star . . . . Major General

Staff or field officers wore on their tunics lace which was either gold or silver in colour, depending upon the regimental button colour. The stars indicating rank were either in gold or silver—the colour opposite to that of the tunic buttons. The lace on both collar and cuffs was 3.3cm wide and the stars indicated:

> Three stars . . Colonel
> Two stars . . . . Lieutenant Colonel
> One star . . . . Major

Subaltern officers had no lace on the collar or cuffs but only stars. These were in gold or silver, corresponding to the regimental button colour:

> Three stars . . . Captain
> Two stars . . . . Lieutenant
> One star . . . . Second Lieutenant

Ensigns wore on the tunic collar a strip of gold lace and a silver plated star. Other cadets had a strip of gold lace and white celluloid stars.

Senior NCOs wore silver lace on their tunic collar together with silver stars. Sergeants had a strip of yellow silk lace and three white celluloid stars. Corporals wore two white celluloid stars and lance corporals one white star of white celluloid.

One of a series of military uniform drawings dating from the period 1869-72. At that time the army wore jack boots, but these were phased out during the 1880s. This Infantry private soldier is wearing the blue blouse, the old pattern equipment and the calf-skin pack.

INFANTRY · COMMON ARMY
1 · Line Infantry uniforms

Tunic

The colour and design for all ranks was the same, but officers' tunics were made of a finer cloth. The tunic was dark blue in colour, single breasted and fastened by six buttons of correct colour—either white or yellow metal—and embossed with the regimental number.

Tunic collar and cuffs for all ranks were of regimental facing colour and, in addition, Other Ranks had shoulder straps and shoulder rolls of that colour. Officers' tunics had neither shoulder straps nor rolls but were piped in regimental colour along the lower edges of the skirt, down the front of the tunic and around the pockets in the rear of the skirt.

There were two buttons set at waist level on the rear of the tunic for Other Ranks. Two shaped flaps on the rear skirt of officers' tunics were fitted with three buttons.

The cuffs on the tunics of German regiments were of the simple turn-back type, but those for Hungarian regiments formed an inverted chevron. In addition, Hungarian cuffs carried a 'bear's paw' decoration of cloth for the rank and file, and of gold or silver bullion lace for officers. The colour of the lace agreed with that of the regimental button colour. There was a small button located at the back of each sleeve, just above the cuff.

The stars and lace indicating rank were shown on the stand-up collar of the tunic collar for all ranks up to that of major. Officers above that rank also showed their status by wearing bands of lace on each cuff as well as on the collar.

The tunic was not only full dress, parade dress and 'walking out' dress, but also the army's service dress. The grey uniform which was introduced in 1909 then became service dress, leaving the blue tunic for ceremonial occasions or for 'walking out'. A black cloth, edged with white and known as a stock, was worn round the neck behind the stand-up collar.

Overcoat

All overcoats were made of a blue/grey cloth. For officers this was in a finer grade of material than that for Other Ranks.

The garment was double-breasted and fastened by one of two rows of five buttons (six buttons for officers.) Two pockets were fitted diagonally on the front skirts and were flapped. From a point just under the shoulder blades of Other Ranks' tunics, the back of the coat was full cut so that it formed two pleats. To hold these in place the garment was half-belted and the rear skirt of the coat was slit to a height of 15cm.

Other Ranks wore shoulder straps; officers did not. All ranks carried a paroli on the overcoat lapels. That for the officers was topped by a small button. Officers also had their coats piped in regimental colour. On the rear skirts of their coats were two pockets, each covered by a 2.5cm wide flap. The collar was of dark blue velvet and on the left side of the garment was a slit through which the sword hilt projected.

Trousers

In the Common Army there were two patterns: slacks which were worn by German infantry regiments, and tight-fitting trousers worn by the Other Ranks of Hungarian regiments. Officers and cadet officers of both German and Hungarian regiments wore slacks.

The colour for both patterns of leg covering was light blue and the trousers were fitted with pockets, set diagonally and flapped. These were placed on the front of the garment.

Other Ranks in Hungarian regiments wore trousers fitting close to the leg and which ended at the foot in a strap which passed under the sole of the foot. The trousers were then worn inside the lace-up boots. Hungarian pattern trousers were decorated with inverted 'Austrian' knots made from yellow and black cord. The same pattern cord was piped down the outside of each leg.

Officers and certain senior NCOs were allowed to wear slacks of a dark blue/grey cloth. These were known as salonhosen and were worn only as undress. Salonhosen were piped down the outside of the leg in red or green (for Jaeger units). Summer pattern trousers were in twill or duck.

Headdress

The full dress shako was an eliptically shaped cap in stiff black felt fitted with a visor, top and chin strap of black patent leather. The inside of the visor was in natural brown leather. On the upper surface of the visor of officer pattern shakoes there was a border of gold lace running round the outside edge. The width of that border was 1.3cm.

The cap badge displayed the Imperial eagle in gilded metal for officers and in yellow metal for Other Ranks. Set above the eagle and projecting above the crown of the shako was a rose of woven golden wire for officers, or of brass for Other Ranks, as described above.

The full dress shako carried bands of lace to indicate rank.

Lance Corporals
A circular cord in yellow wool flecked with black.

Corporals, battalion buglers or battalion drummers
A 4cm wide band of woollen material, patterned in zig-zags and with a black line on the outside edges.

Sergeants and regimental drummers
A 4.6cm wide band of woollen material divided by a central, thin, black stripe. Officer cadets wore the same pattern lace but the material was of Imperial yellow silk.

Pioneer of an Infantry regiment in field service marching order. Note the water bottle that he carries and the shoulder roll on his right epaulette.

Lieutenants

A 4cm wide band of bullion lace.

Captains

A 4.6cm band of bullion lace.

Field Officers

A 6.6cm wide band of bullion lace divided into three sections by two lines of black material.

Undress Shako

This article of dress was worn by officers. It consisted of a body of dark blue or black felt fitted with a visor and a chin strap of black patent leather. The crown of the undress shako was lower than that of dress or parade cap, and the cap was much simpler in appearance.

The visor carried the lace border 1.3cm wide but there was no Imperial eagle badge, and the rosette was smaller in design and set lower—flush with the crown. The chin-strap buckle fitted in the centre of the body of the shako and immediately above it was placed a small gold button. Between that button and the rosette on the crown of the cap was fitted a double length of black-flecked gold cord. Around the bottom of the undress shako was fitted a gold cord, 3mm in diameter.

Other Ranks Undress Head-covering

Until the introduction of the pike grey uniform in 1909 the cap worn by infantry units on non-ceremonial occasions was the blue field cap of the type which will be described in the field service dress section of this chapter.

Below

Left

Werner Auer, Sergeant in the kuk Infantry Regiment No 47, wearing the 1909 pattern pike grey field service dress. The breast cords indicate a marksman's aiguilette. The unusual pattern cap was winter issue.

Right

The full dress shako of a Field officer of a kuk Infantry regiment. Front view showing the cap plate and the bullion rose with the Imperial cypher.

(Scherer collection).

INFANTRY · COMMON ARMY
2 · Jaeger Units

Officers of Jaeger and Landwehr units wore a pike grey tunic with grass green collar, cuffs and pipings. The tunic was single-breasted and was fastened by six plain yellow metal or gilded buttons.

Feldjaeger officers carried the battalion number on their tunic buttons in the same way as the rank and file.

Landesschuetzen

The uniform originally designed for the Landesschuetzen rank and file was a blouse, dark brown in colour with green collar patches. Officers had grass green facings. The garment was fastened by six buttons of yellow metal.

The trousers to this uniform were dark grey and those for officers carried the standard green stripes, of Jaeger units.

In 1889 the officer uniform pattern was changed to that worn by rifle regiments of the Austrian Landwehr but not until 1894 did the Other Ranks receive tunics in place of the blouse.

Identification of Landesschuetzen units was through the regimental number in roman numerals which was worn on the shoulder straps of the tunic by both officers and men. Landesschuetzen officer uniforms were unusual in that they were fitted with shoulder straps.

Trousers

Trousers for Jaeger units were in pike grey for Kaiserjaeger, Feldjaeger and Landesschuetzen, while the Austrian Landwehr wore dark blue/grey trousers.

Officers of both the Jaeger and the Landwehr carried two wide green stripes down the outside leg.

Headdress

A plumed cap was worn by all Jaeger, Landwehr and Landesschuetzen units. The shape of the cap was that of a curly-brimmed bowler hat and the material was of stiffened felt. Patent leather edged the brim, and the chin strap was of patent leather.

A decorative cord was carried round the base of the crown and fastened at the back of the cap. For officers this cord was of gold, and for rank and file in green cord. On the left side of the cap was carried a distinctive plume of dark-green cock feathers which fitted into a metal holder. That holder was fitted behind the horn cap badge which was the distinctive device of all Jaeger and Landwehr units.

Overcoats
Pike Grey. Officers' coats were piped in green.

Below
Tunic of a Lieutenant in 3rd Landesschuetzen Regiment. The edelweiss badge on the collar indicates that the role of the Landesschuetzen was an alpine one. (Scherer collection).

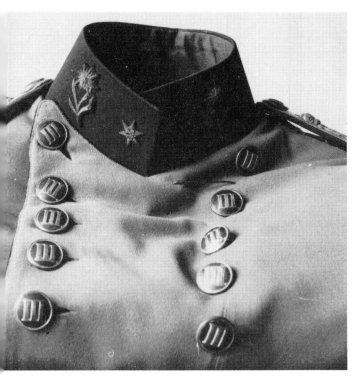

Soldier of a Jaeger unit. The patches on his grey uniform would have been in green.

Rifleman's cap of an Officer in 1st Feld-jaeger Battalion.
(Scherer collection).

|||||||||||||||||||||||||||||||||||||||||||||||||||||||||||||||||||||||||||||||||||||||||||||

INFANTRY · COMMON ARMY
3·Bosnia-Herzegovinian Regiments

|||||||||||||||||||||||||||||||||||||||||||||||||||||||||||||||||||||||||||||||||||||||||||||

Full dress for non-Muslim officers of Bosnian regiments was the shako of Common Army pattern. Muslim officers and the rank and file wore a madder red fez with an 18.5cm long black woollen tassel fastened to a cloth rosette on the top of the crown. The fez was both parade and field service headdress and after 1909 the colour for the field service headdress changed from madder red to pike grey.

The tunic and blouse was of Common Army pattern for German regiments. The facing colour for all four Bosnian regiments was alizarin red; the button colour was yellow metal and the regimental number was embossed.

The trousers of the Other Ranks were cut very full to the knee, but below this and extending down to the ankle they fitted tight to the calf. To hold them in place on the calf two yellow metal buttons were shown on the outside of each leg and just below the knee level, these supplementing the five hooks and eyes which were fitted. A 3.5cm wide linen strap was fitted at the bottom of both trouser legs so that they were held inside the boot.

Bosnian Jaeger
Standard Jaeger uniform but with a red fez.

|||||||||||||||||||||||||||||||||||||||||||||||||||||||||||||||||||||||||||||||||||||||||||||||||||||||||||||||||||||||||||||||||||||||||||||||||||||||

INFANTRY · LANDWEHR
Austrian Landwehr

|||||||||||||||||||||||||||||||||||||||||||||||||||||||||||||||||||||||||||||||||||||||||||||||||||||||||||||||||||||||||||||||||||||||||||||||||||||||||

Neither the Austrian Landwehr nor the Hungarian Landwehr (Honved) was tied to tradition in the matters of facing colours so that their respective High Commands were able to restrict those colours to three: two for the Austrian Landwehr, and one for the Honved.

Shortly after the Landwehr was raised, the officers of the Landwehr Jaeger battalions wore standard Jaeger uniform: a rifleman's cap, pike grey tunic fastened by white metal buttons, grass green facings and blue/grey trousers. Other Ranks wore a blue/grey field cap and a pike grey blouse fastened by white metal buttons. Collar patches and shoulder straps were of grass green facing cloth. Other Ranks trousers were blue/grey.

The Landwehr infantry battalions of that period wore the same type of uniform as that of the Common Army infantry. Officers had a shako, dark blue tunic with white buttons, blue/grey trousers with red piping. Other Ranks had the same field cap as that worn in the rifle battalions. The dark blue blouse was fastened by white metal buttons embossed with the battalion number. The tunic had patches of scarlet—the facing colour of Landwehr infantry—and the battalion number in white cloth was worn on the shoulder strap. Trousers were of blue/grey cloth piped in red.

There were two battalions, Nos 79 and 80, which deviated from standard pattern. Those units were from Dalmatia and were classified as Rifles. The officers wore the rifle cap, a dark blue tunic with white metal buttons and with scarlet facings. Other Ranks did not wear the Jaeger cap but a scarlet field cap. Their uniform was a dark blue blouse, waistcoat, and trousers with red pipings. The two Dalmatian battalions conformed to standard pattern during 1883.

In 1892 the differences between infantry and rifle battalions of the Landwehr were abolished and all battalions wore the same uniform type. This was, for officers, the rifleman's cap with a pike grey tunic fastened by white metal buttons; trousers were dark blue/grey in colour. Other Ranks wore a blue/grey field cap but were issued with a pike grey blouse fastened by white metal buttons. There was now only one facing colour: grass green.

Two years later, in 1894, all ranks were issued with the rifle cap, a pike grey tunic and blue/grey trousers.

||||||||||||||||||||||||||||||||||||||||||||||||||||||||||||||||||||||||||||||||||||||||||||||||||||||

INFANTRY · LANDWEHR (HONVED)
Landwehr (Honved)

||||||||||||||||||||||||||||||||||||||||||||||||||||||||||||||||||||||||||||||||||||||||||||||||||||||

Until the year 1885 the infantry of the Landwehr (Honved) had worn a short, blue, unpiped blouse with red trousers of Hungarian pattern. Honved officers had worn a tunic with sleeves embroidered with 'Austrian' knots in gold cord. They had also worn round the waist not the traditional sash of Habsburg officers, but a barrelled sash of ancient-Magyar pattern.

In 1885 a new uniform was introduced and all ranks wore a Hussar type attila in dark blue cloth with breast cords, sleeve knots, pipings and, where appropriate, shoulder straps. The breast cords for Other Ranks were in red; for officers gold flecked with red. The attila was fastened by olivets of regimental pattern: white or yellow metal.

The trousers worn by officers were of standard pattern and carried red piping down the outside leg. Other Ranks had the standard Hungarian type of close-fitting trousers with red cording and thigh knots.

Overcoats were of standard pattern and carried a paroli in red. Officers' greatcoats were also piped in that colour. Buttons were of yellow metal—gilded for officers—and showed the regimental number.

The full dress shako for Honved infantry was the standard blue cloth headdress fitted with a gilded rose. The central field of that device showed the Imperial cypher and the crown of St Stephan. The gilded cap plate displayed a shield with the coat of arms of Hungary and the motto, 'For King and Fatherland' in either Magyar or Serbo-Croat. For Other Ranks the shako had yellow metal fittings.

The field cap was red in colour and had the regimental number in red cloth on the right side of the cap.

A final pattern of full dress was introduced. This was of dark cloth, double-breasted and fitted with two rows of eight gilded or yellow metal buttons. The five rows of breast cording were removed but the top and bottom of the collar, as well as the cuffs, were piped in red. Piping of the same colour was on the shoulder straps for Other Ranks, and officers had the front edge, skirts and rear pockets piped.

There was also a dark blue blouse on issue for all ranks. This garment was fastened by gilded or yellow metal buttons bearing the regimental number. The collar and cuffs were piped: in red for Other Ranks, and in red flecked with gold for officers.

Officers retained the barrelled sash, and Other Ranks wore a black leather waist belt, the buckle of which carried the Hungarian coat of arms.

CAVALRY · COMMON ARMY

Cavalry uniforms
1· Dragoon Regiments of the Common Army

Tunic

The tunic was a garment of light blue cloth, single-breasted in design and fastened by six buttons of regimental colour. The stand-up collar and cuffs were in regimental facing cloth. The tunic had no external pockets but there was a concealed one in the left rear skirt. Two buttons of regimental pattern were set at waist level, just above the rear skirt.

In common with other mounted units, the dragoon tunic carried no shoulder straps or epaulettes, but there was on the left shoulder a strap made of double thickness attila cord which fastened to a small button set an inch from the collar. There were two other small buttons on the tunic: one each at the back of the sleeve just above the coloured cuff.

Officers' tunics were made from a fine cloth and were piped in regimental facing colour. Their shoulder cords were of black-flecked yellow silk. For ensigns the strap was of yellow silk.

Lambskin-lined Winter Tunic

This garment, of tunic cloth, was so cut that it could be worn over the standard tunic without discomfort. It needed to be generously cut because it was lined in the body and in the skirts with lambskin; white for Other Ranks and black for officers.

The double-breasted, winter tunic was fitted with two rows of eight buttons. The front skirts were rounded and lined with cloth along the free edges. In the back skirts there were inset pockets fastened by a button. Another button was fitted at the waist seam where it joined the back skirts. The two tailed flaps in the rear skirts were fastened by three large tunic buttons. Officers' tunics were piped along the free edges up to the waist button level and on the pocket flaps. Each of the front skirts had an inset pocket set diagonally and covered with a two-tail flap.

Inside the cuffs, which were of regimental facing cloth, there was a lining of black lambskin. Badges and distinctions on the cuff were the same as those worn on the standard tunic. The button on the tunic cuffs was also to be found on the winter tunic, as was the button set on the left shoulder and to which a cord was fitted. These cords were of yellow wool (for Other Ranks), yellow silk (for ensigns) or bullion (for officers). All three types of cord were overlaid with black flecking.

The turn-down collar on the winter jacket was faced with lambskin and was fitted with a clasp and a black cord. On the inner side of the collar

Officer pattern shako of the Landwehr (Honved). Front view. The shako plate shows the arms of Hungary and above them the crown of St Stephan. The royal cypher in the centre of the rose does not read FJI but IFJ, this being the Hungarian style. (Scherer collection).

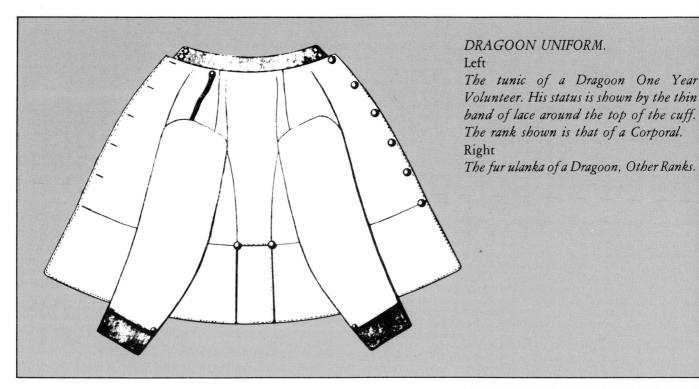

there was a throat cord of light blue wool for Other Ranks, yellow silk for ensigns and gold cord for officers. One end of the cord had an olivet; the other had two slings.

A second throat cord was fitted with an olivet and sling on the right-hand cord and with a loop and three slings on the left. Officers' cords were of sufficient length that when the coat was fastened the cord could be wound round the outside of the collar and fastened by loop and olivet at the front of the throat. Cords on Other Ranks' winter tunics were carried inside the coat.

The lambskin-lined jacket could be worn as a surcoat or could be draped from the left shoulder. When carried draped, the throat cord was fastened in such a way that the edge of the fur collar was held on the wearer's shoulder.

Overcoat

The long-skirted overcoat worn by dragoons was cut on the lines of that worn by the infantry but was coloured dark brown. There was a sword slit on the left side of the overcoat at waist level.

Trousers

All ranks wore breeches of madder red cloth. For Other Ranks these were cut full above the knee so that they fell in folds over the top of the high boots. The trouser legs below the knee tapered strongly to hold the breeches in place. For ease in dressing or undressing each lower leg had a 20.3cm slit which was fastened by zinc buttons. The trousers had two thigh pockets, set diagonally.

A spare pair of breeches worn for riding practice in barracks was reinforced by a double seat of madder red cloth.

Officer patten trousers were cut to a proper breeches shape and were made of a fine madder red cloth.

Above
Left: *Other Ranks pattern helmet.*
Right: *Side view of same.*

Right: *Officer pattern helmet.*

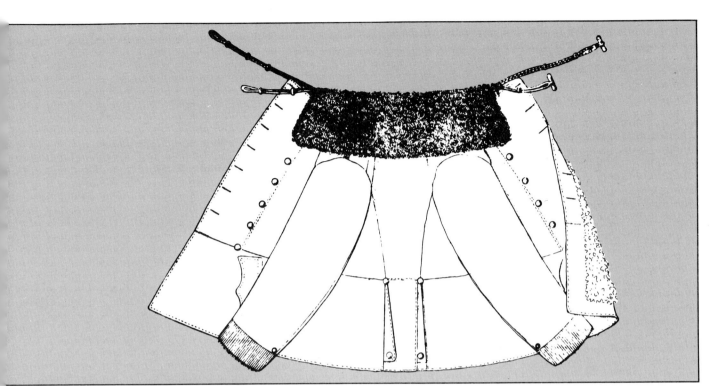

Boots

Butcher boots were worn with the madder red breeches. These boots were of black leather and rose high in the leg to just below the knee. To the heels of the boots spurs were fitted. These were in highly polished mild steel whose shaft carried a 15 point rowel. The spur arms fitted round the heel of the boot and were pierced to carry the screws which kept the spurs in position.

Helmet

The most distinctive feature of the dragoon uniform was the high-crowned helmet. This changed little in design between 1850, when it was first introduced, and 1905 when the last pattern was issued.

The Other Ranks' helmet was a semi-spherical leather skull piece to which was fitted a visor, a neck guard and a comb. All these were of tin plate. The external surfaces of the helmet were black lacquered. The underside of the visor was coloured green and that of the neck guard was painted black.

The visor and neck guard sloped downwards and their free edges were covered with tambac. The helmet comb was made of two tin plate shapes which were held one inch apart by a wooden inlay. The metal rims of the comb were tambac edged. The whole length of the comb crest from the neck guard to bottom of the cone was brass. The helmet cone was concave. The comb crest was fastened to the upper part of the leather skull and to the neck guard by seven domed brass rivets.

On either side of the leather skull was fitted a brass rosette (for officers this rosette was further embossed with a lion's head). This served a double purpose. Around it were fitted a pair of brass splints rising from the rosette to join together at a point just below the comb.

The other function of the rosettes was to secure the ends of the chin strap. For Other Ranks the outer side of that strap was made up of brass scales, alternately two or three pointed. Officers' chin straps carried a design of matt laurel leaves and highly polished laurel berries. The strap was in two halves, one end fastening on the left side of the helmet and the other on the right. These two halves were joined either by buckle and tongue or by a tambac slip.

The helmet could be worn with the strap either underneath the chin or resting on the visor. The strap was lined with soft leather for those occasions when it was worn under the chin.

The chief difference between the headdress worn by officers and those by Other Ranks was that the comb of the officer pattern helmet showed, on the gilded metal side panels, a relief of a lion fighting a snake. Decorating the inside of the concave cones there were a number of designs in relief, including crossed flags, the crown and the Imperial cypher. The helmet worn by sergeants and ensigns carried three narrow, tambac lines on the side panels of the comb.

The helmet plate for all ranks was the Imperial eagle fitted on the front of the headdress in such a way that the crown on the head of the bird touched the base of the cone and the bird's tail feathers rested on the top of the visor. The fittings of officers' helmets were of gilded metal; those of Other Ranks in brass.

Equipment

The brown leather waist belt fastened by a two-pronged buckle: dragoons who were issued with a carbine fitted their belt in such a way that the buckle rested on the left hip so that the two ammunition pouches could be positioned directly in front of the body. Where a pistol was also carried a supporting strap held the hand gun close to the body.

In addition to the pouch for carbine ammunition there was another for pistol cartridges. Both were of leather and both fitted onto the waist belt by means of a loop at the back of the pouch. The pistol ammunition pouch had inside it little leather containers for the cartridges.

The cartridge belt and case which was worn by officers was more than just a container for ammunition. It was the distinctive emblem of an officer in the mounted arm. The red morocco leather box was 15.2cm long, 5.1cm wide and 8.9cm deep. All external surfaces were covered with elaborately chased silver plate. On the lid was the Imperial cypher and the side pieces were decorated with trophies of war. The box held eighteen rounds of ammunition.

The belt which carried the box was made of 3.8cm wide red moroccan leather, highly decorated with bullion lace. The belt passed over the left shoulder, underneath the shoulder cord and was fastened on the right hip. The box rested in the small of the back. The two ends of the cartridge-case strap were a buckle and a strap of silver-plated metal.

HUSSAR UNIFORM

The front and back view of a Hussar attila. The broad band of lace around both cuffs indicates a trade distinction. In this case the wearer is an NCO armourer. The inverted chevrons show length of service.

||||||||||||||||||||||||||||||||||||||||||||||||||||||||||||||||||||||||||||||||||

CAVALRY · COMMON ARMY

2 · Hussar Regiments of the Common Army

||||||||||||||||||||||||||||||||||||||||||||||||||||||||||||||||||||||||||||||||||

Tunic or Attila

The tunic worn by hussars was known as an attila and was issued in two types: standard and winter.

Standard Attila

This was made of tunic cloth in a regimental colour—either dark or light blue—and was decorated with breast cords which terminated in a trefoil. A rosette was fitted onto the cord just before the trefoil. The uppermost of the five breast cords extended from shoulder seam to shoulder seam and passed just below the join of the collar. The second cord was at about armpit level and ran the entire width of the chest. The remaining cords were set at intervals and diminished in length as they followed the line of the chest down to the waist.

The front skirts, each of which was lined in blue calico for Other Ranks, were rounded and each was fitted with a diagonally placed pocket. The piping which decorated these was continued along the seams in the rear skirts and up the seams at the back of the attila towards the shoulders. The same piping extended downwards to form an inverted 'Austrian' knot on each side of the central seam of the rear skirt.

For Other Ranks the split cuffs, fastened by two hooks and eyes, were piped with a cord which passed round to the front of the cuff to form an 'Austrian' knot. Hooks and eyes fastened the front of the attila and the stand-up collar, which was piped at the top and at the bottom. A shoulder strap of double cord was worn on the left shoulder and held in place by a small button. Olivets, which were used as additional fastenings to the attila, were smooth and of regimental colour.

Attila cords for Other Ranks were 6mm thick and made of yellow wool flecked with black. Officers' cords, 9mm thick, were of gold, flecked with black silk. Ensigns had cords of black and yellow silk. Rosettes of appropriate material were shaped to form a black field with alternate black and yellow (gold) circles.

On officers' attilas the skirts were lined with scarlet cloth, olivets were shaped to resemble twisted cord, and the shoulder strap fastened by a rosette and not a button. Cuff decoration for subaltern officers was an 'Austrian' knot. For field officers, cuff decoration was an elaborately decorated triangle of lace, coloured according to the regimental colour of the olivets.

Winter-issue Attila

This was made of tunic cloth of regimental colour and was decorated with the cords and rosettes identical to those carried on the standard attila. The winter garment was lined with lambswool: white for Other Ranks and black for officers. Black lambskin also trimmed the front edges and skirts of the attilas worn by all ranks.

For Other Ranks, at the front centre of the cuffs there was an insert of lambskin trimming shaped to form a rectangle rounded at the top. The black lambskin collar was cloth-backed and fitted with a throat cord and clasp of the pattern already described for Other Ranks in dragoon regiments.

All long service and other decorations worn on the standard attila were to be found on the winter issue garment and were placed in such a way that they lay under a clover leaf design piped on the winter attila cuffs. The fur rectangle on the cuff was thereby not hidden. Officer pattern winter attilas were trimmed with and lined with black lambskin. The gold throat cords, flecked with black silk, were sewn onto the underlay of the collar and were long enough to fasten at the throat after having passed round the outside of the collar.

The cuff decoration for subaltern officers was like that on the standard attila, an 'Austrian' knot. For field officers the decoration was in the shape of an elaborately decorated, pointed triangle, in lace of the same colour as that of the olivets.

Trousers

These were of madder red cloth and were close-fitting. Piping ran down the outside seam of each leg and on each thigh there was piping in the shape of an inverted 'Austrian' knot. The piping was of yellow and black cord.

There were two diagonally-placed pockets set below the trouser band on the front of the trousers. The bottom of each trouser leg was slit on the

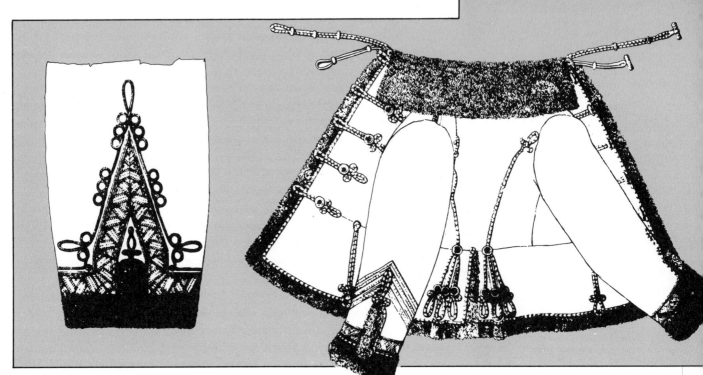

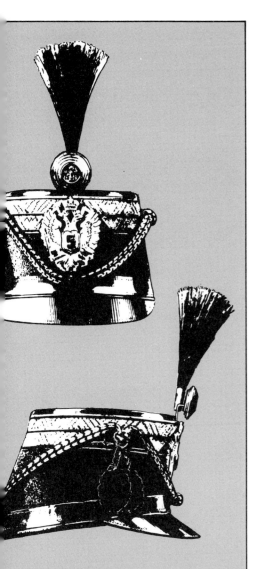

outside and was fitted with a cloth foot strap.

Clothing regulations stated that trousers worn on normal duties, *ie* not for parade purposes, could be double-faced on those surfaces which came in contact with the saddle.

Boots

The hussar 'shismen' were cut lower at the calf than on the shin. The front of the boot was scalloped and decorated with a band of material. Below the scallop was set an oval boss, in black and yellow, 2.5cm in diameter.

With these hessian pattern 'shismen' straight-shafted button spurs were worn.

Headdress

Parade Shako

The felt body was reinforced by a steel spring and was covered round the welt with cloth of regimental colour. The crown of the shako, a narrow band which ran round its base, together with peak, were all of black patent leather. The patent leather chin strap was fastened inside the shako by stirrup buckles. The left strap was fitted with a fastening buckle.

At the front centre of the shako body was a plume and a tambac rosette which showed the Imperial cypher and crown. Behind that rosette was a receiver into which fitted a black horse-hair plume 12cm in height. The tambac cap plate showed the Imperial eagle whose breast was pierced with the regimental number in arabic figures. A black patent leather underlay fitted behind the shako plate emphasised the number.

The shako was decorated with vitez koetes, or cap decorations. These were a 7mm square cord, 34cm long and coloured black and yellow. The cords were laid side by side and fitted round the shako, being supported by hooks set in the crown of the headdress. Both cords terminated in a rectangular woven tassel, 4cm in diameter and fitted in such a way that they lined up with the base of the shako.

The rosette, plume and cap cords (vitez koetes) were removed in wet weather or on active service and were then secured inside the shako. A foul-weather covering of american cloth in regimental colour was then worn over the parade shako.

Headdress worn by officers of hussar regiments differed from that worn by Other Ranks in that the inside of the peak was lined with green leather and the peak rim with patent leather. The cap plate, rose and chinstrap buckle were all of gilded metal. Cap cords were of gold flecked with black. The bullion decoration at the end of each cord (vitez koetes) was fitted with an extension 4.6cm in length and shaped like an acorn. The upper decoration showed the Imperial eagle and the lower one the Imperial cypher.

Hussar regiments of the Austrian service had, traditionally, worn a shako as headdress, although there was a three-year period, between 1864 and 1867, when a different type of hat was worn. This was the kusma, a low fur cap fitted with a busby bag and the standard vitez koetes cords. An eagle feather was a further decoration.

The felt-bodied shako, which was re-introduced during 1868 and which remained on issue until 1918, was a cut-down version of the 1850 pattern headdress.

CAVALRY · COMMON ARMY

3 · Ulan Regiments of the Common Army

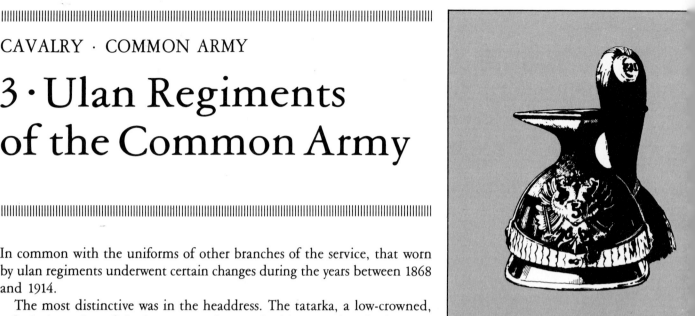

In common with the uniforms of other branches of the service, that worn by ulan regiments underwent certain changes during the years between 1868 and 1914.

The most distinctive was in the headdress. The tatarka, a low-crowned, soft-cloth version of the lancer cap, decorated with an eagle's feather, was withdrawn and replaced by the more familiar high-crowned shakpa, with its distinctive square top.

Ulan regiments were also issued with a cold-weather overgarment to protect them in the bitter Polish winter. This cold-weather surcoat, cut along the lines of the standard tunic, was fur-lined and proved to be so practical a garment that it was issued to all cavalry regiments and was then adopted by other bodies, particularly officers of the General Staff.

ULAN UNIFORM
Above left:
Other Ranks pattern shapka.
Above right:
NCO pattern.
Right:
Officer pattern.
Left:
Other Ranks ulanka: This one displays a broad band of lace on both cuffs, indicating a Sergeant Armourer. The inverted narrow chevrons set above it indicate more than nine years' service.
Right:
The fur ulanka: Officer pattern. The gold bullion fringe between the buttons of the rear skirt was called a 'waterfall'.

Ulanka

This single-breasted cloth garment was lined with blue calico for Other Ranks and with madder red material for officers. It was fastened by ten large buttons of regimental pattern placed at equal distances from the throat to the waist seam.

The rear skirt was divided and each half was folded with three pleats. Each skirt was fitted with a two-tailed cloth flap set with three large buttons. The breast pockets were horizontal and the front skirt pockets were set obliquely. The pocket flaps were two-tailed.

The sleeves had a tailed cuff in regimental facing colour, above which was a small button of regimental pattern. The reinforced stand-up collar was in regimental facing colour and the free edge of the tunic, skirt and pockets flaps, the seams in the back of the tunic, and the seams at the back of the sleeves, were all piped in that colour. On the left shoulder was a strap of double cord fastened by a small button. Shoulder straps for ensigns were of silk.

Tunic buttons were semi-domed and made either of tambac or of nickel alloy. Between the waist buttons at the rear skirt of officers' tunics was fitted a gold lace border and a double row of bullion fringe.

Winter-pattern Ulanka

This was a double-breasted garment made of tunic cloth and lined in the body and skirts with white lambswool for Other Ranks or with black lambskin for officers. The upper edge of the front panels was scalloped so as to form three points and on each of the front panels was a row of seven large buttons

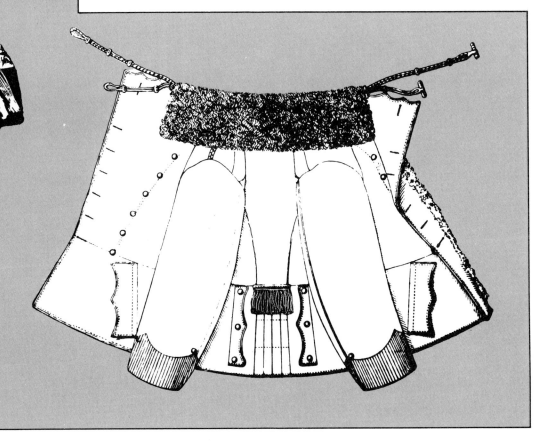

of regimental pattern. The distance between the two rows of buttons when the fur ulanka was fastened was 18cm at the top and 7cm at the bottom.

The front edges of the skirts were rounded and the two rear seams formed pleats on each of which was a pocket covered by a flap fastened by three large buttons. Between the pleats in the back skirt was a strip of lace from which hung three rows of twisted fringe in yellow wool for Other Ranks, in silk for ensigns and of bullion for officers. The two diagonally-set pockets at the front of the skirt were covered with a two-tailed flap of tunic cloth.

The turn-back cuff had tailed facings and a small button was set above the cuff, at the back of the sleeve. The inside of the cuff was lined with black lambskin. A small button fastened a strap of double thickness cord to the left shoulder. This cord was of yellow wool flecked with black for Other Ranks, of silk for ensigns and of gold cord for officers.

The fur ulanka was piped in the same fashion as the standard garment and the turn-down collar was faced with black lambskin. The throat cords were worn as described in the section on dragoon uniforms and the badges or lace on the winter ulanka were of the same pattern as those on the standard garment.

Shapka

The shapka was in two parts: a black-painted leather skull and an upper part of waterproofed felt reinforced with steel wire and shaped so as to form a narrow waisted section. Those upper parts were covered with cloth in regimental colour. Above the narrow waisted section there was a rectangle of board covered with black leather. A strip of the same material covered

the seam which joined the upper section of the shapka to the skull part.

The tambac shapka plate in the form of an Imperial eagle was fitted so that the tail feathers rested on the visor. A shield on the eagle's breast was pierced with the regimental number, emphasised by a backing of black patent leather. On either side of the shapka were tambac splints formed round a convex rosette and shaped to form a concave triangle.

When the chin strap was worn under the chin its two parts were fastened by a buckle and tongue, but more usually it rested on the visor where it was held together by a tambac clip. The outer face of the chin strap was decorated with metal scales alternately two or three tailed. The chin straps on officers' shapkas were similar in pattern to those described for dragoon officers.

The shapka carried a horse-hair plume in black for all ranks, except for trumpeters, who wore red plumes. To keep the plume in position a section of the front left edge of the rectangle was cut out and a brass container fitted, into which the plume was fastened. On the outer side of the plume support the Other Ranks had a tambac rosette bearing the Imperial cypher and, at the back of the support, a wire sling to hold the traditional greenery. A tambac chain, seventeen links long, secured the plume and the chain fastened to a spring clip on the left side of the shapka.

Rank insignia was shown by bands of lace in the fashion already described. Lance corporals' shapkas carried a cord which was fitted to the black leather strip round the skull. The shapkas of other NCOs were fitted with lace which covered the seam where the skull fitted to the upper section. They were also trimmed with cord along the length of the diagonals of the rectangle and along the seams which joined the cloth cover. For ensigns this cord was of silk and the visor of their helmet was bound with black patent leather. For Other Ranks the visor was bordered with tambac.

Officers' shapkas had a visor which was edged with patent leather and a band of gold lace. A matt gold cord with a central black line covered the seam where the visor joined the skull section. The cloth-covered rectangle on officer pattern shapkas was quartered by gold cord flecked with black. The rose which was set in the horse-hair plume was of gold bullion and the black velvet field was embroidered with the Imperial cypher in gold. To hold the plume in place there was a gilt chain and three lions' heads.

||||||||||||||||||||||||||||||||||||||||||||||||||||||||||||||||||||||||||||||||||||||||||||||||||||||

LANDWEHR ULAN REGIMENTS

The Landwehr Ulan regiments wore a similar uniform to that worn by the Ulan regiments of the Common Army. The crown of the shapka was madder red for all regiments and the white metal buttons bore the regimental number.

Far left
Full dress shapka of an Officer of the 5th Ulan Regiment. Front view, showing the cap plate, the chain to retain the horse-hair plume and the rose.
(Scherer collection).

Left
Lancer cap (shapka) of an Other Rank in the 8th Ulan Regiment. Front view, showing the chin strap, helmet plate, horse-hair plume and brass rosette.
(Scherer collection).

|||||||||||||||||||||||||||||||||||||||||||||||||||||||||||||||||||||||||||||||||||||

CAVALRY · LANDWEHR

Tirolean and Dalmatian Mounted Rifles

|||||||||||||||||||||||||||||||||||||||||||||||||||||||||||||||||||||||||||||||||||||||||||||

The Tirolean and Dalmatian Mounted Rifles formed part of the jaeger establishment and wore uniforms of the same pattern as those regiments.

The cap was that issued to jaeger units, that is to say, a high-crowned felt body, shaped like a bowler hat and having a curved brim bound in patent leather. On the left side of the cap was a receiver for the 29cm long bunch of cock feathers. These were fitted in such a way that they formed a cascade falling towards the back of the cap. The badge which held the feathers in place showed a hunting horn in gilded metal for officers and of yellow metal for Other Ranks. Worn within the wind of the horn was the single-headed eagle for Tirolean units and the Imperial eagle for the Dalmatian squadrons.

On their undress shako, officers of the mounted rifles units carried a small golden horn. That device was fitted onto a pair of gold loops at the front of the shako. On the field service cap it was placed below the rosette.

The tunic was single-breasted, pike grey in colour and fastened by plain white metal buttons. The collar, cuffs and piping were grass green. A cold-weather fur jacket of the pattern issued to cavalry units was worn by the Tirolean but not the Dalmatian units. Throat cords on that garment were gold for officers and green for Other Ranks.

All ranks wore blue/grey slacks piped in grass green. Officers also wore riding breeches, boots and spurs as well as salonhosen which were piped in green.

Overcoats were of standard pattern, pike grey in colour. Those worn by officers had a velvet collar and were piped. The paroli was grass green.

CAVALRY · LANDWEHR (HONVED)
Landwehr (Honved) Hussar Regiments

This uniform was the standard hussar pattern uniform with a number of distinctive differences.

There was one standard colour for attilas and this was dark blue and one olivet colour—yellow. The attila cording was cherry red for Other Ranks and gold flecked with cherry for officers. In most respects the style and placing of the breast piping was the same as that for Common Army regiments except that for Landwehr units these were shorter in length and ended in short acorns and not in trefoils. On the fur-lined garment the cording was the same length for both Common Army and Landwehr (Honved) units.

The other piping on the attila was that of Common Army tunics but the 'Austrian' knots were simpler in design on Honved clothing.

Throat cords were cherry red for Other Ranks and gold worked with cherry for officers. The winter attila were lined and trimmed with white lambskin. Officers' coats were trimmed with white but were lined with black lambskin. The intention to standardise the lining to black for all ranks of Honved hussar

Shako of a Subaltern Officer in a Landwehr (Honved) Hussar regiment. Right side view. The picture shows clearly the elaborate cap cords and bullion knots which decorated the shako.
(Scherer collection).

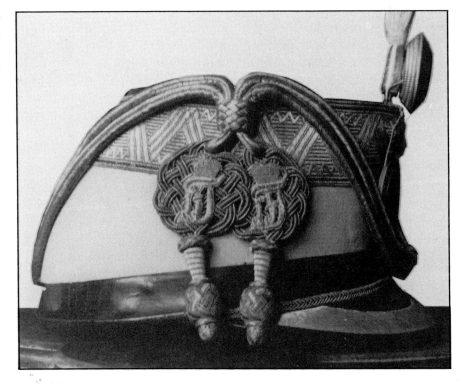

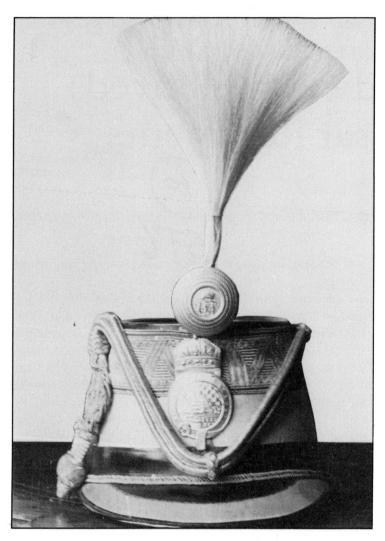

Officer pattern shako, Landwehr (Honved) Hussar regiment. Front view. The white plume, the shako plate and the royal cypher identify it as a Landwehr (Honved) unit.
(Scherer collection).

regiments was not realised, nor was the intention to change the colour of the Honved shako plume from white to black.

The shako had Honved pattern cording and the crown was coloured to identify regiments, in Common Army fashion. The cap plate did not show an eagle but, instead, the Hungarian crown and the royal cypher together with a shield displaying the arms of Hungary and the motto, either in Magyar or in Croat: 'For King and Country'.

Honved Landsturm Hussars

The uniform was similar in design to that of the Landwehr (Honved) regiments but the olivets were coloured white metal for all squadrons on the Landwehr establishment. Shakoes were not coloured regimentally but had a single colour—madder red.

Trousers, the attila and boots were of Common Army pattern.

Field Cap

Landwehr (Honved) hussars regiments displayed their regimental number in yellow metal on the field cap.

Landsturm units carried figures in white cloth on the right side of their field cap.

Sergeant of the Field Artillery. The shoulder crescents on his brown tunic could have been in red, the same colour as that shown on his collar patches.

Artillery uniforms

Parade Tunic

The design of this garment was that of the German infantry tunic, except that the artillery garment was in dark brown. There was one single facing colour for the whole artillery arm and that was scarlet.

Buttons fastening the tunic were of yellow metal and embossed with the brigade number in the case of field artillery units, or with the regimental/battalion number for fortress artillery formations.

Undress Blouse

This was of standard pattern but coloured brown and fitted with collar patches in scarlet. Other Ranks of the field artillery were not issued with a blouse.

Overcoat

This was of infantry pattern and fitted with scarlet parolis.

Special distinction

Senior NCOs of both the field and the fortress artillery carried on the outer garment a distinction made of five small balls in red wool, together with a set of cords.

Trousers

There were two different patterns on issue to artillery units. The field artillery pattern was similar to that worn by dragoons, being full cut in the leg and folding over the high boots.

The fortress artillery wore slacks of German infantry pattern but carried down the outside legs a crimson stripe 5.3cm wide. Officers carried a double stripe. The colour for both patterns of trousers was the same: light blue.

Footwear

The boots worn by field artillery units were of dragoon pattern, and the fortress artillery wore ordinary jack boots.

Headdress

Parade Shako

The parade shako was similar in design to that worn by the infantry with

Left

Right side view of a shako of an Officer of the Artillery. The lion's head device to hold the retaining chain is repeated on the left side of the headdress. The chain held in place the horse-hair plume positioned at the front of the shako.

(Scherer collection).

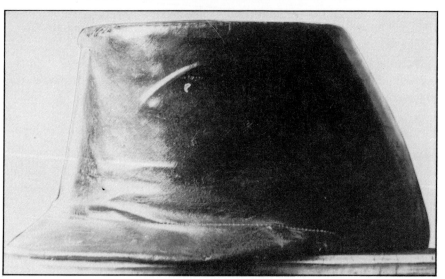

the addition of a plume of black horse-hair, a metal retaining chain and two lions' heads, fitted one on each side of the shako.

The 28cm long horse-hair plume was fastened at one end to the rose at the front of the shako. The free end of the plume then swept down the left side of the headdress and was held in position by a chain 37cm long. The two ends of the chain fastened to the lions' heads by hooks. A large oval ring in the centre of the chain held the horse-hair plume in position at the front of the shako.

The 'fall' of the plume would have covered much of the eagle shako plate and that device was made smaller so that the whole of it was visible. The breast of the eagle carried, in relief, the brigade number (for field artillery regiments) and the regimental or battalion number in the case of fortress artillery units.

Dress regulations stipulated that the parade shako was to be worn by horse artillery units even on active service.

Above

Full dress shako of an Officer of the Artillery. Front view, showing the retaining chain, horse-hair plume and rose.

(Scherer collection).

Left

The foul-weather oilskin cover worn in the Service to protect the headdress. Note that when the foul-weather cover was in position the cap rose was removed.

(Scherer collection).

Field Service Cap

This was of the same pattern as that worn by the infantry but the colour was light blue.

|||||||||||||||||||||||||||||||||||||||||||||||||||||||||||||||||||||||||||||||||||||||||||||||||||

General Officers
and Staff

|||||||||||||||||||||||||||||||||||||||||||||||||||||||||||||||||||||||||||||||||||||||||||||||||||

General Officers

General Officers wore 'German' dress, but those who had been colonels of Hungarian hussar regiments at some time during their service were entitled to wear the special and very colourful General Officers' 'Hungarian' dress.

German Dress: Gala

A black cocked hat with falling plumes of green, vulture feathers. The hat was bordered with General Officer pattern gold lace and carried a rosette with the Imperial cypher. This type of headdress served the General Officers in German dress on those occasions when gala, full dress and service dress were specified.

The double-breasted, white cloth tunic was fitted with two rows each of eight buttons of General Officer pattern. The skirt was lined with scarlet cloth, and cloth of that colour was also used for the facings on collar and cuffs as well as for the tunic piping.

Trousers were of scarlet cloth and carried down the outside of each leg a double row of General Officer pattern gold lace 2cm wide and a line of gold piping showing between the two rows.

German Dress: Service Dress

The tunic was pike grey, double breasted and fastened by two rows each of eight buttons. Collar patch and piping were in scarlet.

The blue/grey trousers and/or breeches bore a double stripe of red lace between which there was scarlet piping.

German Dress: Full Dress

A double-breasted light blue tunic with a double row of eight buttons. The collar, cuffs and pipings were of scarlet. Salonhosen with a double stripe of scarlet lace were worn with this tunic.

The overcoat was of standard pattern with a scarlet cloth lining, pipings and parolis. Buttons were of General Officer pattern.

Variations in German Dress: Gala

Certain officers of very senior rank wore uniforms which differed from those described above and which identified the post they held.

Left
One of the members of foreign Royal Houses given the rank of Colonel-in-Chief of an Imperial regiment was Nicholas, The Tzarevitch and Heir to the Russian Throne. He is wearing the old pattern, white tunic showing the rank insignia of a Colonel. The Tsarevitch was Colonel-in-Chief of 61st Regiment and the device shown on the cuff identifies the unit as Hungarian.

Right
General The Archduke Franz Ferdinand in the undress uniform of a General Officer, c1890.

The Chief of the General Staff wore in gala a tunic of dark green cloth with a collar and cuffs of black velvet piped with scarlet. Trousers were blue/grey with General Officer pattern lace in a double stripe, as already described.

General Adjutants wore a dark green tunic with a black flecked shoulder cord of gold lace to hold the sash which was the insignia of their office. With this type of tunic, dark green trousers with gold lace stripes were worn. The Inspector General of Artillery wore a dark brown tunic with light blue trousers and General Officer pattern lace stripes. The gala uniform of the

The barrel sash of bullion and black silk cord worn by General Officers in Hungarian dress.

Chief of the General Staff and of the Inspector General of Artillery also served those officers as service dress.

Hungarian Dress: Gala

This was a very elaborate version of Hussar uniform. The headdress was a marten fur busby, 14cm high and fitted with a scarlet bag. The cap cords were square shaped and of gold thread, double laid and plaited so as to form a chain seventeen links long. At one end there was a slide fitted with a gold button; at the other two ends, overlapping discs each 5cm in diameter and carrying a tassel 7cm long. The upper disc bore a gold embroidered Imperial eagle and the lower disc was plain.

At the front of the busby there was a 24cm tall plume of egret feathers fitted into a holder of woven gold thread flecked with black silk. A collar of black feathers, 3cm high, covered the join between the egret plume and the holder.

The scarlet cloth attila was lined with red silk and had breast cords of gold bullion. The olivets and rosettes were covered with gold bullion thread. The pipings and other decorations on the attila were of standard pattern but were finished in bullion thread. There was no shoulder cord.

The fur attila of white cloth was lined with scarlet silk and was of standard hussar officer pattern, but with a 4cm high stand-up collar of marten fur. There was an inner and an outer throat cord. The inner one was square, double cord with a sling at one end and a gold thread toggle on the other. The outer cord was of double laid chain and the toggle was covered with gold bullion thread.

Hussar pattern, scarlet cloth breeches carried on each thigh an inverted 'Austrian' knot made of General Officer pattern lace. Down the outside leg were two stripes of similar patterned lace, 2cm in width.

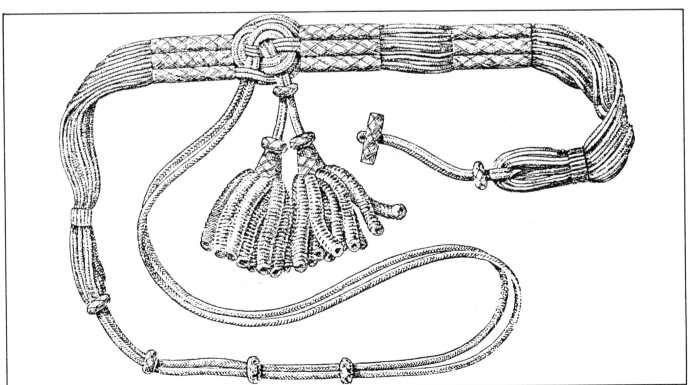

The Hungarian pattern boots, the shismen, were made of soft leather decorated with gold lace and a golden rosette. With them were worn gold spurs of hussar pattern.

Hungarian Dress: Service Dress

Headdress was a standard black hussar shako.

The pike grey attila had a collar and cuffs of scarlet facing cloth and the garment was lined with the same material. Pipings and cords on the service dress attila were of the same pattern as those on the scarlet attila of gala dress, but were of gold flecked with black and not of plain gold.

Trousers were of blue/grey cloth and carried the double red stripe with piping showing between the stripes. Grey riding breeches, which were worn with simple shismen, also carried the General Officer scarlet lace.

Hungarian Dress: Full Dress

A black hussar shako with a gold lace peak was worn by General Officers in full dress. The gilded eagle cap badge and rosette were standard, officer pattern but the cap cords were in gold, square and in double thickness, plaited into a chain of fifteen links. Each end of the chain was fitted with a disc and a tassel.

A plume of green vulture feathers, 12cm in height, decorated the front of the shako and this plume fitted into a holder at the rear of the rosette where it was held in position by a piece of whalebone. The spread of the plume was 9cm.

The pike grey, fur attila was trimmed with mink and lined with scarlet cloth. In style it was similar to the white fur attila of gala dress, but had a turn-down collar. The attila cords were gold with black flecking.

The overcoat was the dark brown, cavalry officer pattern, but lined with scarlet and had parolis and piping of that colour.

Trousers were of blue/grey cloth with the standard piping and scarlet stripes. When on parade or mounted, blue/grey riding breeches were worn and these, too, carried the scarlet stripes.

Officers of the General Staff

All officers of the General Staff wore the same uniform type.

In full dress a cocked hat with falling plumes of green, vulture feathers was worn.

Tunic and blouse were bottle green in colour. Common Army officers on the General Staff and those of the Landwehr wore a double-breasted tunic fitted with a double row of eight buttons. The tunic collar and cuffs were in black velvet piped with scarlet. Scarlet cloth lined the skirt of the tunic. The blouse carried collar patches of black velvet piped in scarlet and parolis of that pattern were worn on the blue/grey overcoat. Buttons on the greatcoat and on the tunic were of plain yellow metal.

General Staff officers of the Landwehr (Honved) wore the standard Honved shako covered with a bottle green cloth and fitted with an upright green plume.

The dark green cloth attila had a black velvet collar and cuffs. With this garment the Hungarian barrelled sash was worn.

The elderly Archduke Rainer, Colonel-in-Chief of 59th Regiment, in gala uniform.

||||||||||||||||||||||||||||||||||||||||||||||||||||||||||||||||||||||||||||||||||||||||||

Field Service Dress

||||||||||||||||||||||||||||||||||||||||||||||||||||||||||||||||||||||||||||||||||||||||||||||||||

The destructive power of modern weapons coupled with their increased range and greater accuracy forced military authorities to accept the principle of the 'empty battlefield' and the need to equip their armies in a shade of colour which may not have been complete camouflage but which was, at least, unobtrusive.

The Imperial High Command introduced as the colour for the army's battle dress the pike grey which the jaeger of the Common Army wore. The decision to uniform the army in that shade was taken in 1907 and by 1909 it had become regulation issue for the uniforms of General Officers, the various Staff Corps, the foot regiments of the line, Landwehr and Landwehr (Honved) forces as well as to the field, mountain and fortress artillery units. The cavalry alone retained as battle dress the colourful parade uniforms.

With certain exceptions, which are listed below, the pike grey uniform consisted of a cap, blouse, trousers and greatcoat.

The Blouse/Tunic

There were two patterns of garment. A summer blouse in linen or twill which was fitted with a turn-down collar and the winter version which was cut on the lines of a simplified parade dress tunic. Neither type was fitted with coloured shoulder straps or rolls. The facing colour which identified a regiment were reduced on the field service dress to two oblong patches of cloth, one on either side of the collar join. On those patches, each of which was 7cm by 4cm in size, were worn the rank distinctions and, where appropriate, specialist insignia, such as the machine-gunner's badge. For those units whose regimental facing colour was grey, the collar patch was backed by a brown cloth frame 3mm wide.

The blouse was fitted with four external pockets: two breast and two hip. Each of these pockets was flapped and fastened by a button of regimental pattern hidden beneath a fly flap. The blouse, too, was fitted with a fly front which concealed buttons of regimental pattern. The only visible buttons were those which fastened the shoulder straps. Other Ranks wore shoulder straps and a small roll of grey cloth was fitted to the right shoulder strap to prevent the rifle slipping from the shoulder.

The blouse was regulation wear on route marches, in camp or on manoeuvres. It could also be worn as off-duty or walking out dress.

In marching order a pike grey cotton stock was worn with the winter issue blouse. The summer tunic with its rise and fall collar needed no stock and

Lieutenant of a German Infantry regiment in field service order. He is wearing a blanket en bandoliere, a map casse on the right hip and binoculars on his waist belt.

Two field service pattern caps. The top one is the standard Other Ranks Infantry issue (with peak) and bears the patch of the 315th Landsturm Battalion. The lower cap is the Calvary or Artillery pattern, Other Ranks issue, and bears the stencilled letters and numeral showing it to be from the 5th Honved Hussar Regiment. (IWM).

that piece of material was often used as a neck shield against the sun. The summer blouse was worn in conjunction with linen or twill summer pattern trousers.

Overcoat

The field service greatcoat was a grey variant of the parade dress garment. Those units which did not wear greatcoats—Landesschuetzen and Bosnian formations—were issued with grey cloaks fitted with a hood.

Trousers

The trousers of the field service uniform were unpiped, except for those worn by jaeger and Landwehr officers, Staff or General Officers. Certain troops wore grey versions of the trouser style worn as their parade dress.

Thus, Hungarian regiments retained their tight-fitting pattern leg coverings complete with grey cord thigh knots, while the artillery, the Landesschuetzen and Bosnian units wore their trousers tight round the calf but baggy above the knee. Artillerymen, when off duty, could dispense with wearing the leather gaiters which formed part of their uniform. The Kaiserjaeger and other jaeger wore high buttoned linen gaiters on active service, while mountain units, specifically the Landesschuetzen, fitted thick socks over the bottom of their trouser legs.

The standard infantry pattern trousers were fastened at the ankle by a reinforced cuff of material which was closed by a pair of buttons to act as a short gaiter.

Headdress

The standard field service headdress was a low-crowned, peaked cap of pike grey tunic material. Ear flaps were fitted and were worn folded upwards in clement weather. When the flaps were folded upwards the cap was fastened at the front by two small buttons of regimental pattern. In bad weather when the ear flaps were used the buttons fastened under the chin.

Other Ranks' caps had a black composition peak. For regimental officers that peak was covered with pike grey cloth. Officers' caps carried a small bullion rosette; Other Ranks had a round brass disc pierced with the Imperial cypher. The jaeger horn was worn, where appropriate, on officers' caps.

The field service headdress was worn with marching order and was standard dress for drill and musketry parades. Officers also had a field service shako of standard design but in pike grey cloth. The bands of lace denoting rank were not worn with this pattern headdress.

Muslims in Bosnian units wore a field grey version of the red fez with a grey tassel.

Staff Officers wore a distinctive low-crowned kepi, completely round in shape and of tunic material.

On active service in cold climates two other head coverings were on issue. The first of these was a knitted woollen cap-comforter which often replaced the peaked cap when in the field. The cap-comforter was frequently fitted with a standard rosette. The second type of head-covering was a flannel or linen toque worn as a balaclava helmet under the field cap.

Decorations worn on the Cap

With the exception of the Jaeger horn cap, badges to identify a unit were not worn in the Austrian service. At the outbreak of war, however, there began the practice of wearing commemorative badges. The designs, shapes and materials from which these were made were many, but the greatest number of these unofficial devices were made of a metal alloy. The subjects chosen as motifs ranged from more or less elaborate badges showing army, corps or divisional allegiance, to reproductions of the faces of members of the Imperial family or of senior officers of the service. Commanders of allied armies and devices commemorating battles and offensives were also popular subjects.

Without doubt the most attractive badges were those semi-official devices worn by officers of cavalry regiments. These were specially designed, usually oval in shape and made of enamelled metal, the colour of the enamel often being that of the regimental facing colour. An inlay of enamel in the initial letter, H D or U, identified the branch of cavalry, and a numeral the respective regiment. In contrast to the other semi-official or completely unofficial badges which were worn on the side of the cap, the cavalry devices were carried on the front of the cap and usually between the two buttons.

PLATE 41

3rd CAVALRY

4th CAVALRY

8th CAVALRY

9th CAVALRY

10th CAVALRY

When the Cavalry adopted grey field service dress, it was no longer possible to identify a regiment by the cut of its tunic, buttons and facing colour. To overcome the problem, officers of the regiments commissioned regimental badges. These were made of silver and enamelled copper and though they were unofficial, they were worn with pride, either at the front of the undress shako between the sling at the front of the headdress or above the left breast pocket. The following pages show some of these unofficial badges (*IWM*).

PLATE 42

1st HUSSARS

2nd HUSSARS

3rd HUSSARS

4th HUSSARS

8th HUSSARS

11th HUSSARS

12th HUSSARS

13th HUSSARS

The dark blue background on the 8th Hussar badge shows the colour of the attila and the light blue letters and numeral on the badge of the 2nd Hussars indicates that the colour of their attila was light blue.

PLATE 43

Her Imperial Majesty
The Empress Zita was
appointed to become
Colonel-in-Chief of the
16th Hussars by The
Emperor Karl.

14th HUSSARS

16th HUSSARS

**LANDWEHR ULAN
5th REGIMENT**

7th ULAN

8th ULAN

Mounted Rifles (Reitende
Schuetzen) was the title
given to the former
Landwehr Ulan
regiments.

**MOUNTED RIFLES
1st REGIMENT**

11th ULAN

12th ULAN

PLATE 44

6th DRAGOONS

9th DRAGOONS

**7th HORSE ARTILLERY
HALF REGIMENT**

**25th INFANTRY
DIVISION**

OTHER RANKS
Field service cap
rosette

MACHINE GUNNERS
Cap badge

**OTHER RANKS
MACHINE GUNNERS**
Collar badges

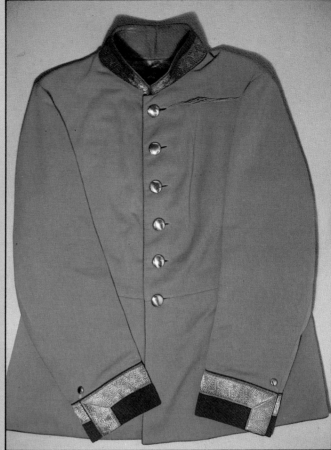

Above left:
45 Jaeger Officer's overcoat. Note officer pattern parolis and yellow metal buttons. (*IWM*)

Below left:
46 Field service blouse, Other Ranks in a Jaeger unit. Note the roll on the right shoulder to prevent the rifle slipping. The thread on the left shoulder strap is the British Army's sealed pattern label. (*IWM*)

Above right:
47 Front side of a tunic; Colonel of Kaiserjaeger. (*IWM*)

Below right:
48 Front side of a tunic; Lieutenant of the Artillery. The brown tunic and red facings of the Artillery were traditional in the Habsburg Army. (*IWM*)

Dragoon tunic, Other Ranks.
Left: 49 Front view, to show the buttons (Kompassen) the shaped cuffs and the shoulder sling. The scarlet cuffs and piping, together with the white metal buttons, identify the regiment as 11th Regiment.

50 Rear view, to show the skirt and back piping. (*IWM*)

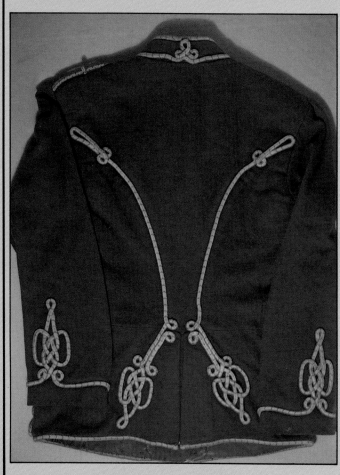

Above:
51 Common Army Hussar attila, front view, to show the breast cords and the sleeve decoration.
Left:
52 Common Army Hussar attila, rear view, to show the piping on the back and in the skirts. (*IWM*)

PLATE 53

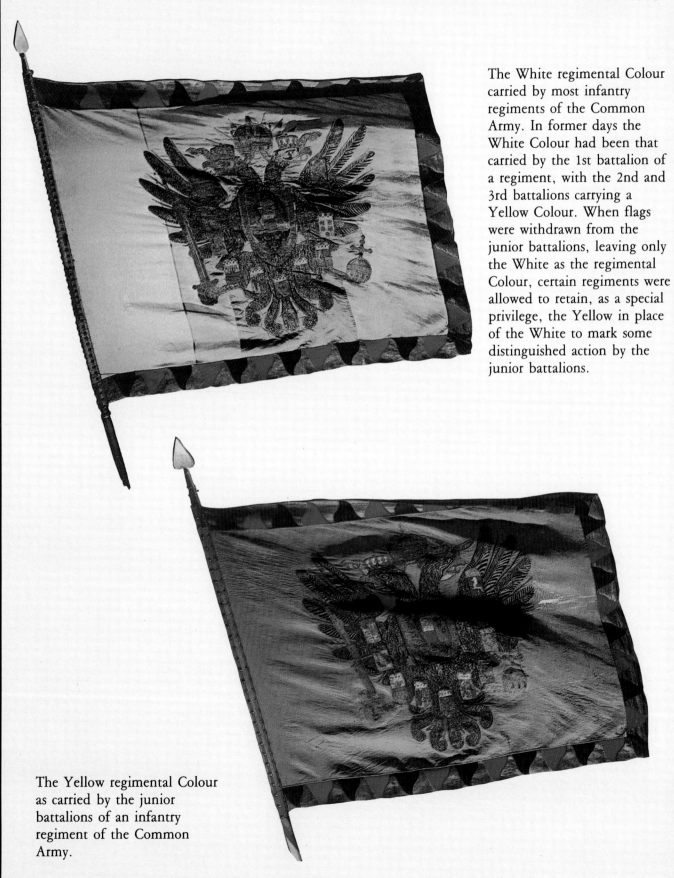

The White regimental Colour carried by most infantry regiments of the Common Army. In former days the White Colour had been that carried by the 1st battalion of a regiment, with the 2nd and 3rd battalions carrying a Yellow Colour. When flags were withdrawn from the junior battalions, leaving only the White as the regimental Colour, certain regiments were allowed to retain, as a special privilege, the Yellow in place of the White to mark some distinguished action by the junior battalions.

The Yellow regimental Colour as carried by the junior battalions of an infantry regiment of the Common Army.

PLATE 54

The regimental flag
of the 2nd Regiment
of the Tiroler
Kaiserjaeger.

The Austrian Imperial
double-headed eagle
taken from the
centre-piece of a
Yellow regimental
Colour.

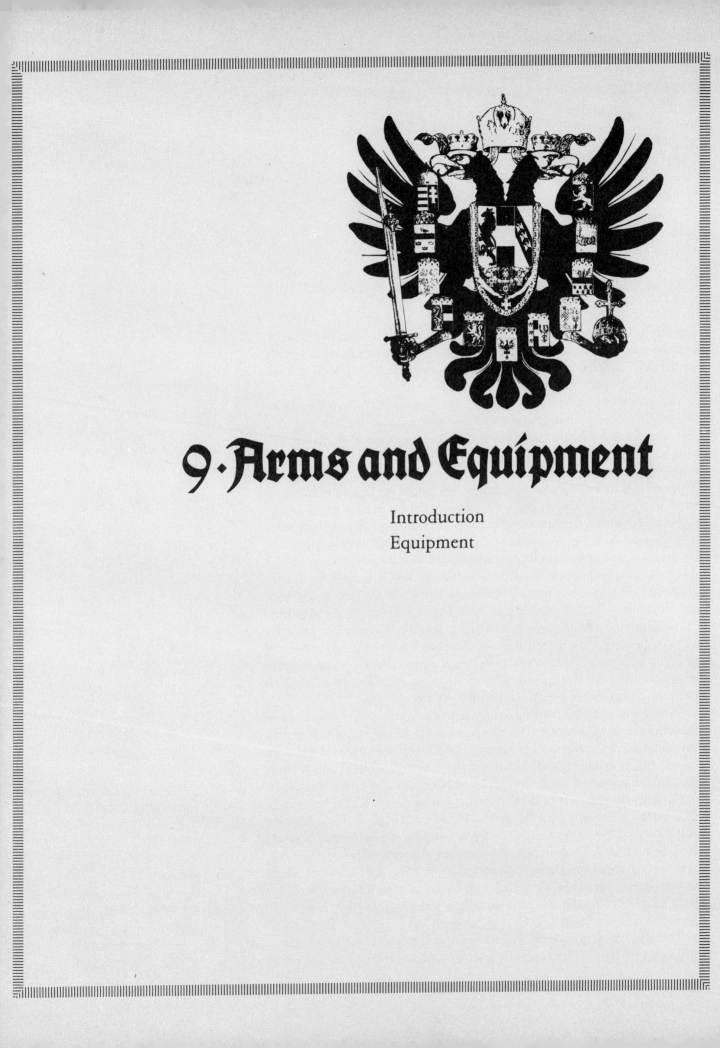

9·Arms and Equipment

Introduction

Equipment

||||||||||||||||||||||||||||||||||||||||||||||||||||||||||||||||||||||||||||||||||||||||||||||||||||||||||||||||||||

Weapons

||||||||||||||||||||||||||||||||||||||||||||||||||||||||||||||||||||||||||||||||||||||||||||||||||||||||||||||||||||

The extensive natural resources in iron and coal, an efficient railway network and the natural skills of its peoples gave the Empire an arms industry able to meet not only the demands of its own armed forces but to supply those of less well-developed countries.

That statement requires qualification. The development of new weapons was inhibited by parliamentary control of the military budget and as a consequence two Austrian inventions, the machine pistol and a caterpillar tracked armoured vehicle—the tank—were lost to the army.

Economies were made by the military through the standardisation of weapons and in issuing arms which were no longer on first line supply to third line units. It was not usual in the Imperial Service for every soldier to be issued with a firearm—even among the fighting troops. There were many whose weapon was just a bayonet but no rifle. Other military formations, such as the Landsturm, were issued with whatever weapons had not been scrapped. Some Landsturm battalions which actually went into action and fought in the first battles on the Eastern Front were issued with the single-shot Werndl, which had passed out of service decades earlier.

Although the needle gun was introduced into the Prussian Army as early as 1841, it was not until 1867 that the Austrian Lorenz rifle was converted to become a breech loader by using the Wenzl system. These interim firearms were retained until the introduction of the single shot Werndl rifle which fired an 11mm bullet over distances of 2,000yds.

During the 1880s the need for a magazine rifle to arm the infantry became a paramount consideration. The Austrian Service solved the problem with the adoption of the Mannlicher system. The Mannlicher rifle fired the same calibre bullet as the Werndl but the use of a new propellent and a hard-lead bullet improved upon the results obtained by the earlier weapon.

Concern was then felt by the military authorities at the additional weight of ammunition which the infantryman would need to carry. The magazine rifle increased the rate of fire and to compensate for this extra rounds would have to be issued. To overcome the problem of increased weight the rifle bore was reduced from 11mm to 8mm and a new propellent was used. These innovations reduced the weight of each round of ammunition which was then adapted to fit the standard issue firearms: the M86/90, the M88/90, the M90 and the M95.

The M86/90, a variant of the original 11mm weapon, was improved by fitting a new type of barrel and by several other minor changes. The 88/90

The Officers' Machine-Gun School at Bruck an der Leitha, 1913. The weapons are Schwarzlose machine guns with which the army was equipped at the outbreak of war. Note the pack animals which were used to bring the guns and ammunition forward.

was declared obsolescent during 1902, was withdrawn from line units and intended for issue to Landsturm infantry units. A variant of the rifle, the M88/90 was originally built to fire a black-powder cartridge but the introduction of smokeless powder made the weapon obsolete.

An improvement of the 88/90, the M90, was designed to fire ammunition using the new propellent and was replaced by the M95, which was not only lighter in weight, but to which certain improvements had been made to the breech.

Mannlichers were straight-bolt magazine-fed weapons and, in addition to the rifles described above, there were also carbines whose development followed very closely that of the standard firearm. The M95 carbine differed from that of the M90 only in the sighting arrangement, and the M95 Stuetzen only in the fitting of a wooden upper forestock and in the sling attachment. The carbine was not fitted with a bayonet because its distribution was principally to the cavalry and to the horse artillery. The Stuetzen was intended chiefly for issue to mountain troops but during the course of the First World War the Stuetzen was taken over by cavalry units and the carbine by mountain detachments.

The Austro-Hungarian Army was the first to issue automatic repeating pistols and as early as 1908 the Imperial cavalry had been issued with the Roth-Steyr or M7. This hand gun replaced the army revolver, 1870/1874, 11mm Gasser, which had been the regulation issue weapon. Officers of the cavalry and other mounted arms carried the 9mm Gasser-Kropatschek six-shot revolver.

Regulations demanded that all officers carried a pistol on active service but the choice of firearm was left open. The pattern recommended for infantry officers was the Gasser-Kropatschek until the M7 and the M12 replaced it.

The M7 was manufactured by two companies; one in Steyr and the other in Budapest. The gun fired a 7.99mm bullet and had several unusual features. The chief of these was the way in which the magazine was loaded. A charger holding ten rimless bullets was placed into the top of the pistol and pushed down into the magazine. When the charger was removed the pistol was both loaded and cocked. A safety device ensured that when a shot was fired a new round was chambered but the action was not automatically cocked. Pressure on the trigger was needed to cock the piece and a second pressure to fire it.

The M7 weighed 2lb 4oz and had an overall length of 9½in.

The M12, also known as the Steyr Hahn, was the most common pistol in use in the Austrian Service during the First World War. It fired a 9mm cartridge and was basically the same type of weapon as the M7. It differed in being shorter by ¾in and in being lighter by 2oz.

The magazine, which held eight rounds, was unusual in that it was fitted with a release catch. When this was activated the whole contents of the magazine were ejected in a single operation. The 9mm round which the M12 fired was not only a very powerful one but was unique to that weapon, being made of a length that fitted only the Steyr Hahn.

Mannlicher Magazine Rifle M95

Weight without bayonet	8lb 6oz
Length without bayonet	4ft 2in
Length with bayonet	4ft 11in
Calibre	8mm
Sighted up to	2,133yd

The foresight of the M95 was of the barleycorn type. The five-round magazine, which was loaded by a clip of cartridges, was a fixed metal box. The magazine and trigger guard were in one piece, with the magazine being open underneath in order to allow the empty clip to fall out.

Mannlicher Magazine Carbine M95

Weight	6lb 11oz
Overall length	3ft 4in
Calibre	8mm
Sighted up to	1,968yd

The Mannlicher carbine, which was similar in construction to the M95 Rifle, was the weapon on issue to mounted troops. So that the piece could be carried slung and lying flat to the wearer's back, the lower sling was fitted on the side of the butt and not underneath it in the standard way. Bayonets were not issued with the carbine.

Mannlicher (short) Rifle M95

The short Mannlicher magazine rifle (the Repitirstuetzen) was on issue to technical troops. The weapon was identical with the Mannlicher carbine, except that the piece was fitted with a bayonet and that the sling was fitted in the standard way.

One of the means of raising money for war charities was the sale of Vivat bands. These were of silk, designed by well-known artists and skilfully printed. This picture shows the Vivat band with the motif of a 30.5cm mortar.
(IWM, Dept of Art)

Edged Weapons

Swords, whether of infantry or cavalry pattern, were used to cut or thrust and consisted of three main parts: blade, scabbard and hilt.

Swords for infantry officers were made of polished steel with a slightly curving blade, 32in in length and which fitted inside a polished steel scabbard. For the greater part of its length the blade was channelled and its point was double-edged. The wooden grip was covered with fish skin bound with silver and the guard was slightly flattened. The combined weight of the sword and scabbard was 1lb 14oz.

The sword issued to NCOs, musicians, artificers and medical personnel was designated 'Infantry sabre M61'. This was made of unpolished steel with a pronounced curve in its 30in long blade and which fitted into a leather scabbard with a brass shoe. In every other respect it was identical to the officer pattern weapon.

The sword carried by both officers and NCOs in mountain units was of standard pattern but had a blade only 24in long. The officer pattern sword guard was pierced so as to form an eagle and an Imperial cypher. The guard on the NCO pattern side-arm was unpierced.

The standard pattern cavalry sabre was the M69 which had a blade 33in in length; in polished steel for officers and in unpolished steel for Other Ranks. This cutting and thrusting weapon was made up of a blade with tongue, hilt and scabbard. The weight was 4lb 9oz, that of the sword alone being 2lb 11oz. All later patterns of cavalry sabre developed from the original

Regiments which bore the name of His Majesty the Emperor were usually honoured by a commemorative medal which was then affixed to the regimental Colour. In the case of Field Howitzer Regiment No 8, the award of a medal would have been inappropriate as artillery units did not carry Colours. As the mark of royal distinction the barrel of each artillery piece in the regiment was cast emblazoned with the Imperial monogram, as shown here.

M69 design. The blade was double-edged for one-third of its length and channelling ran from the point of the blade where the double-edging began to a point just below the guard. A development of the M69 was the M77, which had less of a curve in the blade and a guard which was that less decorative but in every other respect was identical to the M69. It was found that the M77 was not suitable as an offensive weapon, being unable either to beat down an enemy trooper's parry or to carry through a deadly thrust. A replacement piece was required. The M4 cavalry sabre was another variant of the M69, and although the blade was not channelled it was a weapon lighter in weight than the M77.

Artillery Weapons

M96 Field Gun

The standard artillery weapon of the field and horse artillery, as well as of the mountain artillery, was the M96 Field Gun.

Calibre	9cm	Weight of HE shell	16lb
Length of gun	81ft 10in	Weight of shrapnel shell	14lb 5oz
Weight of gun	9cwt 38lb	Track width (field and	
Weight of carriage	11cwt 29lb	horse artillery)	5ft
Muzzle velocity	1470ft per second	Track width (mountain	
Maximum range	4170yd	artillery)	3ft 9in
Rate of fire	6 rounds per minute		

Three shots of the 30.5cm Mortar, the production of which had been kept secret from Parliament who would otherwise have scrapped the project. The 30.5cm was one of the best artillery pieces in service in the world and some pieces were supplied to the German Army in 1914 to help smash the French and Belgian forts. Above right: The very mobile piece, which could be broken down into three loads, ready for the road. Right: The gun being prepared for a firing position.

Brüssel.
Österreichische Kanonen in der „Caserne d' Artillerie".
(Mit diesen Kanonen wurden Namur und Maubeuge bombardirt.)

33

The steel-bronze M96 had a Krupp breech action and a spade recoil. The weapon with which the horse artillery was equipped weighed 174lb less than the standard Field Gun.

M99 Field Howitzer

The M99 Field Howitzer was the standard piece of ordnance on issue.

Calibre	10.5cm	Muzzle velocity	500ft per
Length	4ft 5in	(minimum charge)	second
Maximum elevation	43 degrees	Maximum range	6,600yd
Maximum depression	10 degrees	Track	5ft 5in
Weight	7cwt 53lb	Rate of fire	6 rounds
Weight in action			per minute
(howitzer and carriage)	19 cwt 21lb	Weight of shell	32lb
Muzzle velocity			
(maximum charge)	1,017ft per second		

M99 Mountain Gun

The M99 Mountain Gun was the standard weapon on issue to alpine units. Such units were also issued with the M96 Field Gun on a narrow gauge track, as described above.

Calibre	7cm	Muzzle velocity	1,030ft per second
Length of gun	3ft 3in	Maximum range	5,400yd
Weight of gun	2cwt 24lb	Rate of fire	5 rounds per minute
Weight of carriage	3cwt 96lb	Weight of HE shell	10lb 8oz
Track	3ft 1in		

The Mountain Gun M99 broke down into three loads which were carried on mule back. The first load was the gun barrel and breech, the second animal carried the front part of the carriage. The third carried the rear part of the carriage and the gun wheels.

30.5cm Heavy Gun Howitzer.

|||||||||||||||||||||||||||||||||||||||||||||||||||||||||||||||||||||||||||||||||||||||||||||||||||||||

Equipment

|||||||||||||||||||||||||||||||||||||||||||||||||||||||||||||||||||||||||||||||||||||||||||||||||||||||

Infantry

The infantry equipment described below was the M1888 pattern which came on general issue during 1896. The leather parts of this equipment were of brown hide artificially blackened on all external surfaces.

The leather waist belt was fitted with a metal buckle impressed with the emblem of a double eagle. The belt fastened by a claw on one end of the belt fitting into a clasp fixed on the inside of the buckle.

That waist belt was the foundation to which the other pieces of equipment were fitted. The principal piece was a double knapsack of brown cowhide lined with canvas, strengthened with brown leather and stiffened by a detachable wooden frame, concave shaped so as to fit the wearer's back.

The knapsack was divided into two separate parts and was fitted with a variety of rings and buckles to which the equipment pieces, as well as an overcoat and a tent half, were attached.

The lower and smaller part of the knapsack was known as the cartridge sack and contained fifty rounds of ammunition, one tin of preserved meat and one meat and vegetable ration. The upper part of the knapsack held the soldier's personal equipment, a further ten rounds of ammunition, foot bandages (which were issued in place of socks in most European armies of the day) and the rifle cleaning equipment. It was usual for a blanket to be the uppermost item in the large knapsack and this was folded so that it showed below the cowhide flap. The overcoat was rolled and strapped round the outside of the pack. Other straps fastened into position an alloy cooking utensil and a two-part mess tin.

The smaller knapsack formed part of a soldier's battle equipment and was carried by him into action. The upper part was left behind with the rest of the baggage.

A haversack of waterproof canvas was carried on the left hip by all ranks except those personnel who wore a sabre. The haversack was then carried on the right hip. The haversack held a water bottle, knife, fork and spoon, a bread ration, tobacco and other personal items. Grooms, bandsmen and stretcher-bearers were issued with two haversacks, one of which was in lieu of cartridge pouches. Also carried on the left hip was an entrenching tool complete with leather case to which was attached a bayonet in its frog.

At the front of his body the infantryman carried two ammunition pouches each of which held twenty rounds. A new pattern equipment, the 1909, was introduced but had not come into general issue by 1914. In that pattern the ammunition pouches were smaller and held only ten rounds each. They were issued in pairs and each infantryman wore two pairs, fitted one pair on either side of the belt buckle. The other equipment pieces were the several supporting straps.

Each man armed with a rifle carried part of a tent and three tent pegs. The remainder portered six pieces of tent pole.

The total weight carried by the infantry soldier, including clothes, arms, ammunition, equipment and portion of tent, was in excess of 60lb.

Cavalry

The basis was the waist belt which was fastened by a tongue and prong method. There were two calibres of ammunition on issue and, thus, two types of ammunition pouch were needed, for that which held the M1891 Mannlicher carbine could not take the Mannlicher rifle ammunition. Each cavalryman was issued with two pouches of correct pattern for the weapon he carried. These were fitted on the waist belt and positioned at the front of the body. Those men who were armed with a revolver had to fasten the belt in such a way that its buckle was positioned on the left hip.

The cavalryman's kit was carried in two large leather wallets connected by a strap and carried at the front of the saddle. A cornsack with a cloak or òvercoat on top was strapped to the rear of the saddle. In addition to his own equipment the cavalryman had also to deal with that of the horse. This consisted of the bridle with bit and bridoon, the breastplate, a saddle of the M1883 pattern, a horse blanket, two girths and two wallets. Cornsack, haversack, nosebag, two shoe pockets, a canvas water bucket (one for every two horses), footshackles, mess tin, cooking utensil (one for every two men) and an axe (one for every seven men). Each man carried a water bottle and a swimming sack for crossing small rivers.

The total weight carried by a horse fully equipped and with a rider was about 21 stone.

10 · Traditions, Regimental Days, Music, Flags and Standards

Traditions

The Imperial Army was not encrusted with much tradition for the committee under the Archduke Albrecht removed many of the negative influences which had grown up during the centuries of the army's existence. Mention has already been made of the abolition of the almost feudal powers of the colonel-in-chief of a regiment but among the other visible changes were the reduction in the number of Colours carried by a regiment and the total abolition of regimental bands in cavalry units.

Yet enough traditions remained to be a link with former days and to bind the old established regiments and the newer-raised regiments together. One act which helped in that respect was the Army Order signed by the Emperor Franz Joseph on 13 May 1888, at a ceremony during which a statue to the Empress Maria Theresia was unveiled in Vienna. Franz Joseph's proclamation ordered that certain regiments were to carry 'for all time' the names of former monarchs, former great soldiers and former army leaders. In the same Order the Emperor ordered each regiment to select for itself a special day which

The Ringstrasse, Vienna, 16 October 1913, during the ceremonies to commemorate the Battle of Nations at Leipzig in 1813. Regiments which fought at Leipzig participated in the ceremonies and one of these is marching past The Emperor Franz Joseph and senior officers of the army.

The tall Archduke Eugene, The Hoch and Deutschmeister (note the Grand Master's Cross on his left breast) seen with The Archduke Joseph, Vienna (probably 1908, at the ceremonies commemorating the Emperor's Diamond Jubilee). The Archduke Eugene is in the General Officer (German) pattern uniform, while the Archduke Joseph is wearing the Hungarian dress uniform of a General Officer.

would be celebrated as its 'regimental day'. These are listed on pages 209-212.

To certain units of the army the Emperor awarded a medal which was usually pinned to the regimental Colour. In the case of cavalry regiments, which carried no Colours—another of Albrecht's reforms—the medal was pinned to the trumpet cloth of a specially presented instrument. The 8th Field Howitzer Regiment carried not only the commemorative medal awarded for the Emperor's Golden Jubilee, but was also allowed to carry the Imperial cypher on its guns.

The regimental Colour of the 50th Regiment carried a unique distinction: a golden medal awarded to the regiment for faithful service during the year of unrest, 1848.

There were certain regiments which had traditions connected with their Standards. The 2nd Battalion Yellow Colour was carried by the following regiments in place of the White Colour: 2nd, 4th, 39th, 41st, and 57th. In each case this special distinction honoured the bravery of one of the junior battalions of the regiment. From 1892 the 38th Infantry was also granted this privilege. The 10th Feldjaeger Battalion carried a specially presented signal horn, which, by Imperial decree, was accorded the same honours as a regimental Colour. This distinction was to honour the part played by that battalion in the battle of Monte Berico.

Although Grenadiers had been abolished even before the war with Prussia, one regiment, the 42nd Infantry, was given the privilege of playing *The Grenadier March* to commemorate the gallant part it played in the Battle of Wagram.

The 8th Dragoons, too, had a unique honour which recalled an event in 1619. The Emperor was rescued from his dissident ministers by the timely arrival of the 8th Dragoons and as a mark of special favour the colonel of the regiment had the right to enter the Imperial presence without announcement. The regiment also had the right to recruit inside the courtyard of the royal palace and to post away any of its soldiers who had been convicted of a serious military crime. Thus, no man of the 8th Dragoons was ever sentenced to life imprisonment or executed. Another Dragoon regiment, the 14th, was the only cavalry unit which was allowed to retain its guidon and the men of that regiment also had the distinction of being allowed *not* to wear moustaches.

In matters of dress there were several national distinctions to which mention has been made. The single purely regimental dress distinction was that held by 2nd Ulan Regiment whose officers and men carried a white metal or silver chain on the shapka and not the gold chain as worn by the other ulan regiments.

The parade march of the army was a variant of the German goose-step,

Senior officers of the Army and Navy, as well as senior Court officials, proceeding into St Stephan's Cathedral, Vienna, for the Feast of Corpus Christi, which was one of the principle events of the Vienna social scene. The troops lining the route are German Infantry. The dark uniformed figure in the foreground is a soldier of the Bodyguard Infantry Company. The uniformed men in spiked helmets among the crowd are Viennese policemen.

Above

The Archduke Franz Ferdinand in naval dress, for the launching of an Austrian battleship. On the right is an Officer of Kaiserjaeger.

Above right

The Emperor's birthday was a day of celebration for the whole army. These officers of the General Staff of the Corps stationed at Lemberg ride back to their quarters after celebrating Mass to honour the Sovereign's birthday.

the difference being that the leg was not raised so high. The marching pace was between 110 and 120 paces to the minute, each step being between 70 and 80cm in length.

Some ceremonial practices which were retained included saluting with the hand. This custom had been taken into the Austrian Service about 1790 and replaced the practice of raising the headdress in salute. Officers who wore the cocked hat, as well as those off duty, continued to raise their hats but by 1868 that custom was abolished. Thereafter, the headdress was no longer removed on parade except to take the oath of allegiance or for prayers.

In 1898 the form of salute in which a rifle is held vertically in front of the body in the position known as 'present arms' was discontinued in the Austrian Service. From that year the method of saluting with a firearm consisted of gripping the small of the butt with the rifle slung from the right shoulder. While the right hand gripped the small of the butt the left hand was placed so as to cover the bayonet. The movement of the soldier's head and eyes to look at and then to follow the inspecting officer constituted the salute. Other ranks on horses, carts, limbers and in vehicles saluted their superiors by turning the head towards the officer to whom compliments were being paid. One unusual practice in the Austrian Service was that of saluting with the left hand while carrying a rifle slung from the right shoulder. This form of salute was usually paid to the dead at funerals.

Regimental Days

It is usual in the armies of the world for their constituent regiments to commemorate some outstanding event or date in their history and to celebrate this as the regimental day. Listed below are the dates elected by those units of the Austro-Hungarian Army which are covered in this book.

Not all the dates chosen recall a battle. The earliest regimental day was 5 June 1619, chosen by the 8th Dragoons to commemorate the occasion when the regiment rode into the Hofburg in Vienna and saved the Emperor from his rebellious ministers. A more happy occasion to be remembered was 4 August 1843, chosen by 11th Dragoons to celebrate the day on which Franz Joseph became the Colonel-in-Chief. Two of the four regiments of Bosnian infantry selected 7 October, for it was on that day in 1908 that the Province of Bosnia-Herzegovinia was formally annexed to the Austrian crown.

The selection of commemorative dates covers the military history of the Habsburg Empire up to the 19th century. There were regimental days recalling the wars against Turkey when Austria defended Europe against Islam. The war with Prussia in 1757 was commemorated by five regiments, one of which, the 14th Dragoons, also carried special privileges connected with the battle of Kolin. One battle of the Napoleonic age was recalled in the choice of Aspern 1809, by sixteen regiments which fought during that short campaign. The great battle of Leipzig was commemorated by three infantry and one dragoon regiment and the struggle at Wagram by two regiments, one of which, the 42nd, so distinguished itself that it gained the right, unique among the Imperial infantry regiments, of playing the *Grenadier March*.

The victorious campaigns in Italy during 1848/49, conducted by Radetzky, included the names of five battles, one of which, Novara, was commemorated by four infantry regiments. The less fortunate war—that engineered by Louis Napoleon and provoked by Italy in 1859—was commemorated by the battles of Magenta, Solferino and Melegano respectively, which were selected by eleven regiments.

The alliance between Prussia and a French/Italian coalition brought about the disastrous campaigns of 1866. While Austria was successful in the south against the Italians and the French, the northern army in Bohemia suffered a crushing defeat. Forty of the regiments which faced the Prussians selected that battle as their regimental day. Ten regiments of that total chose Trautenau and five others Wysokow. It is significant that eight of the nine regiments which commemorated the battle at Koeniggratz were from the artillery, recalling the self-sacrifice of the gunners in covering the retreat of the Austrian infantry from the stricken field. From the campaign in the south thirty-three regiments celebrated the battle of Custoza and six selected the victory at Lissa.

The last occasion the Imperial Army went out on active service during the 19th century was for the war against the Bosnians when that province was annexed in 1878. The fighting against the insurgents endured until 1882 and the bitterness of service there was commemorated by ten regiments.

It is, of course, understandable that regiments raised in the final decades of the 19th century would have no battle to commemorate, but there were others on the infantry and cavalry establishments whose record of service should have allowed them to select a special day on which their forebears had fought and achieved, if not always victory, then always honour.

NO	REGIMENTAL DAY	COMMEMORATING THE BATTLE	REGIMENTAL MARCH	NO	REGIMENTAL DAY	COMMEMORATING THE BATTLE	REGIMENTAL MARCH
INFANTRY REGIMENTS							
1	27 June	Trautenau 1866	*Tratenau* by J. Preis, 1866	25	21 May	Aspern 1809	
2	18 June	Kolin 1757	*Trautenau* and *Alexander* by J. Persius, 1814	26	21 Oct	Caldiero 1805	
				27	6 Feb	Oeversee 1864	*Gablenz* by C. Stenzl
3	22 May	Aspern 1809	*Erzherzog Karl* composer unknown	28	24 June	Custoza 1866	
				29	24 June	Custoza 1866	*Laudon* by J. Fuchs, 1888
4	18 June	Kolin 1757	*Pfalz Neuburg Teutschmeister* by J. N. Fuchs	30	3 Feb	Oeversee 1864	
				31	22 May	Aspern 1809	
5	24 June	Custoza 1866	*Monte Croce* by H. Grimm	32	6 Sept	Bassano 1796	*Maria Theresia* by J. N. Fuchs, 1888
6	29 Sept	Koniginhof 1866		33	23 March	Novara 1849	
7	24 June	Custoza 1866	*Custoza* by L. Stasny, 1866	34	3 Feb	Storming of the Koenigsberg 1864	
8	22 May	Esslingen 1809		35	24 June	Solferino 1859	
9	4 June	Magenta 1859		36	24 June	Custoza 1866	*Phillipovic* by Friedrich Schmidt
10	22 June	Blumenau 1866					
11	8 June	Melegano 1859	*Friedlander* by J. Pitschmann	37	16 Oct	Leipzig/Lindau 1813	
12	16 June	Kolin 1757		38	19 Aug	Sarajevo 1878	
13	27 June	Trautenau 1866		39	24 June	Custoza 1866	
14	4 June	Magenta 1859		40	18 Oct	Leipzig 1813	
15	22 May	Aspern 1809	*Ja wid Nassau* by F. Scheibenreither, 1849	41	21 Nov	Baudin Odziak 1878	
16	23 July	Sona 1848		42	6 July	Wagram 1809	*Wagram* by J. Wiede
17	7 Aug	Jajce 1878		43	24 June	Custoza 1866	*Jovanovic* by K. Seber
18	22 May	Aspern 1809	*Reisinger* composer unknown	44	21 May	Aspern 1809	*Erzherzog Albrecht* by K. Komzak, 1888
19	18 Oct	Leipzig 1813		45	6 May	St Lucia 1848	
20	27 June	Wysokow 1866		46	None		
21	22 May	Aspern1809	*Gyulai* composer unknown	47	23 March	Novara 1849	*Somma Campagna* by A. Tischler, 1848
22	14 Aug	Banya Luka 1878	*Lacy* by G. Sebek	48	14 Aug	Novi 1799	
23	27 June	Trautenau 1866	*Szlankamen* by L. Schlögel	49	13 May	Schwarz Lackenau 1809	
24	27 June	Trautenau 1866	*Strauch* by Emil Kaiser, 1808	50	24 June	Custoza 1866	*Olliosi* by F. Lehar (senior), 1866

NO	REGIMENTAL DAY	COMMEMORATING THE BATTLE	REGIMENTAL MARCH
51	22 May	Aspern 1809	*Splenyi* composer unknown
52	23 March	Novara 1849	
53	24 June	Custoza 1866	*Trenk Panduren* by von der Trenk, 1741
54	24 July	Somma Campagna 1848	*Alt Starhemberg* by J H. Fuchs, 1888
55	22 May	Aspern 1809	
56	23 July	Somma Campagna 1848	*Daun* by J. N. Fuchs
57	27 June	Oswiecim 1866	*Josias Coburg* attributed to Michael Haydn, 1792-3
58	27 June	Trautenau 1866	*Wallonen* by W. Asboth, 1763
59	24 June	Solferino 1859	*Rainer* by Hans Schmid
60	21 May	Aspern 1809	
61	16 April	Sacile 1809	
62	30 April	Caldiero 1809	
63	24 June	Custoza 1809	
64	14 July	Biskupic 1866	
65	24 June	Custoza 1866	
66	24 June	Custoza 1866	
67	None		
68	17 Sept	Nova Broka 1878	
69	22 July	Blumenau 1866	
70	23 March	Novara 1849	
71	26 Feb	Crunij Klamac 1882	
72	26 June	Podol 1866	
73	None		*Lymfjord* formerly *Dormus* by S. Scharoth, 1864
74	None		
75	24 June	Custoza 1866	
76	24 June	Custoza 1866	
77	28 June	Skalitz 1866	
78	21 Sept	Senkovic Bandin Odziak 1878	
79	16 May	Malborgeth and Predil 1809	*Jellacic* composer unknown
80	None		
81	None		
82	None		
83	13 May	Schwarze Lackenau 1809	

From Infantry Regiment 84 to 95: None

NO	REGIMENTAL DAY	COMMEMORATING THE BATTLE	REGIMENTAL MARCH
96	17 May	Malborgeth Predil 1809	
97	None		
98	None		
99	22 May	Aspern 1809	*99th Regiment* by R. Hunyacek
100	None		
101	None		
102	None		

KAISERJAEGER REGIMENTS

NO	REGIMENTAL DAY	COMMEMORATING THE BATTLE	REGIMENTAL MARCH
1 to 4	24 June	Custoza 1866	*Kaiserjäger* by K. Muhlberger

FELDJAEGER BATTALION

NO	REGIMENTAL DAY	COMMEMORATING THE BATTLE	REGIMENTAL MARCH
1	21 May	Esslingen 1809	
2	21 May	Esslingen 1809	
4	11 March	Monzambano 1814	
5	28 June	Skalitz 1866	
6	27 June	Wysokov 1866	
7	24 June	Custoza 1866	
8	3 July	Swiebwald 1866	
9	6 Feb	Oeversee 1864	
10	10 June	Monte Berico 1848	
11	25 July	Somma Campagna 1848	
12	27 June	Trautenau 1866	
13	4 June	Magenta 1859	
14	None		
16	27 June	Trautenau 1866	
17	27 June	Wysokov 1866	
18	None		
19	24 June	Custoza 1866	
20	3 July	Koeniggratz 1866	
21	24 June	Custoza 1866	
22	None		
23	4 June	Magenta 1859	
24	None		
25	27 June	Wysokov 1866	
27	None		
28	27 June	Trautenau 1866	
29	28 June	Muskyberg 1866	
30	3 July	Swiepwald 1866	
31	19 Aug	Sarajevo 1878	
32	26 June	Huehnerwasser 1866	

BOSNIAN-HERZEGOVINIAN REGIMENTS

NO	REGIMENTAL DAY	COMMEMORATING THE BATTLE	REGIMENTAL MARCH
1/3	7 Oct	Annexation of Bosnia 1909	

CAVALRY REGIMENTS

DRAGOON REGIMENTS

NO	REGIMENTAL DAY	COMMEMORATING THE BATTLE	REGIMENTAL MARCH
1	25 March	La Fere Champenoise 1814	
2	21 June	Tokay 1673	
3	None		
4	23 April	Regensburg 1809	
5	16 Oct	Leipzig 1813	
6	27 June	Wysokov 1866	
7	17 Aug	Belgrade 1717	*Lothringer* by L. Ganne
8	5 May	The Hofburg in Vienna 1619	*Pannenheimer* by Michael Haydn
9	18 June	Kolin 1757	*Erzherzog Albrecht* by K. Komzak
10	12 Sept	Quesnoi 1793	
11	4 Aug	Announcement of the Emperor as Colonel-in-Chief 1843	
12	24 June	Solferino 1859	
13	12 Aug	Berg Harsany 1687	*Prinz Eugen* Arranged by Leonhardt
14	18 June	Kolin 1757	*Windischgrätz* by G. Mahr, 1867
15	24 June	Custoza 1866	

HUSSAR REGIMENTS

NO	REGIMENTAL DAY	COMMEMORATING THE BATTLE	REGIMENTAL MARCH
1	24 June	Custoza 1866	
2	20 March	Arcis sur Aube 1814	
3	22 April	Egghuehl 1809	
4	21 March	Lyon 1814	
5	15 Aug	Novi 1799	*Radetzky* by J. Strauss the elder
6	22 May	Aspern 1809	
7	26 July	Volta 1848	
8	21 May	Aspern 1809	
9	18 June	Kolin 1757	
10	24 June	Solferino 1859	
11	26 June	Nogaredo Versa 1866	
12 to 15	None		
16	6 July	Wagram 1809	

ULAN REGIMENTS

NO	REGIMENTAL DAY	COMMEMORATING THE BATTLE	REGIMENTAL MARCH
1	24 June	Oswiecim 1866	*Kronprinz Rudolf* composer unknown
2	21 May	Aspern 1809	*Schwarzenberg* by Theodor Kaschte, 1814
3	22 May	Aspern 1809	*Erzherzog Karl* by Emil Kaiser
4	None		
5	24 June	Tishnowitz 1866	
6	29 Oct	Caldiero 1805	
7	18 June	Wisternitz 1758	
8	None		
11	None		
12	24 June	Custoza 1866	
13	24 June	Custoza 1866	

ARTILLERY REGIMENTS

FIELD GUN REGIMENTS

NO	REGIMENTAL DAY	COMMEMORATING THE BATTLE	REGIMENTAL MARCH
1	24 June	Custoza 1866	
7/8/9/10	3 July	Koeniggratz 1866	
11/12	24 June	Custoza 1866	

Field Gun Regiments 13 to 35 had no special commemorative day

NO	REGIMENTAL DAY	COMMEMORATING THE BATTLE	REGIMENTAL MARCH
36	3 July	Koeniggratz 1866	
37	22 July	Blumenau 1866	
38	19 Sept	Bihac 1878	
39	19 Aug	Sarajevo 1878	

FIELD HOWITZER REGIMENTS

NO	REGIMENTAL DAY	COMMEMORATING THE BATTLE	REGIMENTAL MARCH
1	4 June	Magenta 1859	
2	None		
3	3 July	Koeniggratz 1866	
4	24 June	Custoza 1866	
5	27 June	Trautenau 1866	
6	27 June	Wysokov 1866	
7 to 9	None		
10	24 June	Custoza 1866	
11	22 May	Aspern 1809	
12	3 July	Custoza 1866	
13/14	3 July	Koeniggratz 1866	

NO	REGIMENTAL DAY	COMMEMORATING THE BATTLE	REGIMENTAL MARCH
HORSE ARTILLERY HALF REGIMENTS			
1	None		
2	None		
4	24 June	Custoza 1866	
5	27 June	Trautenau 1866	
10	24 June	Custoza 1866	
HEAVY HOWITZER HALF REGIMENTS			
1/3	None		
4	24 June	Custoza 1866	
5/6/7/8	None		
9	24 June	Custoza 1866	
10 to 14	None		
MOUNTAIN ARTILLERY REGIMENT			
1/2/3/4/5/6/7/8/9/10/11/12/13	None		
14 Tirol and Voralberg Kaiser	21 July	Bezzecca 1866	

NO	REGIMENTAL DAY	COMMEMORATING THE BATTLE	REGIMENTAL MARCH
FORTRESS ARTILLERY REGIMENT			
1	17 May	Malborgeth und Predil 1809	
2	20 July	Lissa 1866	
3	None		
4	19 July	Lissa 1866	
5	19 July	Lissa 1866	
6	None		
FORTRESS ARTILLERY BATTALIONS			
1	20 July	Lissa 1866	
2	None		
3	19 July	Lissa 1866	
4	18 May	Malborgeth und Predil 1809	
5	20 July	Lissa 1866	
6 to 10	None		

Men of a 'German' kuk Infantry regiment, probably the 4th Infantry, the 'Hoch und Deutschmeister', marching past The Emperor Franz Joseph, during the celebrations to commemorate the centennial of the battle of Leipzig—Vienna 1913. Note that no carrying sash or cup was issued, so that the whole weight of the flag had to be carried by the NCO Ensign.

Music

Military music was one of the great unifying forces within the Austro-Hungarian Empire. Military band music was particularly popular. In this photograph musicians of a Hungarian kuk Infantry regiment are giving a performance in the Prater in Vienna.

If the regimental Colours may be considered as the regiment's soul then the regimental band and the music it played was the pulse. Any record of the Austro-Hungarian Army would be incomplete without reference to the very important part which music played in the development and in the life of that army.

The Habsburg Empire was fortunate that in its territories were to be found some of the most musical races in Europe. Vienna attracted the most gifted so that the city was not only the capital of a large Empire, but in the middle decades of the last century had become the musical capital of the world.

For graduates from the Conservatory of Music there were posts to be found as military bandmasters where they would be well paid while they studied to equip themselves for more academic works in their chosen career. The post of a military bandmaster, particularly of a crack infantry regiment, was eagerly sought. Both Lehar and Johann Strauss were once thus employed,

and other military bandmasters went on to careers in classical music. There were some who conducted symphony and philharmonic orchestras in later life.

On the military plane, although musicians had accompanied armies from the very earliest days of warfare, it was not until the middle decades of the 18th century that the composition of a regimental band assumed a formal shape. The musicians were within the competence of the colonel-in-chief and it was he who usually paid for them. The case of the 'Hoch und Deutschmeister' regimental band illustrates this. When it was first formed in Milan during May 1748, the regimental treasure chest did not have sufficient funds to provide instruments for, or to pay the salaries of, the thirty-six piece orchestra. The Colonel-in-Chief, Colloredo, supplied the money out of his own pocket and the band of that regiment went on to achieve worldwide fame for the extent of its repertoire and for the excellence of its playing.

Until the privileges connected with the post of colonel-in-chief of a regiment were abolished, the powers of the colonel were almost feudal and it was he who decided the speed at which his regiment marched. There grew up in the Austrian Service a situation in which some regiments marched at 104 paces to the minute while others marched at 110. Such a situation could not be allowed to continue and a standardisation of the marching pace was introduced during 1851 as 100 paces to the minute.

On the battlefield, too, there was a need for bodies of troops to move in step and at a standard pace. To meet this demand there grew up a standardisation in the music played by regimental bands and an Inspector of Military Music was appointed to control this. The Austrian War Office, notorious for the care it exercised in the control of public funds, laid down that the band of an infantry regiment would consist of forty-eight professional musicians. For jaeger and cavalry the establishment was twenty-four bandsmen. The sum allotted by the Ministry to pay for the bands was insufficient even to purchase the instruments and a regimental levy provided the funds for these. The ordinary bandsmen were, of course, soldiers and received their standard pay. The bandmaster, however, was not a soldier but a uniformed civilian who was employed on a civil contract and whose salary was paid for by the officers of the regiment.

Such crack infantry regiments as the Kaiserjaeger or the Deutschmeister were able to offer bandmasters' contracts to very talented musicians who, in turn, immortalised in music the regiments by which they were employed. Marches were composed for their regiments by such men as Ziehrer, Komzak and Leonhardt. But even among the rank and file of a regiment there was considerable musical talent to be found. Fritz Kreisler, for example, served as an infantryman, and Wilhelm Jurek wrote the most famous of all Deutschmeister marches while serving as corporal with the 7th Company of that regiment.

Austrian military bands and the music they produced soon achieved international recognition, not merely for the excellence of the compositions themselves but, more importantly, for the band's interpretation of the work. On one occasion an enquiry from a German music critic as to why there was such a very noticeable difference between the playing of the same march by a German and then by an Austrian military band, produced the answer: 'Your German musicians play only the notes. Our Austrian musicians play what lies between the notes.'

The band of a German regiment, probably kuk Infantry Regiment No 4, playing the guard back to barracks after the Guard Changing ceremony at the Hofburg, Vienna c1906.

The band of a Landwehr (Honved) Infantry unit, c1986. The Austrian Landwehr had no regimental bands on establishment although the buglers, trumpeters and drummers could be brought together to provide music.
(Kalman collection)

A distinction must be made between marches which were composed for the regiment and those to which the regiment marched past on parades. The Deutschmeister infantry regiment was one formation about which, or for which, more than one hundred pieces of music were written. Despite the excellence of many of these, the tune to which the regiment marched past on ceremonial occasions was based on motifs from the 12th and 17th centuries.

The appended table which shows the regimental days also lists the march past music of a number of units. Those for which no special piece of music had been composed used any one of the standard marches in the army's band book. It will be noted that much of the music listed below was written for infantry regiments. This is because, concurrent with the great increase in march composition during the latter decades of the 19th century, the bands of cavalry regiments, together with the post of Inspector General of Music, were abolished. Among the other changes produced by the reforms of Archduke Albrecht was a change in band uniforms. The over-elaborate styles of earlier decades were discarded and although the traditional 'swallows' nest on the shoulder were retained these, too, had been discarded by the end of the century. Bandmasters, although not commissioned, carried officer pattern sabres with a silver acorn sword knot. In addition to rank stars, bandsmen and the bandmaster wore a lyre device on both sides of the tunic collar join.

One feature of Austrian military bands in the late 19th century was the regimental animal which pulled the cart on which the big drum rested. The drum beast, usually a pony, accompanied the regiment even when it went out on active service. It was the practice for bands to play the regiment into battle and to accompany the battalions even in the charge. It will be understood that among the unarmed musicians and the regimental drum beasts losses were often abnormally high. During the battle of Cholm the

Deutschmeister band marched into the attack with the leading companies of the regiment and suffered total loss. At Tratenau the band of 1st Infantry Regiment suffered a fifty per cent casualty rate, and even in the opening battles of 1914 the bands continued the tradition of playing the regiment into battle. Unacceptably high losses led to that practice being discontinued but the musicians were kept to maintain morale, for it was considered that the regimental band was as much essential to the upkeep of morale as were tobacco and alcohol.

The long period of peace in Europe lasting, without serious interruption, from 1870 to 1914, brought into prominence the ceremonial aspects of the army and it was during those last decades of Imperial splendour that military music in Austria reached its zenith. The great military parades were features of the Vienna season and the Spring Parade, attended by the Emperor and the whole court, was the high point of the social year. There was the fiercest

The outbreak of war in 1914 produced a wave of patriotic feeling. That feeling was particularly strong among the Poles and Ukrainians who hoped that a successful war against Russia would bring freedom to their own countries. The volunteer units which they raised formed part of the Austrian Landwehr organisation and, unusually for that force, also formed regimental bands. This photograph shows one of the bands of the Legion.

competition among the regiments to provide the best music, and intense partisanship on the part of the massed spectators. The 1897 parade, for example, was a glittering one in which eleven bands took part. There were 19,000 men on parade, together with 3,500 horses and 92 pieces of ordnance. One other important date in every military year was 18 August, the Emperor's birthday, which was always celebrated by every unit of the army and for which a number of marches were written. One theme often used in marches was the national anthem and four famous ones used the opening bars of that hymn. The first of these was the *Franz Joseph Jubel Marsch* by Johann Strauss the younger, and the *Kaiserjäger* by Muhlberger. Novotny's *Alle Ehren ist Österreich voll* used the first bars of the anthem as a background slow march to the main theme which is in quick time. The fourth march to use the national anthem was Komzak's *84th Regiment March* and that composer also wrote the *Kaiser Marsch* in 1898 to commemorate the Emperor's Golden Jubilee.

At the turn of the 19th century the Archduke Karl carried out research into the subject of military music, particularly into those pieces played during the most important ceremonies of Tattoo and Retreat. The composer of the original pieces could not be traced, for their origins went back for more than two centuries and had been formally adopted as ceremonial music as early as the beginning of the 18th century. New versions of both *Retreat* and *Tattoo* were composed by Leonhardt, the senior bandmaster of the army in 1854, using the original themes and the new compositions were first played in camp at Olmutz during that year.

The bugle calls of the Austrian service, particularly those of the cavalry, were very finely written and it has been said that if armies could win victories for the excellence of their bugle calls, then Austria would never have lost a battle.

Throughout the centuries of Austria's military history there had been a guard-changing parade in the Burg in Vienna and a number of composers had written music for that ceremony. On 11 November 1918 the Emperor's Guard was changed for the last time and the piece of music which marked the passing of Imperial glory was Czibulka's *From the banks of the Danube*. The guard does not now change in the Hofburg but the memory of the golden Habsburg years is not yet dead. There is still in Vienna a band of expert musicians which is called the Deutschmeister and in Tirol another group of civilians who keep alive the name and the memory of the Kaiserjaeger. More enduring than those are the marches themselves recalling the centuries of Imperial rule and for as long as good marches are played the Empire is not dead.

The band of the 1st Regiment of the Kaiserjaeger in Innsbruck 1908, waiting for the arrival of the Emperor.

|||||||||||||||||||||||||||||||||||||||||||||||||||||||||||||||||||||||||||||||||||||||||

Flags and Standards

|||||||||||||||||||||||||||||||||||||||||||||||||||||||||||||||||||||||||||||||||||||||||

From the earliest days of warfare armies carried flags. In battle they distinguished friend from foe; they formed a rallying point in the confusion of a mêlée and in times of crisis their presence among the soldiers inspired them to rise above a natural fear of death. In time the regimental Colour became a mystical symbol, the soul of the regiment, an object made venerable through the sacrifice of those who had died fighting beneath it. The capture of an enemy's Colour on the battlefield was an act to be richly rewarded. Conversely, the loss of one's own Standard to the enemy was a terrible disgrace, hardly to be borne.

Over the centuries the scale of distribution of flags or Standards extended to company level. Then, in common with most military forces, the Austrian Service reduced the number on issue. By the time of the war with Prussia each Austrian line infantry regiment carried three. The first battalion carried the White or regimental Colour. The other two battalions each carried a Yellow Standard.

One of the reforms brought in by Archduke Albrecht's committee was the withdrawal of the Yellow flags, leaving only the White to serve as the regimental Colour. There were, however, certain regiments whose junior battalions had particularly distinguished themselves in past battles. To recognise those deeds of bravery the 2nd, 4th, 39th, 41st and 57th Regiments all had the distinction of carrying the Yellow Standard and not the White.

All line infantry Colours were of standard shape, size and design with a field measuring 176cm in length and 132cm in depth. Three sides of the flag floated free. The fourth was fixed to the staff by four rows of gilded nails. Bands of silk or paint in red, silver, black and gold spiralled round the 284cm long flagstaff, rising from the shoe to the gilded metal spearhead which was engraved with the Imperial crown and cypher.

Colours for the Common Army units were made of a double layer of pure silk. The devices displayed on the obverse and the reverse were embroidered or hand painted. The two decorated sides, separated by a layer of silk, were then sewn together, the border was fitted and the flag nailed to the staff. The nailing of the field to the staff symbolised the birth of the new Standard and the occasion was carried out at a drumhead service. The senior officers of the regiment, commencing with the colonel-in-chief, banged the nails into place.

The White Colour bore on the obverse field a figure of the Blessed Virgin Mary set in a mandola and bearing a corona of twelve silver stars. The Virgin

In the first months of 1915 the 2nd Regiment of Kaiserjaeger was presented with a new Colour. Here the Colour is dipped during the playing of the national anthem. Although the presentation was made in February 1915, and therefore lies outside the parameters of this book, it has been included to show this unusual event.

was depicted standing on a cloud and trampling down the serpent of evil. The reverse displayed an Imperial eagle upon whose breast was a shield with the arms of Habsburg, Austria and Lorraine. Surrounding the shield were the neck chains of the knightly Orders of the Golden Fleece, St Stephan, Leopold and the Iron Crown, together with the neck ribbon of the Maria Theresia Order.

Descending from either wing of the eagle were the coats of arms of the kingdoms and provinces of the Empire. On the eagle's right wing were those of Hungary, Galicia, Lower Austria, Upper Austria, Salzburg and Styria. On the left wing the shields of Bohemia, Istria-Dalmatia, Siebenburgen, Moravia, Silesia and Carinthia-Carniola. Upon the widespread tail was set a shield bearing the arms of Tirol.

The Yellow Colour carried on both the obverse and the reverse the eagle as described above.

The Colour carried a 10cm border of varicoloured triangular flames. For Common Army regiments these were coloured in red, silver, black and gold. Honved regiments carried red, white and green flames for Hungarian units and flames of red, white and blue for Croat regiments.

Since regimental Colours were of standard pattern it was not possible to identify the unit to which they had been presented except by checking the banderoles. These were broad sashes, streamers and bows of pure silk in regimental facing colour, fixed to the head of the flagstaff. Upon them were embroidered the most important dates and/or places in the life of the regiment. The embroidery was of either gold or silver bullion thread and matched the regimental button colour. As the banderoles were often produced regimentally and sometimes were embroidered by the ladies of the regiment, they did not always conform to the set pattern, either in design or length.

In inclement weather, or when not on parade, the Colour was rolled and carried enclosed within a black oilskin bag which bore the inscription 'Infantry Regiment No . . .' in large white letters. When the Colour was uncased the oilskin bag was worn like a sash, from shoulder to hip, by the NCO who carried the flag. There was no provision for a carrying sash or supporting cup. The bearer thus bore the full weight of the flag at all times, holding it against his body with the right hand and using the left hand as a support.

Colours for Landwehr infantry regiments were designed but never issued. The design would have shown on the obverse the Imperial eagle upon whose breast was set the arms of Austria, Habsburg and Lorraine bordered by the chain of the Order of the Golden Fleece. The reverse would have borne the Imperial cypher with an Imperial crown in each corner. The border would

Two prints showing left, the reverse and right, the obverse of the guidon carried by 14th Dragoon Regiment. When the practice of carrying Colours by Cavalry regiments was abolished by the Albrecht committee, the 14th Dragoons alone were permitted to retain theirs. A full description of the guidon of the 14th Dragoons is to be found on these pages.
(HGM)

have been that of Common Army pattern. The size of the field would have been 165cm long by 134cm deep and the staff 298cm in length.

Honved regiments were issued with Colours. These had a white field and upon the obverse was a shield displaying the arms of Hungary, supported by two flying angels and surmounted by the crown of St Stephan. On the reverse was the royal cypher together with a legend in Magyar which read: 'I have one God and one King. For the one I die, to the other I pray'. The flagstaff was crowned by a halberd and not a spearhead.

On 11 October 1915 an Imperial memorandum on the question of regimental Colours for the Common Army appreciated that their design no longer truly represented the structure of the Empire. It was, therefore, proposed to issue Standards of a new design. The new flag would have borne on the obverse the Austrian eagle together with the Hungarian arms and the legend in Latin 'Indivisible and Inseparable'. On the reverse was to be the Imperial cypher and in alternate corners the Imperial and the St Stephan's crowns. The border was to carry not only the Common Army's red, silver, black and gold flames, but also flames in green so as to incorporate the national colours of Hungary. The new Standards were never brought into service and the only one produced is held in the Heeresgeschichtliches Museum in Vienna.

Feldjaeger units of the Common Army carried no Colours for their was a light and mobile role for which the carrying of a Standard on the battlefield would have been impractical. One battalion, the 10th (Kopal) did have bestowed upon it a signal trumpet which, by Imperial decree, was accorded the same honours as a Colour.

Among the cavalry regiments only the 14th Dragoons was allowed to retain a Colour as a regimental distinction. This was the traditional swallow-tail guidon. The field of this was 96cm long and 57.5cm deep. There was a border

embroidered with gold leaves from which hung a fringe of bullion lace. The reverse of the Standard was of green brocade and bore a representation of the capture of Prussian cannon together with the superscription *'Que n'y en avoit il davantage'*. The red brocade obverse bore the Imperial eagle wearing the chain of the Golden Fleece. The spearhead carried on the obverse a monogram and on the reverse an Imperial eagle.

There were many units in the Austro-Hungarian Service which carried unofficial Colours or Standards, particularly the Standschuetzen units and although these were based on Common Army design they often bore local names and slogans. Such unofficial flags are outside the scope of this work.

The Colour accompanied the regiment when it went into the field in 1914, and was usually carried into the attack. It was soon clear that the losses suffered by the ensigns and the escorts was unacceptably high and, with reluctance, the order was given for flags to be withdrawn from the front line. This order was not always obeyed and in some units Colours were carried in action until 1916.

Landwehr (Honved) regimental Colour.

Epilogue

A BYSTANDER who watched the funeral procession pass on the bright cold December day when they buried Franz Joseph would have been well aware that, with the Emperor's death, an era had come to an end. The old Monarch was dead. Only those who were themselves very, very aged could remember a time before he had come to the throne. Franz Joseph had become Emperor in 1848, the year of revolution and a time of national crisis. Now, in 1916, death had taken him from the scene and, once again, there was a crisis situation: a great war.

Seen from military viewpoint Austria was in a strong position in that year of 1916. Her armies stood everywhere on enemy soil. On the Eastern Front the allied hosts of Austria and Germany had shattered the Russians and the Roumanians. On the Southern Front the Italians had been flung back and in the south-east the Serbs had been eliminated. The war was by no means at an end but for the central powers there was every confidence of a victorious outcome. For the civilians life was, it was true, a monotonous grey existence but to our watcher in the streets of Vienna, who saw the Emperor pass, it must have seemed that final victory must surely come.

Our observer in Vienna, two years later, seeing the young Emperor, Karl, at the Mass to celebrate the Feast of Corpus Christi, would have been reassured that the Habsburg Empire was still strong. In the religious procession there had been the glitter of peacetime uniforms, the pomp and the radiance which for centuries had attended upon Habsburg ceremonies; and yet, only five months later and the glory had passed away. Those new nations which had been born out of the dissolution of the Habsburg Empire had called their soldiers home. Only the German/Austrian regiments and a few others: Croats, Slovenes and Bosnians, chiefly, had stayed loyal; and these would soon all be in the barbed wire compounds of prison cages. With the death of the Empire the tripartite armies; kuk, kk and ku, had been destroyed.

*   *   *

To visit a great military cemetery anywhere in Western Europe is to be made aware of the terrible losses that were suffered at national level in the First World War. Those who visit Austria will find, if they walk through village churchyards, examples at a much more personal level of the cruel cost of war. Churchyard walls are often lined with the framed photographs of soldiers, villagers, who lie in foreign soil. The young faces staring out of the frames are those of local lads, and from the dates carved below their pictures it is possible to identify the battle in which they fell in action. And the same family names are found repeated two, three, four or even five times. There are war memorials too, on which are carved the chilling figures which show how severe were the losses that the villages suffered.

Today, children play around the village war memorials in Austria. The stone statues showing embattled and stern-faced soldiers standing in heroic poses, or depicted dying a glorious death in a war fought nearly three-quarters of a century ago, have little significance for their descendants. The soldiers, it would seem, are totally forgotten. And yet in a sense those men of the old army can never fade from mind totally and completely. The marches of the regiments recall them. For as long as *Radetzky* is played it will always link those who hear it, even though they may be unaware of the connection, to those soldiers of the Imperial armies who once marched unflinchingly

Young NCOs and men en route to the Eastern Front in the opening stages of the First World War, August 1914.

into the fury of battle following the insistent tattoo of its drum rolls and responding to the brazen call of its trumpets.

And what now remains to show that once four hundred years of military service had passed by? The battlefields remain as do the memorials. Of these none can be more chilling in its impact nor make the point of patriotic sacrifice more clearly than that one in Klagenfurt which reads: 'From this spot on 10th August 1914 the Imperial and Royal Feldjäger Battalion No. 8 went off to war, with a strength of 38 officers and 1222 non-commissioned-officers and men. Of that number 38 officers and 1221 non-commissioned-officers and men fell in battle.'

Bibliography

Adjustirungs und Ausrustrustungsvorschriften fur das k.k. Heer. (Wien 1878)
Adjustierungsvorschrift fur das kuk Heer. (Wien 1907)
Das Heerwesen der oesterreisch-ungarischen Monarchie. Karl Gluckmann (Wien 1897)
Uniformen, Distinktionen und sonstige Abzeichen der gesamten oestarr.-ungar. Wehrmacht. (Leipzig 1904)
Geschichte der kuk Wehrmacht. Band 1 and 2. Wrede, A. (Wien 1898-1901)
Normen fur die Trainausrustung des kuk Heeres. (Wien 1896)
Verordnungsblatt fur das kuk Heer. Jahrgang 58 and 59. (Wien)
Schematismus fur das kuk Heer. 1906 to 1913/14. (Wien 1907-14)
Die oesterreich.-ung. Armee. Moritz Ruhl (Leipzig 1898)
Oesterreich-Ungarns letzter Krieg. 1914-1918 (Wien 1932)
Aus meiner Dienstzeit Conrad von Hoetzendorff. (Wien 1921)
Oestrreich-Ungarns Anteil am Ersten Weltkrieg. Rudolf Kiszling (Wien)
Heerwesen. 1914. 1917. Schmid (Wien 1914-17)
Gliederung und Entwicklung der Batterien der oesterreich.-ungarisch Feld und Gebirgsartillerie im Weltkrieg. 1914-1918. Sobicka, G. (Wien 1924)
Gliederung der bewaffneten Macht oesterreich-ungarn. 1883. (Wien 1883)
Gebuehrvorschriften fur das kuk Heer. (Wien 1895)
Instruktionsbuch fur die Reserveoffiziers-schulen. Teile. 1 to 8 (Wien 1909)
Dienstreglement fur das kuk Heer. (Wien 1909-12)
A Magyar Kirelyi Honvedseg Tortenete. 1868-1918. Berko (Budapest 1828)

As well as battalion, regimental and Divisional histories, including the kuk No 4 Deutschmeister, 47th, 94th, 99th Kaiserjaeger, 10th Feldjaeger Kopal, Dragoner No 6, Husaren No 9, 29th Division and the Edelweiss Division.

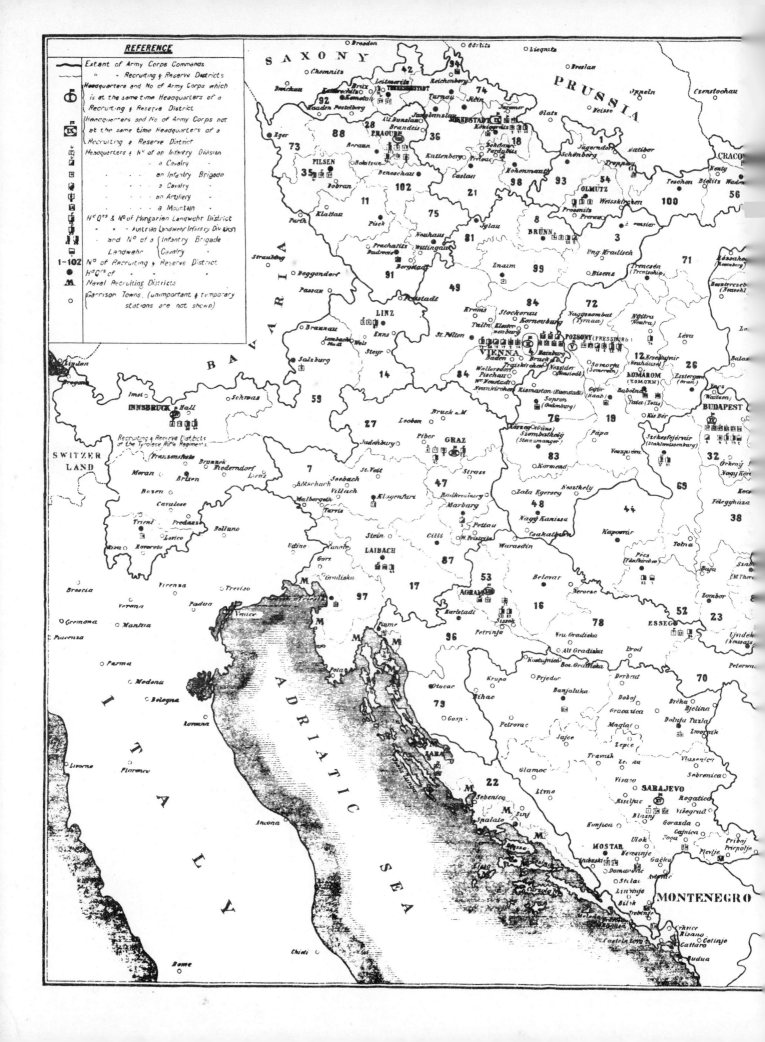